Praise for *Sigh, Gone*

"In actuality and on the pages of this memoir, Tran's life goes off-road, defying reading plans or most other kinds of plans, which makes *Sigh, Gone* a congenial read for our chaotic time."

—Maureen Corrigan, NPR's *Fresh Air*

"As the title implies, *Sigh, Gone*, with its wistful pun on the erstwhile capital city of his native country, is built around Tran's devotion to and curiosity about language—the friction between English and Vietnamese, the Western literary canon he fell in love with, the said and the unsaid both within his family and in the wider world. The book powerfully explores themes of assimilation, racism, complex and abusive family dynamics, and the challenge of coming into one's own. In other words, *Sigh, Gone* is like all great works of literature—it asks big questions, universal in their specificity."

—*Los Angeles Review of Books*

"[*Sigh, Gone*] recounts in stunning detail [Tran's] coming-of-age in white, small-town America . . . [and] in laying out his childhood around themes and metaphors, Tran makes his own Great American Memoir."

—*The Seattle Times*

"A heartfelt and ambitious memoir." —*Portland Press Herald*

"*Sigh, Gone* is more likely to launch a broken-down kid on a mission to read 150 great books—for free, at the local library. Put Phuc Tran's book in the hands of a bunch of teenage punks goofing off in English class and see what they do with it." —*PopMatters*

"[A] funny heartbreaker . . . This wry and unsparing coming-of-age memoir recaps the tumultuous childhood and turbulent adolescence of a bookish Vietnamese immigrant raised in a blue-collar American town." —*Shelf Awareness*

"*Sigh, Gone* provides a vivid and eye-opening look at yet another legacy of the American War in Vietnam: what life was like for Vietnamese children and their families who escaped from their homeland and were transplanted in small-town USA." —*The Veteran*

"Riveting." —*Lincoln Journal Star*

"The United States was already a better country because Phuc Tran refused to change his name. Then he went even further in changing this country by giving us this bold, funny, and profane memoir: a portrait of a young punk refugee and of heartland America itself, each of them as defiant and compelling as the other." —Viet Thanh Nguyen, author of Pulitzer Prize–winning *The Sympathizer* and *The Refugees*

"I like to think that had I been born a much cooler, male, Vietnamese version of myself, *Sigh, Gone* is the book I would have written. This glorious memoir is a reminder of the transformative power of literature and a tribute to friendships, music, and the unique kindness of Americans. I loved it!" —Firoozeh Dumas, *New York Times* bestselling author of *Funny in Farsi* and *Laughing Without an Accent*

"I started reading this book and couldn't stop. Phuc Tran has written the Great American Nerd-Punk Boyhood Memoir, a story that's rollicking and laugh-out-loud funny while also offering a piercingly profound look at race, the challenges of assimilation, and the inherently defiant act of growing up. Earnest, observant, and diamond-sharp, this is a new voice of unmistakable talent. I'll follow this writer anywhere."

—Sara Corbett, coauthor of *New York Times* bestseller *A House in the Sky*

"In *Sigh, Gone*, Phuc Tran offers a searing, trenchant, and hilarious chronicle of adolescence. His memoir seethes with all the shame and rage, loneliness, and longing born from cultural dislocation; thrums with all the fears and half-truths, anti-triumphs, and confused desires of that vicious American journey we call 'assimilation.' With this book, Tran not only puts himself on the literary map: he rips the map to pieces and tapes it back together as he—forever the bookish young punk—sees fit. The result: a refugee story of the most modern kind, told entirely on the author's own terms."

—Jaed Coffin, author of *Roughhouse Friday*

"I want to gift this book to my witty friends, my well-read friends, my punk friends, and my Asian American friends. I also want to gift it to my witty, well-read, punk Asian American friend who will be so thrilled to know that a book has finally been written to show the world that, yes, we can be all these things all at once, in all its mash-up glory. *Sigh, Gone* is a painfully—and I mean *painfully*—funny book that seems to have collected all our best and worst memories and turned them into a story told by a smart narrator who will not let us go. His voice will grab you by the hand and remind you that, for many of us, childhood was really no laughing matter."

—Cinelle Barnes, author of *Monsoon Mansion*

"A powerful memoir that proves the transformative power of music and literature . . . Tender and even comic, it is, in his own words, 'a misfit's memoir,' exchanging estrangement and adversity for hard-won accomplishment."   —The Center for Fiction

SIGH,
GONE

SIGH, GONE

GONE

| A MISFIT'S MEMOIR
| OF GREAT BOOKS,
| PUNK ROCK,
| AND THE FIGHT
| TO FIT IN

PHUC TRAN

FLATIRON
BOOKS
NEW YORK

SIGH, GONE. Copyright © 2020 by Phuc Tran. All rights reserved. Printed in the United States of America. For information, address Flatiron Books, 120 Broadway, New York, NY 10271.

www.flatironbooks.com

Designed by Michelle McMillian

The Library of Congress has cataloged the hardcover edition as follows:

Names: Tran, Phuc, 1974– author.
Title: Sigh, gone : a misfit's memoir of great books, punk rock, and the fight to fit in / Phuc Tran.
Description: First edition | New York, NY : Flatiron Books, 2020.
Identifiers: LCCN 2019047906 | ISBN 9781250194718 (hardcover) | ISBN 9781250194725 (ebook)
Subjects: LCSH: Tran, Phuc, 1974– —Childhood and youth. | Tran, Phuc, 1974– —Books and reading. | Vietnamese Americans—Pennsylvania—Carlisle—Biography. | Immigrants—Pennsylvania—Carlisle—Biography. | Refugees—Vietnam—Ho Chi Minh City—Biography. | Racism—Pennsylvania—Carlisle—History—20th century. | Vietnam War, 1961–1975—Refugees. | Carlisle (Pa.)—Race relations—History—20th century.
Classification: LCC F159.C2
LC record available at https://lccn.loc.gov/2019047906

ISBN 978-1-250-82661-9 (trade paperback)

Our books may be purchased in bulk for promotional, educational, or business use. Please contact your local bookseller or the Macmillan Corporate and Premium Sales Department at 1-800-221-7945, extension 5442, or by email at MacmillanSpecialMarkets@macmillan.com.

First Flatiron Books Paperback Edition: 2022

10 9 8 7 6 5 4 3 2

For Sue

CONTENTS

PROLOGUE

The Picture of Dorian Gray

Fuck that kid.

That's what I thought when I first saw Hoàng Nguyễn in eleventh grade. Hoàng never did anything to me, and he *certainly* never said anything to me. God, he hardly looked at me except when we passed in the hallways, me on my way to physics, him on his way to wherever. We'd glance at each other, give a quick nod, and move on, swept along in the rapids of our hallways. But fuck that kid.

Hoàng was a fun-house mirror's rippling reflection of me, warped and wobbly. I hated it. I was Dorian Gray beholding his grotesque portrait in the attic, and I was filled with loathing. My disgust for Hoàng was complicated and simple at the same time: I was *the* Vietnamese kid at Carlisle Senior High School. Just me. Fuck that new Vietnamese kid.

Nestled in the Susquehanna Valley town of Carlisle, Pennsylvania, Carlisle Senior High School sprawled as a monolithic mid-century modern block of types: archetypes and stereotypes. Industrial gray lockers ringed its hallways, the compartments narrow enough to repel most of your textbooks but wide enough to collect the trash and detritus from your backpack—your own personal landfill. Linoleum floors, classrooms with chables (the combo chair-tables of the seventies), blackboards, American flags, loudspeakers from which the *wah-wah-wah* of adult-speak would drone. Our school district was so large that the juniors and seniors had their own separate high school—the so-called Senior High School—and the freshman and sophomores had their own underclassmen high school building.

Carlisle High School stocked its seats and bleachers with a familiar cast from the eighties: the athletes who towered above the rest of us; the cheerleaders who lay supine beneath them; the geeks with their physics books under their arms; the preps with their Tretorns, Swatches, and impeccable Benetton sweaters; a handful of black kids with MC Hammer pants and tall, square Afros, tightly faded; punks and skaters with their leather jackets and black Converse; a few swirly hippies; the rednecks with their oily palms and cigarettes and trucks. Carlisle High School was another cultural cul-de-sac built with the craftsman blueprint of John Hughes, the Frank Lloyd Wright of teen malaise.

Overwhelmingly white, Carlisle's population offered all the rainbows of Caucasia. The town's main employers were Dickinson College, the Army War College, a smoky stack of factories, and the service industries that had sprung up to support the aforementioned trifecta.

In the spirit of public education, we progeny were all in the mix together: the itinerant army brats; the ivory sons and daughters of professors, doctors, and lawyers; the greasy offspring of waiters, cooks, and factory workers; and the token refugee family. The Trần family blended right into the mix like proverbial flies in the ointment. That is to say: we didn't.

Carlisle's glitter was unmistakably eighties, but its structure was straight from the postwar era, bricked together by the mortar of the fifties. We had a downtown Woolworth's with a chrome luncheonette counter and red vinyl stools and a grand movie theater with its incandescent marquee. The four corners of Carlisle's town square were righted by two courthouses and two churches (Episcopalian and Presbyterian). God and Law and Law and God. It wasn't a subtle message to any of us living in Carlisle what was at the heart of the town.

And the pièce-de-résistance: our high school was the town's designated Cold War fallout shelter. The blue-and-yellow radiation placards festooned our hallways, reminding us that we were only a button-push away from nuclear annihilation.

From what I gleaned on television, Carlisle seemed like a slice of American pie à la mode. We bottled lightning bugs on summer nights. Trucks flew Confederate flags. We loitered at 7-Elevens and truck stops. We shopped at flea markets and shot pellet guns. My high school provided a day care for girls who had gotten pregnant but were still attending classes. We stirred up marching band pride and fomented football rivalries. The auto shop kids rattled by in muscle cars and smoked in ashen cabals before the first-period bell. We were rural royalty: Dairy Queens and Burger Kings.

This was small-town PA. Poorly read. Very white. Collar blue.

So where did the immigrant Vietnamese kid fit into all of this?

By junior year, I had spent the last eleven years of school clawing my way to acceptance, at least in my own mind. As the only Asian kid in my classes and school through eighth grade, and then one of the very few in high school, I had been taunted and bullied in those early years. The blatant playground racism I bore in elementary school dipped below the surface in middle and high school, but it was always rippling under the social currents.

I believed that I was bullied because I was Vietnamese, so I did the math for my survival: be less Asian, be bullied less. Armed with this simplistic deduction, I tried to erase my otherness, my Asianness, with an assimilation—an Americanization—that was as relentless as it was thorough.

My plan for assimilation was a two-pronged attack, top-down and bottom-up. The top-down assault was my attempt at academic excellence.

In the trenches of high school warfare, honor roll and National Honor Society shielded me: even if I felt like a social pariah in my classes, at least I would have a better vocabulary than these philistines.

I realized that there was *some* prestige in being smart, or at least appearing smart. Sounding smart was not the same social Teflon as being good-looking or athletic or funny, but hell, if someone could give me some props for being good at school, I would take nerd props over no props at all. I got zero props for being Vietnamese or bilingual or a refugee. Operation Sound Smart commenced: I read voraciously, I studied tirelessly. I read as much (or at least name-dropped as much) of the Western literary canon as I could. Of course, I was a teenager—what the hell did I really know?—but my drive was as tenacious as my ignorance was deep. Being an intellectual gave me some clout in the classroom. And basking myself in the esteem of my classmates, I felt the warmth of their respect in sharp contrast to my cloaked envy of them. They belonged in a way that I never could, and their regard for me was sweet and sour. How Asian.

Then I hit the jackpot. Triple cherries. Working at my town's public library as a library page, I bought a discarded copy of Clifton Fadiman's *The Lifetime Reading Plan*.

In *The Lifetime Reading Plan*, Fadiman listed and summarized all the books that he thought educated, cultured Americans should read over their lifetime, beginning with the Bible and ending with Solzhenitsyn. *The Plan* listed the books and presented Fadiman's synopses of the books' merits and his justification for their obvious place in the Western canon. His introduction was unapologetically American, classist, and white—and I loved it. *The Plan* would be the most powerful cannon in my war for assimilation.

I now possessed the de facto manual for educated white men. Fadiman's list of must-read books was a cheat sheet for those who wanted to be (or in my case, appear to be) erudite. In no particular order, I read what I could, sometimes with Fadiman as my docent, sometimes not:

Flaubert, Twain, Kerouac, Brontë, Kafka, Camus, Ibsen, James, Thurber, Shakespeare.

But in the course of reading great books, *something* happened. My reading molded me, the tool hammering its hand into shape. By some miracle—and by miracle, I mean great teachers—I pushed past the shallowness and stupidity of my own motivations. I fell in love with the *actual* literature and the *actual* ideas of great literature. As an immigrant, as a Vietnamese kid, as a poor kid, I had collected so many scarlet letters of alienation that I connected profoundly to the great works.

As I read, I began to understand that all the great works wrangled with big questions, *important* questions: our place in the world, the value of our experience, the fairness and meaning of our suffering, our quest for love and belonging. Universal themes bound these great works together, and they bound me to their oaky, yellowed pages like Odysseus lashed to the mast of his ship. I felt a connective and humanizing resonance in books: I wasn't *alone* in my aloneness. I wasn't alone in my longing for love. I wasn't alone in my fear of being rejected, my fear of never finding my place, my fear of failing. The snarl of my journey was untangled and laid out clearly by books.

In the great classics, there were so many moments for me to divest my age, my town, my skin, so many moments to be part of a universal conversation. Homer sharpened my mind's edge. Dickinson gave me winged hope. Thoreau made a whole cabin for me.

With my academic assault underway, the second prong of my attack commenced: Operation Look Punk. You know one way to show that you fit in? By *not* fitting in. It's a weird, counterintuitive trick—a social trompe l'oeil, if you will.

Here's an analogy: In drawing, the way that you show perspective— the way that you make something look real—is by making things bigger in the foreground and smaller in the background. While the paper lies flat and two-dimensional, the *exaggeration* of certain aspects of the draw-ing makes the objects *appear* to have a third dimension. The medium has no depth, but the content does.

How do you do that in the social milieu of high school? You pick a subculture. Exaggerate some part of yourself, draw attention to it, and then all the other things will fade into the background. If you're a Viet-namese kid in a small Pennsylvania town and you're getting your ass kicked because you're Asian, what does this mean? You go punk rock. Like, you go FULL PUNK. Get the leather jacket. Shave part of your head. Wear ripped-up flannel. Bleach your hair.

With my academic survival ensured in the classroom, my bottom-up assault was designed for social standing outside the classroom, and I pinned my safety on eighties punk culture.

Now the rednecks don't want to kick your ass because you're Asian; they want to kick your ass because you're a social freak. Being a freak because of my weird clothes and hair was a respite. These were things that I had chosen—these were things that all my punk friends had cho-sen. Fighting rednecks because you were a punk was far better than fighting because you were Asian, and fighting with allies was far better than fighting alone.

Being an outsider because of my race was a burden that I didn't choose. There was nothing I could do about it. On the surface, I seemed to be another angry teenager, but my anger wasn't just swayed by ju-venile impulses. I hated myself. I hated my parents. I hated my town. I hated the racism that made me hate myself. But through punk, I found my tribe. A group of people with whom I could bond over new skate tricks or the new Fugazi record or going to punk shows. We punks got to skip over superficial things like race and ethnicity. We talked about important things like where to get beer and how to pay for tattoos. For a kid whose days at school and nights at home were littered with the land mines of physical violence and emotional abuse, punk rock was close enough to love.

If you catch me in my off-guard moments, I'll tell you that at some points in my life, I wanted to be white. It's not a proud feeling, but it's not a feeling that comes from the shame of being brown. It's a tired feeling. Tired of the crushing racism. Tired of not belonging. It's the exhaustion from fighting for your right to exist. Getting called a *chink* at any age is painful, whether you're five, fifteen, or thirty-five. Damn it, I'm not even Chinese, but that didn't matter.

Punk alleviated that exhaustion—or at least I thought it did. In my spiked leather jacket, Subhumans T-shirt, Doc Marten boots, and ever-changing haircuts, I forged the portrait of a kid who belonged, a kid who fit in by not fitting in, and even if that portrait ultimately turned out to be flat and shallow, it had the illusion of depth.

In Oscar Wilde's supernatural novella, *The Picture of Dorian Gray*, the protagonist Dorian Gray maintains his physical beauty while a mysterious painting of himself, which he hides in the attic, ages and grows putrid and grotesque. Dorian pursues an immoral and decadent lifestyle, and while his physical appearance remains unchanged, the true corrosion of his soul is reflected in the portrait. The reader understands that the portrait is the real nature of Gray, but Gray's beauty, his physical appearance, is no less real. As the novella unfolds, the reader wrestles with the reality of both Gray and his painting. What was real, his physical body or the painting of his soul? Wilde might say both, and when I read *Dorian Gray*, I recognized immediately the echoes of similar tensions in my life. Was the punk rock version of myself the real me? Or was the real me the one hiding underneath the punk rock?

By junior year of high school, 1990, I had achieved insider status, even if that insider status was with the outsiders. Then fucking Hoàng showed up.

He was fresh off the boat. His English was terrible while mine was impeccable. His teeth were crooked while mine were straight because of orthodontia. He had a bowlegged walk, probably because of early malnutrition from years spent languishing in third-world poverty. Having escaped Sài Gòn, my family had come to America in 1975. It didn't get any more privileged than that. Hoàng's clothes were ill fitting and clearly hand-me-downs.

When Dorian Gray beholds his portrait in the attic and shows his friend Basil the horror of the painting, Basil is sickened. The portrait reflects the rot of Dorian's soul, and it repels Basil just as I was repulsed by Hoàng.

But it wasn't him that I found repugnant. I hated everything he stood for. I hated that he was my portrait if my family hadn't escaped Sài Gòn. Hoàng embodied my alternate reality. Nervous. Smiling. He made me feel a sick cocktail of emotions: shame, guilt, and sadness. He was an unflinching foreigner, walking down the hallways of my high school, oblivious to his foreignness. I hated how unaware he was. There was no art or artifice to his presence or appearance. He seemed grateful just to be in high school, and his gratitude was infuriating. Now kids would lump me in with Hoàng in spite of everything I'd done to rip up and spit out these expectations. Consequently, I spent the last year of high school avoiding Hoàng. By the time we graduated, we had merely exchanged only semaphores of quick nods and glances across a silent expanse.

Recently, I looked at my high school yearbook. My senior portrait is ridiculous. I have a huge Morrissey-style coif, a shitty tight-lipped smirk on my face, and a small skull-and-crossbones pin on my lapel. It's so dated and silly, a picture that is as much a time capsule as it is an artifact of a young man's hubris. I'm an angry teenager in the photograph, and I know every fold and wrinkle of that rage and loneliness.

I flipped the page from my portrait to Hoàng's, then back to mine.

Hoàng Nguyễn's portrait is as plain as it is unremarkable. His hair is short, and it is parted cleanly on the left. He stares just to the right of the camera, dressed in a simple blazer and tie. It's the nicest outfit he probably has, and its simplicity gives the portrait a timeless feel.

You can't look at it and pinpoint it to a specific era or trend. It feels generic, but in its generality, it feels universal. Its lack of guile is stark.

Hoàng smiles. His face is broad, wide, and his eyes—his eyes are full of hope.

| I |

THE PLAGUE

1978, CARLISLE, PENNSYLVANIA

"Ba, what's my name?"

The Bee Gees's "Stayin' Alive," with Barry Gibb's siren falsetto, cut a suave silhouette from the radio's single speaker, the accidental theme song for the Trần family. My father sat at the table, my mother bustled over the stove, and I was saddled upon my rocking horse, corralled in the corner of our eat-in kitchen.

Four years old, I was pondering a playground encounter with a freckly blond boy who had asked me my name, and I didn't know what to say. I didn't know how to answer the most basic playground question: *What's your name?* It wasn't rocket science, but I answered it like the alien I was: "I'm not sure."

It wasn't that I *didn't* know my name. I didn't know *which* name to tell the boy. My family, as with all Vietnamese households, wielded a series of pronouns, nicknames, and endearments for me in addition to my given name, Phúc. I answered to all these monikers as my parents, aunts, uncles, and grandparents summoned me, upbraided me, teased me.

Con. Cưng. Cháu. Em bé. Honey. Sweetie. Kiddo. Baby.

My father shuffled some papers and was scribbling items into a ledger when I asked him. He replied without looking up. "Your name is Phúc. What kind of question is that?"

"No, I mean: What is my name *in English*?" I was hanging upside down from the rocking horse.

My father admonished me in Vietnamese, the lingua franca *chéz nous.* "Don't hang from the horse—you'll knock it over again and get hurt. We can't afford that." He meant the last part. Hunched at the kitchen table. Hacking through a jungle of paperwork. Scratching out a list of how much each paycheck was, how much they needed for bills, and what they could afford to send to my grandparents—his parents—still in Sài Gòn. A secondhand scarlet dictionary lay on the table next to him, thudding open as he consulted it for vocabulary that he didn't understand in the rustling white of bills and checks. *Amount Due. Gross Pay. Net Pay.* (Helpful hint for future English learners: you can't just look up the definitions of *net* and *pay* and put them together.) As he signed checks, he carefully wrote his name the American way. In Việt Nam, names were written and given as Last, Middle, First, but in America, we had to relearn our names backward (First, Middle, Last) to fit in. Do things backward to fit in—a fitting metaphor.

This is the earliest memory I have. Dangling from the horse's legs, bouncing upside down from the springed coils that held them, I was trapped indoors and trick-riding my plastic pony. My two-year-old brother, Lou, was still more accoutrement than accomplice, leaving me a lone ranger for playtime. With a napping baby, I had to find something quiet to do. Hanging upside down on the horse was my best effort at quiet.

My mother was preparing dinner, mincing onions, broccoli, and beef for a quick and cheap stir-fry, and she echoed my father's admonition. "Stop hanging from the horse, you monkey!" *Con khỉ. Monkey.* The sharp edges of her injunctions were always smoothed over with a sweet endearment.

Our apartment's kitchen, my ersatz O.K. Corral, was a twelve-by-nine rectangular combo eat-in kitchen—the apogee of postwar efficiency *and* the nadir of seventies style—a kitchen into which my parents had shoved a secondhand white-and-gold-flecked Formica kitchen table and four matching chrome seats with squeaky patched vinyl upholstery. The kitchen's oak laminate cabinets overflowed with three *nearly* complete sets of donated dishes, utensils, pots, and pans—an incongruous scrum of kitchenware. The rocking horse reared in the corner; past the sink, stove, and refrigerator rumbled the washer and dryer in the back. We ate, cooked, did the dishes, and washed (and dried) our clothes all within twelve feet. How was that for all-American economy? It was barely a four-yard running play, but what a score for our first down in America. A washer and dryer in the tightest end of the apartment. A winning combination.

That 660-square-foot apartment at 214 Walnut Bottom Road was our first home in Carlisle. The apartment complex, Colonial Square Apartments, was owned by one of our sponsors, Bill Hooke, a real estate developer, who had set aside a unit for our nucleus of four. Short-looped emerald-green carpeting padded the entire apartment. Stiff, durable, and easy to clean, the verdant wall-to-wall carpet rolled through every room, a tightly landscaped golf course, a putting green for a family with no sense of the long game. We didn't know that we'd be in this apartment for the next decade.

The unit was outfitted with used furniture that our American host families had assembled for us, the Trầns from the land-of-no-furniture. The Hookes and the Burkholders—American families in the luxury and safety of small-town America—were moved to help nameless refugees from the other side of the world. We received an array of household items, scattershot all over Maslow's hierarchy of needs: pots and pans, clothing, a dictionary, shoes, toiletries, toys, a small black-and-white TV, and the aforementioned plastic rocking horse. Having traversed the globe for four months from Sài Gòn to Guam to Wake Island to Fort Indiantown Gap and finally to Carlisle, Chánh and Chi Trần were grateful for any semblance of stability. They set up a home and were allowed to feel hopeful there on Walnut Bottom Road.

Hanging upside down, I awaited my father's answer to my question.

What's my name in English? This was *more* than just a four-year-old's questions about penises, vaginas, and where babies came from. This was a four-year-old's question about where *he* came from and why something as simple as his name had more than one answer.

Here's a vulgar family secret: *I've said my name wrong my entire life* because of this very moment.

In Vietnamese, my name is phonetically pronounced *fuhp*. It sounds like a baseball clapping into the lithe, oiled leather of a catcher's glove. *Fuhp*. Also, because Vietnamese is tonal (like its northern neighbor, Chinese), there's a rising tone to it, so your voice upswings like a Valley girl if you say it correctly. *FUHp*? The letter *c* at the end of my name isn't even pronounced like a *c* (thanks to archaic orthography and sound changes in the language)—it's a *p* sound.

My question precipitated a flowchart of choices for my father. In that moment, he had to make the decision that many immigrants are burdened with when their mother tongue is not compatible with their adoptive homeland's phonetics. This is the original game of broken telephone.

What are our choices? What do you do when Vietnamese doesn't sound like English? How do you pronounce *Phúc*? Well, I'm glad you asked, Mr. Trần.

Behind Door #1: Approximate the sounds (but stay true to the pronunciation)! *Fuhp*.

Behind Door #2: Make slight adjustments that don't sound like the original but seem to make sense with the spelling! *Fook*.

Behind Door #3: Pick a new name and bury that old name as a vestige of a country lost and forgotten! Americanize it completely! Peter or Paul? John or George?

My dad thought for a few minutes about my query and went with door number two: slight adjustments for English that don't sound like the original name but make sense with the spelling.

He answered my question. Finally.

"*Fook.* I guess your name is *Fook* . . . in English." He went back to the mathematics of survival.

And *Fook* was born. You know the poem about a path that diverges in a wood and you take the one less traveled? That's the one we took. Less traveled but easier to pronounce, as if easier-to-pronounce would make my path any smoother.

The vowel sound was different. No rising tone. Align the *c* at the end of my name with English orthography to make a hard, velar stop instead of the bilabial *p* sound. Vietnamese pegs squeezing into Colonial squares.

I mouthed the name. *Fook?* It didn't feel like *Fuhp* . . . No one said *fook* within the confines of our apartment. My parents and grandparents would never say it this way. *Fook* didn't exist except for out there, on the other side of our green hollow-core door. *Fook* was out there. In the real world. In America. In the real America. I had to get used to him. I had to respond to that name. I had to introduce myself as him. "*Fook?* Okay . . . *Fook.*" It wasn't a question anymore. It was a statement. An assertion. A declaration.

With that small and benign act of linguistic legerdemain, we rechristened *Phúc* with his alter ego *Fook.*

Fuck it. *Phuc* it.

1979

"Dad, what's a Wookiee?" I was lying in my father's lap on the floor of the living room, cradling *The Star Wars Storybook*, C-3PO and R2-D2 in their glossy glory on the cover.

"Let me see. . . . Ah, that's Luke Skywalker." My father read it aloud, enunciating each syllable slowly.

"And who's that?"

"That's Han Solo."

"Who's that?"

"That's Chewbacca. It says he's a . . . Wookiee."

"What's a Wookiee?" Neither of us knew. *Wookiee*? We went to the dictionary, as we always did, to look up words from the American story-books that my parents read us.

Wood . . . Woof . . . Wool . . . Woolen . . . No *Wookiee*. We looked again in the Star Wars book to make sure we were spelling it correctly. *W. O. O. K. I. E. E.*

I asked my father to look yet again. Still nothing.

"I don't know, Phúc. It's not in the dictionary. I don't know what it is."

"Really? Are you sure you're looking it up right?" I was incredulous. "Are you sure it's not in there? Aren't all words in the dictionary?" The dictionary had *all* the other words that we had looked up, and it never occurred to either of us that *Wookiee* was a made-up word, because who would make up a word? Wasn't the point of writing to use real words?

In my pique over *Wookiee*, I had more to complain about. "Also, you know the story *101 Dalmatians*? That dog's name is not Col-o-nel, Dad." We had a secondhand Little Golden Book of the Disney movie that my parents read to us often (as much for them to practice their English as it was to entertain their children).

My pivot from *Star Wars* to Disney surprised my father. He pronounced *colonel* as *call-a-knell*. "What do you mean? That's how it's spelled. *Col-o-nel*. That's pronounced *col-o-nel*."

"No, it's not! At show-and-tell last week, I brought *101 Dalmatians* into school, and I told them that my favorite character was Col-o-nel, and Derek Elkins laughed at me—everyone laughed at me! Derek told me it was pronounced *ker-nel*. It's *ker-nel*, Ba. Not *col-o-nel*." I was annoyed at his not being able to find *Wookiee*, but recounting the humiliation of mispronouncing *colonel* rushed back to my throat. I reddened, and my confidence in my father faltered. No *Wookiee*? I assumed that he couldn't find the word and not that the word didn't exist. Wookiee obviously did exist because it was in the *Star Wars* book. But *colonel*? The dictionary was still in front of us. "Just look it up! Look *colonel* up!"

He did. *COLONEL*. At least he found it (which galvanized my doubt that he was looking up *Wookiee* correctly). The mysterious diacritical marks did not help, but he pieced it together, pointing to the phonetic guide: / ˈkər-nᵊl /. "Well, I don't know what the upside down ə is, but there is an *r* there. Geez, that's strange. I guess it is pronounced *ker-nel*. Huh. English is hard." He shrugged.

Vindication. Increased doubt. "SEE? See? It is *ker-nel*!" I didn't have anything else to say. I needed to trust in my dad's ability to navigate the world at large, and I was already doubting him. He seemed adrift and lost, and I didn't know where to put my doubt. Five-year-olds were supposed to believe what their parents said. Maybe some kids' parents still had the golden nimbus of infallibility, but not my parents and not for me. Not Chánh and Chi.

I placed my disappointment squarely upon my parents without their knowledge. I needed to figure out English, to figure out Carlisle, to figure out my place in it. And I needed my parents to know the answers, because that's what kids need their parents to do: to know the world and to explain it to their kids. Without their expertise, the world felt uncertain and chaotic. How did you say certain words? Even if my parents said that this was how a word was pronounced, how could I be sure?

My early childhood memories are overgrown with thickets of faith and doubt. And in knowing the supposed truth, I furrowed a deep groove in myself for my doubt to root.

When I first read Camus's *The Plague* as a teenager, I read it with the sensational (and juvenile) lens of an apocalyptic survival story. Pestilence! Death! Rats! Camus's prose (in translation, at least) was yeomanlike, plodding steadily like the inexorable march of its disease. But I read it again, and its themes coalesced with our struggles, struggles that I had seen in my parents and in myself: the sinewy strain between faith and knowledge. In *The Plague*, Camus refers to the tension as a menace. As Dr. Rieux realizes that the plague is upon Oran, he no longer can enjoy the simple, ignorant pleasures of life. He knows the truth—the menace of knowing—and his knowledge conflicts with his faith, his desire to believe, his need to hope.

My faith in my parents' competence was withering as I watched them flounder. Misreading a storybook or laboriously translating the news-paper. Navigating the obliquely named sections of the grocery store. Looking for a toilet when it was euphemistically labeled Restroom. They wandered in the ineluctable labyrinth of America.

If they couldn't figure out small stuff like how to read a kids' picture book, how would they navigate the big picture? I already doubted that they could. And if I couldn't believe in my parents, in whom (or what) could I believe? In vain I groped about for an answer, and my doubt in them germinated, nourished by their shortcomings. My doubt con-taminated everything we did—and everything I wanted to believe in.

Faith. Knowledge. Doubt. They weaved in and out of our lives with a baroque intricacy, a background fugue to our stumblings on the stage.

APRIL 1975, SÀI GÒN

I remember none of this, but I know all of it. I know all of it because it is *the* family story.

I was not yet two when my maternal grandparents, Ông Bà Ngoại, made the decision that we were all leaving Việt Nam. My grand-parents both worked for the US embassy, and our family had been monitoring the thundering advance of the Việt Cộng army as closely as they were fretting the quiet unraveling of the Republic of Việt Nam. The call to evacuate came at the end of April, and my mother's parents made the arrangements for ten people: themselves, my mother and father, her sisters and brothers. I was their only grandchild (as my mother was the eldest). My father chose to accompany my mother and me, leaving behind his parents and his two youngest siblings who, without the proper paperwork, were unable to board the American transports. We waited for the bus that would take us to the airfield amid a swelling throng of frantic South Vietnamese. Bus after bus filled as desperate families pushed on, bulging them beyond capacity. We moved up the line, finally at the front, and were ready to board. Our bus pulled up; the doors opened. Half of my family members were already on board when—according to everyone's account—I began to shriek so loudly and inconsolably that our family agreed to deboard the bus.

My grandmother comforted us as we stood in line again. "Let's wait—it's okay. We'll take the next one." As we watched that bus pull away, it was struck by mortar fire and exploded, killing everyone on board. We lay on the ground, cowering. Some bystanders scrambled to the wreckage to help, but it was war, and a losing war at that. With the burning carcass of our bus still in view, we boarded the next bus, not knowing if it, too, would explode and kill us all. But it did not explode.

As we passed a checkpoint, the South Vietnamese military police separated the evacuees into two groups: able-bodied men into one area and women and children into the other. They were conscripting men of fighting age for fodder in their last stand against the North Vietnamese army in Sài Gòn, and all the young men from our cohort were detained. Heartbreak and terror. My father, along with my uncles, was held behind. He watched as my mother and I boarded a helicopter. One of my shoes came off with the push and pull of evacuation. We lifted off, leaving behind my shoe and my father. To where? How could we possibly find one another? The only plan was to escape from Sài Gòn, and in the din and chaos of the evacuation, our family was broken apart.

My mother and I landed on an aircraft carrier, took another helicopter, and landed at another base.

That was the beginning and the end. South Việt Nam collapsed. The army was in retreat. Government officials were fleeing. Even in that ending for us, in the great collapse of Sài Gòn, it was not the end that so many others suffered. It was not crashed planes, abandoned babies, or mass executions. In that end was our beginning. In that death lay the seeds of a new life. We weren't bodies in a shallow grave. We weren't the nude children in the war photos with our clothes burned off. We were fortunate even in the midst of such misfortune.

We landed in Guam, and from there, we were relocated to Wake Island. My mother was distraught. Had my father been killed? Did he manage to escape with my grandmother's connections to the embassy? How would he know where to find us? Thousands of evacuees, wrenched from loved ones, scratched out desperate notes and posted them on walls all across the airfields of Guam and Wake Island. *"If you see this note, please find us at . . ." "We're alive and at the camp at . . ."*

Luck of all luck: my father and uncles were reunited with us, weeks later on Wake Island. He had escaped Sài Gòn, and somehow, four thousands miles away and two weeks later, he arrived on the same island. In a refugee camp full of strangers, strangers uprooted by war, the splinters of our family were reassembled.

We needed to stay together, all twelve of us, and we said this as we filled out paperwork, talking to the camp staff, hoping to be sponsored. Only Ông Bà Ngoại knew English from their work at the embassy, but the army officers spoke too fast and about things they didn't know, using vocabulary they hadn't learned. *Refugee. Relocation. Asylum.*

The Trầns were being sent to Fort Indiantown Gap in Pennsylvania. Where was Pennsylvania? We didn't know; beggars were not choosers. Off to another camp. Upon our arrival, Red Cross volunteers and camp officials greeted us with clipboards and signs in English, which we couldn't read. Lutheran volunteers came from their parishes to help the military. My mother's side of the family was Catholic (my father,

Buddhist, had converted to Catholicism to marry my mother just before their wedding). The Lutherans found us sponsors, the Burkholders and the Hookes, while my family was still wondering what Lutherans were. Who were these sponsors? Were they Lutherans? Where did they live? Carlisle, Pennsylvania. So many names, all hard to pronounce. Our sponsors found us apartments and jobs for the adults, and by the fall, my mother peeled apples at an orchard and my dad drove a cement mixer. It wasn't being a lawyer, as he had been in Việt Nam, but it was a job.

We needed to blend in, adopt our new country as it had adopted us. My parents were navigating all the straits and inlets of living in America, holidays like Halloween and Thanksgiving, driving in the snow, the difference between ketchup and catsup.

Within the first year of arriving in the United States, my mother got pregnant. What was more hopeful (or more stupid) than having a baby as a refugee family? My brother, Louis, was conceived while we were at Fort Indiantown Gap, and he was born in March 1976. Louis was supposed to be named Lú (in accordance with a Vietnamese proverb), but my parents decided to Anglicize it to Louis, an American name with a French wink-wink to Việt Nam's Franco-colonial past. Louis's non-Vietnamese name was a small sliver of the diaspora. The assimilation had unknowingly begun while we were at the relocation camp.

Maybe my brother's birth was the most hopeful thing they could have done. Maybe it divined happy days ahead in America. How would we survive? How would we fit in? Who could say whether the hardest part was behind us or ahead of us?

We were tired and poor. We took one last huddle, knelt for a miracle play as we touched down in Pennsylvania that summer of 1975.

1979

Carlisle Tire and Rubber employed hundreds of workers, manufacturing small-diameter tires for lawn mowers and golf carts; the factory provided regular work, a livable paycheck, and good benefits for high school diploma holders—and recent immigrants.

A year after his arrival in Carlisle, my father shifted from his first, gear-grinding job of driving a cement mixer to the slightly less grinding gig of the tire factory. He had studied for and earned his GED at the local junior high through its night classes, and the equivalency diploma opened the factory doors for him. He worked on the quality-control team, checking tires for defects as they rolled off the manufacturing line. Because the tire factory operated 24/7, my father toggled through a biweekly rotation of a day, night, or graveyard shift. He was gainfully employed with a burgeoning grasp of English.

My father, twenty-nine years old, came home from the factory shifts reeking of freshly extruded tires. He wore the same work clothes several days in a row, and by the third day, his jeans and flannel work shirts smelled of burnt rubber, spattered with the dark spots of adhesives and black latex. Standing at a slight five feet five inches, he had shaggy black hair that was parted on the left, a pronounced underbite, and rogue stubble that sometimes rallied itself into a sparse mustache after a few weeks' growth, only to be repelled by the razor. In photos from these first years in Carlisle, his large dark almond eyes are bright and hopeful. He gives off an air that is a mix of youthful exuberance, American potential, and Vietnamese optimism.

At break time, a few of my father's coworkers at Tire and Rubber sidled up to him. "Hey, Tran. TRAN. How's it going?"

"It okay. How are you?" He didn't know that particular employee's name. He glanced at the name tag. "Oh, you name Mr. MacDaniels?"

The other workers laughed at my father's formality. "Oh, lookie! MacDaniels got a promotion! *MISTER* MacDaniels!"

Laughter? "You not Mr. MacDaniels?" More laughter.

"Oh no, I'm MacDaniels all right." MacDaniels grinned and shot a stern look at his entourage as they quieted. "Say, Tran: Do you know all about our customs here in America? You know, like breakfast and lunch and stuff like that?"

"Yes, sure."

"Christmas? You know about Christmas?"

"Yes, but it called *Noël* in Việt Nam because they French."

"Oh, that's good! Yeah, Noël . . . Right, Noël. And what do you brush before you go to bed, Tran?"

"Sorry?" Maybe my father had misunderstood the question.

MacDaniels bared his teeth and pointed to his pearly whites. "You know. Before you go to bed. What do you brush?" Some of the workers whispered, *He's gonna say it watch he's gonna say it.* "What do you call these?"

Smiling back, my father understood. "Oh yes! Of course. You brush your tit." The circle of workers exploded with laughter. "That wrong?" My father was confused.

"Oh no, you said it just right. *Teeth.* That's right. . . . You said it just fine. *But say it again.*"

"Your . . . tit?" The men behind him were laughing so hard, they had to wipe their eyes. MacDaniels smiled but kept his composure. My father knew they were laughing at him, but he didn't know why. "Don't you brush your tit before you go to bed? Is that wrong?" A bell rang out over the scene. Break time was over.

The circle dissipated as the assembly lines hissed and clanked to life. Saved by the bell. My father trudged back to his quality-control station, and at the second break, he avoided the cafeteria by sitting in his car, an old green-and-black Pontiac. Back to the line when the bell rang.

The abuses of the factory rolled off the assembly line, black and steaming like the tires they were manufacturing, and my father bore them with a stoic resolve, their barbs blunted by his ignorance of English and American social cues. Only a few factory workers targeted him among the many shuffling clock-punchers who were grinding out their paychecks, and their cruelty was offset by the kindness that our sponsors showed our family, week after week. More donations of clothes, family dinners, visits to check in with us.

Years later, my father always talked about the kindness of our sponsors, the incredible generosity of the Americans who helped our family of a dozen refugees. For their entire lives, my parents and grandparents maintained contact with our original sponsors, our annual holiday cards and graduation announcements serving as a declarative that we had made it, that we had been worth the rescue effort.

Random strangers had saved us. And random strangers were cruel to us, too. My father's coworkers were Americans, but not the same Americans who sponsored him. How hard was it for him to maintain his faith in the goodness of America? It was, indeed, harder for him to put his faith in the good ones. Who were the good ones? How could you tell? What could he be sure of?

Camus writes that in the midst of the plague, as the citizens of Oran are dying in droves, Dr. Rieux affirms himself in his work. What do you have control over? And what is beyond your control? As Camus's protagonist, Dr. Rieux offers an answer: when the world is coming apart, you do your job.

That my father and mother could do.

In the uncertain air of their new life in America, they inhaled the work. They lived and breathed work. They counted on it. They believed in it.

APRIL 1979

"Why don't you go play on that playground?" My parents were strolling with me and my brother when they spotted the playground and allowed us to run over to the swings. The playground was modest—just a small five-foot slide, some gymnastics rings, two swings, and a seesaw. My brother, three years old, clambered up the slide ladder as I hopped onto a swing and pumped my way into *Star Wars* orbit. My parents stood by the fence and Vietnamesed quietly with each other while Lou and I played. A little blond boy approached us.

"Why are you in my yard?" He hopped onto the other swing.

I swung past him. "What do you mean? We're just playing." He and I were on opposite arcs, his up to my down, my down to his up.

"This is my yard. I mean, it's okay to swing, but it's my yard."

I looked at the playground, noticing for the first time how close it was to the apartment building and how small it was. It wasn't a playground. It *was* his yard and his swing set.

I jumped off the swing. "Oh, I'm sorry. . . ." I started to run off. "Come on, Lou! This isn't a playground." Trying to leave before my embarrassment could turn into humiliation.

The sliding glass door of the adjoining apartment opened, and a woman with a bleach-blond bob, baby-blue tennis polo, white shorts, flip-flops, pink nail polish, and smooth, muscular legs appeared. A neighbor right out of *Three's Company*, a shimmering vision of network prime time, but we hadn't come and knocked on her door, and she wasn't waiting for us. I stopped, and she walked by me, patting me gently on the back of my head. "Oh, sweetie, you can keep playing. Go ahead. It's all right."

I vacillated, weighing what course of action would be more embarrassing, but my hesitation was broken by the boy's question. "Hey, do you like *Star Wars*?" And with that question, my embarrassment was quickly displaced by *Star Wars*, my otherness replaced by galactic familiarity.

"Yeah, I love *Star Wars*! Wanna play X-wings?" I slid back on the swing next to his and off we soared. His name was Tim. I told him my name a few times as he whipped past me. "Phuc: rhymes with Luke." He nodded affirmatively. Tim was a little younger than me. He liked *Star Wars*, I liked *Star Wars*, and that was enough for a best friendship.

His mother walked over to my parents and smiled widely, extending her hand. My parents shook her hand and bowed simultaneously, and their heads bobbed up and down as my father did most of the Englishing. Her eyes crinkled and she angled her head to one side (the universal posture for I'm-listening-as-hard-as-I-can). I could see my father's head tilting and tipping as he gestured in the direction of our apartment. I heard her say, "Come over anytime." She treated us as though we were like everybody else. With a smile and with kindness. The kindness that kept my parents' faith flickering.

1979, PHILADELPHIA

In those early years in America, my family (in various configurations of aunts, uncles, cousins) visited the grand trophies of the Northeast: Washington, D.C.; Niagara Falls; New York City (where my eldest aunt and her family had immigrated). But Philadelphia was not on the list, and without any friends or relatives there, we never made the two-hour drive east to bask in brotherly love until that year. En route my father drove while my mother read the directions to him, which he had written out ahead of time. My brother and I dozed, played, and fought in the back seat as the turnpike miles whirled away. My parents didn't bother to quiet us, too preoccupied with navigating the highways and exits to North Philly, my father parsing my mother's mangled pronunciations, which he had to retranslate. *What street? FRANG-LING CHREE. What? What street?! FRANG-LING CHREE! FRANG-LING CHREE! What street?! What is FRANG-LING CHREE? Is it Franklin Street? IS IT FRANK-LIN STREET?*

My father didn't say it any better than my mother. And we missed the turn. U-turn. We finally found Franklin and parked on a side street.

"Why are we here again?" I realized they had never told us the reason behind the road trip to Philadelphia.

"To pray for Mom," said my father, pulling back the curtain, no longer hiding us from what they had been keeping from their five- and three-year-old sons. How could they explain to their young children something that they themselves hardly understood? They didn't, and they chose not to disclose anything until they were compelled to, and there, in our Pontiac on the side streets of Philadelphia, they had to tell us the truth. Our innocence and ignorance had nowhere to hide in the narrow confines of our car. "Mom has to have surgery next week. They're going to cut her open to see if she has cancer in her lungs."

"What's cancer?" I asked. Lou deferred the cross-examination to me. "It's a disease."

"Is she really sick? Are you going to get it?"

"You can't get it from her, but we don't know what it is yet."

I turned to my mother. "Má, do you feel okay?"

"I feel okay, dear. I'm tired. And I'm having a hard time breathing." She smiled thinly for us. My mother and father kept it simple. Just the facts.

My father continued. "We drove here to pray for her at a church."

"Why?" We already went to church all the time—and by all the time, I meant every Sunday. "We came to Philadelphia to go to church?"

"We're going to pray to Saint John Neumann. He's a saint. You need to pray to him for Mom." My father's voice strained as he said the last few words, and I felt a tug of fear in my abdomen. My mother was scheduled to go into surgery the following week, and my parents were there in Philadelphia to exhaust their faith in God before they entrusted themselves to the knowledge of doctors. It was their last-ditch effort. The phrase *Hail Mary attempt* is figurative, but my parents' pilgrimage was a literal Hail Mary. Plural, actually. Hail Marys.

In the early summer of 1979, my mother started to have difficulty breathing. A trip to the hospital and several X-rays later, Dr. Castrina told my parents that she had polyps and tumors all through her lungs and trachea. My grandmother, who coincidentally worked at the hospital in Carlisle and had the best grasp of English in our family, had looked up the X-rays herself during her break time and told my father that it seemed dire. Dr. Castrina wrote some things on notepaper for them. In the scarlet Thorndike Barnhart dictionary, my father looked up *Hodgkin's lymphoma. Cancer. Mortality.* In their English, cancer sounded like *cang-say.*

Behind closed doors, my mother and father fretted and planned. Not knowing the Vietnamese words for *pathology* and *diagnosis*, Lou and I blithely watched *The Electric Company* in the living room and played in our bedroom, unaware of our parents' ills and anxieties.

The photos of my father from that time are stark: my brother and I are making faces, sticking out our tongues, but my father's face wears the worry, his eyes grim and heavy. He is staring directly at the camera with a steely look. He's thinking about a life without his wife, burdened with two small children, with the prospect of making ends meet on his $160-a-week salary at Tire and Rubber. The fourth year in his new country.

When I think back to this time, I don't recall my parents' worrying about the cancer's prognosis. I remember all the things in which my parents chose to have faith despite their uncertain future. They exhibited faith in its buoyant, naïve, dumb form: kept saving money; talked about plans for a home someday; hoped for better jobs; prayed for opportunities for me and my brother; prayed a lot in general.

That's why we were there in Philadelphia.

The sooty gray Gothic church stabbed a single sharp spire upward. The stonework and iron fence stoked my imagination, and I nudged Lou. "Whoa—look at that! Looks like a castle!"

My father corrected me. "It's a church." My parents walked ahead, my father limping along next to my mother (a motorcycle accident in Sài Gòn had put him in the hospital for six months and granted him a lifelong hiccup in his gait).

The shrine was brighter and shinier than our Saint Patrick's Church in Carlisle. As we pushed through the veils of candles and smoke, the altar loomed before us. My brother and I knew the protocol for church: no shenanigans or else. We were intimately familiar with "or else," and it was not an idle threat. Lou and I trailed behind our parents, our tomfoolery doubly checked by new and strange surroundings. The shrine was hushed in between mass services, but parishioners were free to enter and pray. My parents walked to the front toward the altar, where the prie-dieux arrayed themselves in perfect, religious order. Behind my parents, I tarried so that Lou and I could sit in a pew, but my parents marched us to the prie-dieux to kneel alongside them.

Then I saw the dead body.

We stood before a long glass case like the jewelry display at the Montgomery Ward department store. But in the place of Seiko watches or zirconia earrings, in this glass case stretched a dead body. And it was dressed up like a bishop.

"What is *that*?" Lou was aghast. "*Is he dead?* Who is he?" We both hesitated—my parents had given us no warning that on our first trip to Philly, we would be kneeling before a corpse.

My father leaned down between us and church-whispered, "That's Saint John Paul Neumann. He was just canonized as a saint. We're going to pray to him now for Mom." He knelt on the prie-dieu and took a rosary out of his pocket.

My mother knelt, and Lou and I knelt alongside them. "Dear God: please help my mom. Dear Saint John Neumann: please help my mom. Thank you." That was the extent of my praying abilities, and I repeated those prayers a few times before my mind wandered over to Saint Neumann's corpse and the waxy mask that covered his face.

My parents' lips fluttered their prayers to God, their rosary beads clicking quickly as they glissandoed from one Hail Mary to the next and on to the next. Lou and I stared at the glass coffin, running our eyes across its landscape of snowy fabric, the intricate embroidery, the ivory gloves. I stared so long at Saint Neumann that I thought I could see a rise and fall in his torso. Was he alive? Was he giving us a sign? I saw a twitch. I thought I saw him twitch. Then I convinced myself that I saw him twitch. Maybe he didn't actually do it, but I believed that I saw it. I stared for so long, I didn't know what I believed anymore.

"Did you see him move?" I asked. My brother shook his head, then immediately doubted himself.

"He didn't move, did he?" A younger sibling's pliability.

My parents finished their rosaries, made the sign of the cross, and stood up. My mother's eyes looked distant. My father's visage was down-cast, having expended all his effort on the prie-dieu, unable to look at the shrine anymore.

Lou was jubilant to be standing. "Are we done? Are we going to go home now?" Our boredom muddied time's passage, and we were unsure whether we'd been praying for thirty minutes or three hours.

"We just need to stop in the gift shop." *Gift shop?* We definitely did not have a gift shop in our church in Carlisle. But we also didn't have a dead body inside a glass case, either. With their dead body and gift shop, Philadelphia Catholics seemed to do things differently.

The cathedral gift shop did not have stuffed animals or snow globes or anything cool, instead vending rosaries, wallet prayer cards, ornate crucifixes, and other devotional items. Lou and I walked around, examining the prayer cards for various saints—the trading cards of Catholicism. I wasn't sure about their value, but how could you put a price tag on salvation? Did people trade these? Did you collect them? Was it a sin to trade three saints for a Jesus if you already had two Jesi? Or was it more like poker? Did Mary and four apostles make a full house of worship?

I was most intrigued by the illustration of Saint Neumann wearing a red hat and cape—far different from the waxy death mask that we had just seen in the shrine. His posture, the raised gesture of his hand, and the rays of light that emanated from his head all gave him a superheroic look, and I recognized the power pose.

My parents came over to usher us out, my mother clutching a small plastic bag that held her purchase. "What did you buy?" I asked.

She halted her careful gait to show us her purchase and pulled out a small, clear plastic case. It was padded with gray foam as if for jewelry, but I couldn't make out what was in it. I held up the plastic box closer to see the contents. Nestled against the foam was a sand-colored shard of wood. "Is that a piece of a chair or something?"

My father took the box from me. "It's a relic. Do you know what that is? A relic is a piece of the saint's body. This is a piece of his bone."

"Whaaaaat?!" My brother and I were aghast. "What do you do with a piece of a saint's bone?!"

"We believe that it has power. He is a saint, after all. We believe this relic has the power to help Mom." My father was firm in his conviction, unshakable. "Here, we got you and Lou these prayer cards." He handed us each a Saint Neumann trading card. Lou and I held our cards as we walked back to the car. I flipped mine over to look at Saint Neumann's "statistics," which were a prayer and his title patronage.

Saint John Neumann, Patron Saint of Immigrants and Sick Children. What about a sick immigrant with children? Close enough.

My mother clutched the bag to her chest as the turnpike guided our Pontiac home. She and Lou nodded off once the car was pinned on I-76 with an hour to go. I stood in the back, putting my chin over the front seat. "Hey, Ba . . . Hey. Hey, Ba." He was silent for a while.

"What is it? You need to sit."

"I will. But why did you ask God to forgive us and to forgive Mom?"

"What?"

"I heard you say that in the church. Why? Why did you ask God to forgive her?"

"Because that's what you do when you need help. You ask for forgiveness."

"But . . . what did Mom do?" He was silent again. "What did she do that she needed forgiveness for?"

"You need to sit. NOW! It's dangerous to stand." My father's rebuke woke my mother, who asked if everything was okay. "It's fine, dear— just go back to sleep. Phúc, SIT DOWN NOW!"

I sat again in the back seat, feeling frightened and alone despite being in the car with the whole family. I felt the fear and isolation of powerlessness. My head on the cold glass of the window, watching everything blur by. I felt the powerlessness of being a child, deepened by the desperation that my parents were feeling. A few hours ago, I learned that my mother might have cancer, that she was getting surgery next week, and that we had driven all the way to Philadelphia to pray for a cure. Praying for a cure or a miracle—which seemed as far-fetched and desperate as could be. Even I understood that, and knowing that terrified me.

In the logic of my mother's theology, which was a muscular, if simple, Catholicism, good things happened to good people, and bad things happened to bad people. That was the nature of justice. That was the nature of God. Even in the aftermath of Việt Nam's civil war, some of my family members clung to this idea of divine or deserved justice. Our family had escaped. We had been rewarded for our probity. We deserved what we got.

If that were true, how did we understand my mother's cancer? Cancer was undoubtedly a bad thing, and my mother had it. Did that make her a bad person? But my mother was the kindest person I knew. Did she deserve cancer? My parents couldn't believe that even if it was their logic: Could bad things happen to good people? To people who didn't deserve bad things? Did God allow that?

For my parents, that was unimaginable. Their blind faith in the power of prayer and the goodness of God was immovable.

While my mother had surgery, we stayed with Ông Bà Ngoại. I don't remember for how many days, but one afternoon, my grandmother told Lou and me that we could go home. We bounded up the stairs at Walnut Bottom Road and saw her. My mother. Frail. Tired. Bandaged.

"MÁ!" Lou and I were beside ourselves with relief.

She Vietnamesed feebly. "Oh, sweetie . . . I'm okay. I'm going to be okay. Be gentle though."

"Where is it? Did they cut you?" No understatements or soft-pedaling. I wanted to see the scar.

"Yes, right here." She opened the top of her shirt and my brother let out a cry. Her neck was bandaged along the bottom of her throat. She lifted the gauze to show us: across the width of her neck was a precise incision that went from side to side, sutured together. It looked like someone had slit her throat (they had), and from the front, her head looked like it was stitched onto her body (it wasn't). Her black hair, falling on either side of her languid face, framed her seam all the more. No one expects to see their mother's head Gothically sewn onto her body à la Mary Shelley.

Despite my worry for her health and her wound, I hugged her gingerly around the waist. "I'm so glad you're home, Má."

From behind, my dad spoke. "They didn't find any cancer. Nothing. No tumors. No polyps. *Nothing*. The X-rays were wrong. Her throat and lungs are fine." We didn't see my father's face, but his voice was shaking, and in his voice, I heard the sharp and distinct confidence of his faith. "They didn't find any cancer, thank God. It's a miracle. *A miracle.*" He meant that last part—he believed it. I didn't know what to believe. I didn't know what a miracle was. I only knew what I could see: that my mother was alive.

My dad sat at the kitchen table, the tape recorder in front of him—a rectangular box with faux wood paneling and a silver speaker. He held me in his lap as he read from the newspaper. He pressed the record button and began reading.

"Thee ree-sen ee-ven in dee Midduh Eest ah affec-teeng dee price of gaz all over dee wuhld . . ." He read on for a few more paragraphs before stopping and rewinding the cassette tape. He pressed play, and his voice, a little higher and squeakier, wobbled out from the perforated speaker part.

He turned to me. "How did that sound? Did I sound like an American?"

"No, not really."

"What word sounded wrong? I think it's pretty good." He wanted to do better.

"Well, I don't know what all those words mean, but the word *world*: you said it as *wuhld*. It's *wer-ld*. There's an *r* in there."

"*Wulhd.*"

"*World.*"

"*Wulhd.*"

"*Whir-ld.* Try saying it like it's two sounds. *Whir. Uld.*"

"*Wuhld.* There! I did it!"

"No. *Whir-uld.*" This went on for fifteen more minutes, then my dad moved on to other difficult words like *street* (he said *chreet*) and *girl* (he said *gull*). Over and over, he would rerecord himself reading, listen to his recording, and jot notes down in his pocket notebook.

"*Wuhld. Wuhld. Wuhld.* Geez . . . English is so hard to pronounce."

"It seems fine, Dad. I mean, I know what you're saying."

"No, it needs to be better. It's not good enough for you to just understand me. My accent is terrible—you sound like an American already. It's great. Okay, it's bedtime. Time for you to brush your teeth." He pronounced the last word with emphatic articulation. *Brush your tee. Th.* It still came out sounding like *tit*, but I knew what he meant.

From the bathroom, I could hear him still practicing as I brushed. "Thee ree-sen ee-ven in dee Midduh Eest ah affec-teeng dee price of gaz all over dee wuhld . . ."

Why was it so hard for him and so easy for me? Why couldn't he just say it the way it was pronounced?

The first bricks had already been laid for me to doubt my father, and my doubt cast a long shadow over my faith in him even as he placed so much of his own belief in the importance of mastering English, in the American dream, in a boundless future for his children.

He had so many things to fuel his faith. We were alive. We had a roof over our heads. We had a sage-green Pontiac. These weren't the compacted dirt roads of Việt Nam. These were the smoothly paved highways of America. Land of the free. Home of the brave.

"Can we stop to get McDonald's?" My grandfather pointed to the Golden Arches in the distance as we drove home from the mall. McDonald's was pronounced *Magk-Doh-Noh*. Did I already mention how hard American consonant clusters are for native Vietnamese speakers?

"Why don't we just go through the drive-through?" My father vetoed the idea of dining in at McDonald's. "We can just get food and eat it at home."

"What does it matter?" my grandfather insisted. "We can all eat in the store. That's fine. We'll do that." According to Vietnamese hierarchy, my father should have deferred, but he didn't.

My father rebutted. "There're too many of us." Too many? Five of us sat comfortably in the car. "They probably don't have room." The Pontiac had pulled into the driveway and idled in the drive-through lane.

"Why don't we go in? It's all the same." My grandfather huffed his annoyance that my father was not deferring, and Ông Ngoại's patriarchal authority was rendered moot by the smooth pleather of the passenger seat. He was not behind the wheel.

"There're too many of us." My father's voice was agitated. "There're too many of us, and people will stare. Who knows what will happen? Do you know how they treat me at the factory? You know how they laugh at me? What will happen when they see so many of us?"

This was the menace of knowing.

I didn't understand the anxiety that my father felt, but I eventually would. That was my inheritance. The anxiety of being stared at. Maybe someone would walk past our table and tell us to go back to our country. Maybe they would be rude to us. Maybe they wouldn't serve us. He didn't want to subject us to that and, in the driver's seat of the Pontiac, ushered us through the timeless tradition of the drive-through. Out of sight at the drive-through, we were like everyone else. That is, until we spoke into the intercom.

The car thrummed as we pulled up to the illuminated speaker, which crackled and barked, haloed in the translucent glow of all the holy glories that McDonald's had to offer. My dad had to repeat his order several times, and he started each time with "Hello. How are you? I would like . . . tree chee-burka, two Bic Mac, tree fend fry. No, tree. TH-REE.

Yes, fend fry. No. Tank you . . . yes, tank you." I repeated our order from the back seat with perfect clarion enunciation.

The aroma of beef-tallow fries and hamburgers warmed the car, and as my uncle Thái held the bags next to me, my father called back to us. "Save the container for the Bic Macs, okay? We can use them for sandwiches for your school lunches." After dinner, we washed and rinsed the yellow Styrofoam containers carefully and set them on the drying rack.

At lunch the next day, I pulled out a pale yellow Big Mac container from my lunch bag, laying it next to a banana and the pint of milk that was handed out to everyone.

Craig crowed his approval. "Holy moly! You got a Big Mac for lunch! You are so lucky!" Other kids chimed in, amplifying the chorus of approval. I beamed.

Then I pulled out a cheese sandwich—a homemade one, not even grilled.

The table's waves of envy reversed into a riptide of laughter as I held my sandwich over the opened clamshell container, the supposed pearl of a McDonald's sandwich now in reality just a square of cheese pushed between two slices of white bread. I ate it wordlessly, staring at the Big Mac container with disgust.

Amid the laughter, Shawn asked if there was really a banana in my banana, and the jokes rolled on from there. *Was there really milk in my milk?*

I had thought that my parents, in their thrift, were ingenious for reusing the McDonald's packaging, but no one else did—at least, no one at Mooreland Elementary School. My admiration for the package soured, and from that point on, whenever my mom packed my lunch in a Big Mac container, I would break it, purposefully pushing my thumb through the top or snapping the clasp so that my parents wouldn't use them anymore for my lunches.

"I guess these aren't as good as they look." My mother tossed another one in the trash.

My father scratched his chin. "That's strange. Mine has been fine for months. I think Phúc is just too rough with them. . . . I can keep using them. Just give him a plastic bag." My father continued using the Styrofoam containers, a small bit of scrimping so that his son could be spared the ignominy of it and be like everyone else.

That was the delusion. We *weren't* like everybody else. I now had the menace of knowing, and it infected everything I did.

I was reminded of it constantly in ways large and small: my parents' wobbly accents as my English became arrow-straight, the long and confusing searches in the grocery stores for simple items, the stares from strangers at the mall. These reminders that my family was not a normal American family—that we didn't look like the rest of our town, that we were from somewhere else—wove into my very fabric a need to belong, a need that was a glittering and slippery yarn. I would never be able to untangle it from who I was and who I wanted to be, and it seemed that if I tugged on this thread, everything would unravel and leave me exposed.

2

CRIME AND PUNISHMENT

Violence—physical violence—simmered as an unstable agent in my family's chemistry. Parents spanked and beat their kids. Siblings struck one another. Cousins punched cousins. Grandparents smacked their grandkids. Pillow fights turned into fistfights. Am I missing anything?

I had no reference for what was normal. Behavior that I now in adulthood recognize as excessive, I accepted wholesale as a child. My family's thermodynamics were volatile and explosive, but this was our reality: violence and the threat of violence darkened the rosy tint of childhood.

Sometimes, violence settled disputes, and sometimes it splintered into more problems. It was how my family expressed their feelings of anger and disappointment and even love. They beat us because they cared for us because they loved us because they beat us.

Maybe you were the victim of violence. Maybe you were the perpetrator. Maybe you were just an innocent bystander. At some point in the Trần family, you would be all three. The troika.

Violence lashed Dostoevsky's *Crime and Punishment* to my childhood. The violence of Dostoevsky's world is woven throughout *Crime and Punishment,* stitched into the very language of the novel's narrative. In his tale about a desperate college student who murders two helpless women, Dostoevsky plunges his reader into a paranoid world where violence hangs thick in the air. The violence and assault of his raw imagery, feverish and unyielding, is indelible. This was a world I knew from experience, a world I had grown up in, a world where violence was potentially everywhere.

NOVEMBER 1979

I was in Ông Bà Ngoại's apartment, watching a rerun of *Land of the Lost,* when I heard my grandmother yelling at my uncle Thái (who was ten at the time). All kids take great interest in the woes of other children, so I immediately abandoned the world of Sleestaks and stop-motion dinosaurs to peer around the corner from the safety of the living room. My grandmother was berating Thái, whose nose was bleeding. His black hair, in an asymmetrical bowl cut, was yanked up and disheveled.

My grandmother was apoplectic, having amassed unstoppable momentum. "That bike was a gift! Why didn't you take care of it?! Do you know how nice the Hookes were to give you that bike?! And now you lose it?!" The timbre of her voice peaked at a fervid pitch.

Wearing oversized rose-colored bifocals, Bà Ngoại, my grandmother, reigned as the undisputed heavyweight champion of the Trần family. At forty-seven years old, she had birthed ten kids over two decades, displaying a will and a uterus of iron. With her black hair in a bun, she powdered her face to lighten her already fair complexion, and her blush, which was actually lipstick rubbed in light circles on her cheeks, gave her a carnival visage. Every morning Bà Ngoại drew thin eyebrows on herself, penciling them slightly higher than her natural brow line. Her high brows gave her a look that—depending on the occasion—signaled alertness, alarm, or surprise. At that moment in her vexation, the high brows gave her an erumpent intensity. She was not looking for a judges' decision. She was in the ring to knock someone out.

Bà Ngoại's ire wasn't the anger of personal damages but the anger of being shamed, a singular dishonor that she and my parents bore heavily. If our elders felt that we kids had done something to embarrass them or to cause them to lose face, our punishment was administered as if the entire town were watching and judging them as parents. Puritanical in its purity and unflinching in its deliverance. The severity of our punishment was commensurate to their own perception of their parenting. That is to say: the *worse* you were beaten or punished, the *better* they seemed to be as parents.

Thái tried to explain. "I didn't lose it—some kids beat me up and *took* it! That's not losing it!" He offered the explanation and—*CRACK*—Bà Ngoại slapped him across the face.

"DON'T INTERRUPT ME!" She punctuated her reminder with another savage blow. Thái's already bloody face now bore the pale imprint of her hand reddening against his cheek. She continued with a withering dismantling of my uncle, who avoided eye contact for fear of another blow. Her every utterance struck the point about how it was an embarrassment to the family. Jolted by the hard slap that she meted out to my uncle Thái, I made an indelible mental note: do not *ever* interrupt Bà Ngoại unless I wanted to be slapped. She stormed out of the room, still the defending champion. Bà Ngoại. Undefeated record. Thái went outside to sit on the apartment steps.

Two of Thái's older brothers, Chương (who was twenty-one) and Chí (who was eighteen) followed him. I slipped along behind them, abandoning *Land of the Lost* altogether. Real drama trumped fake drama. I knew better than to speak—that was the first rule of being one of the younger kids. Talking out of turn got you a punch in the shoulder or a blow across the back of the head.

Thái wiped the blood from his nose, the imprint of his mother's hand still pulsing on his left cheek, a ruddy reminder for us all of the matriarch and her unquestioned authority.

"What happened?" Chí comforted Thái.

"I was riding around the cemetery and some kids knocked me off my bike and took it. They told me to go back to my country." I was bewildered by the details of his story. You could just take something from someone by hitting them? A complete stranger could just walk up to you, hit you, and take your bike? How did you get your bike back then?

The second part of Thái's story was equally baffling. *Go back to your country.* What did that even mean? What country? The one we had lost? That made as much sense as telling us to run back *inside* a burning building because we weren't welcome *outside*. The import of it, the insult of it, was lost on me, and selfishly, I was much more terrified of the first proposition: the bike stealing. Shameless theft without consequence was horrific to consider.

Chí and Chương Vietnamesed with each other quietly and then turned to Thái. "Let's go look for your bike."

"Really?" Thái straightened up.

"Yeah—*Phúc*, you stay here." I didn't argue with Chí, knowing my low place in the hierarchy. My three uncles headed off in the direction of the Molly Pitcher Cemetery, a block away, where Thái had been riding his bike. The cemetery's stone-hewn wall was visible from the top of the apartment steps, so I stood, watching and waiting.

I pondered the idea of random strangers taking things from us. How could I protect myself from it? Did these people look a certain way? What distinguished the nefarious strangers from the benevolent ones? My thoughts did laps on the short track of kinderlogic as I looked past the parking lot toward the cemetery.

After half an hour, I saw my three uncles walking back from the cemetery, and as they got closer, I noted that Chí's face was flush, Chương seemed disheveled, and Thái's crimson nosebleed flashed red. They weren't speaking to one another, and their sluggish pace suggested defeat. But as they got closer, instead their stride strengthened with an air of confidence—defiance even. It was not the limp of defeated boys.

I saw that Thái's stolen bike was being pushed between Thái and Chương. They had taken it back from the other kids, their knuckles bloodied and faces mottled.

Violence had counterbalanced violence. Maybe violence *could* exact justice, and if it wasn't justice, at least violence could recover what was lost. And even if winning wasn't justice, it still felt better than losing. Maybe violence could make things right.

Lou perched at the kitchen table, drinking from a sippy cup. I seized the cup from him to drink some of his juice, a deprivation that immediately caused him to shriek.

"*PHÚC!* STOP IT! I'm trying to cook!" My mother stormed over, wrenched the sippy cup from my hands, and gave it back to Lou. "Leave him alone!" My mother. Twenty-eight years old, barely five feet tall, with long jet-black hair that cascaded to her waist, delicate features, fair complected, and large dark eyes that were emphasized by the striking frame of her hair. Her hands were hardly larger than mine, and her wedding band wobbled loose on her finger. Her eyes always had clouds of worry lingering at their edges regardless of whether she was laughing or crying, worry that I assume sprung from having a child at twenty-two, fleeing Sài Gòn at twenty-four, having another child at twenty-five after a difficult pregnancy, and receiving a cancer prognosis shortly thereafter.

Of course, I didn't leave Lou alone. I grabbed the sippy cup and pinched him on the arm before running around the corner. It wasn't even a matter of my wanting a drink now. I felt like pinching my little brother. I was shrieking and yelling as I ran around the apartment, when my mother marched around the corner and grabbed the cup again.

"I SAID STOP IT!" It was a game now. Game on. I could smell rice boiling over and charring on the stove. "Look what's happening now!" she yelled as she noticed the rice pot clanking and clacking. My mother's worst profanity was *trời đất ơi—oh my heavens*. I could hear her muttering *trời đất ơi* under her breath as I made a third attempt at pilfering Lou's sippy cup.

I snatched the cup and sprinted to my bedroom. Victory. I could hear my brother crying again as I hid, giggling. The juice was all but gone, but I chewed on the hard plastic top, too busy to care or notice.

I didn't even see the blow coming.

A burst of white flashed in my eyes like a camera bulb, and a dull burn seared the left side of my head, near my eye. My mother had rolled up a magazine, and with her improvised cudgel, she had struck me as hard as she could on the left side of my head. *THWACK.* "Give Lou back the cup! *Trời đất ơi!*" Her blow capitalized the seriousness of her demand. Game over. She snatched the cup from me, grousing while she stomped back to the kitchen to cook.

In the woozy wake of the blow, I held my head and wept on the bedroom floor until my mother barked at me for dinner. When I rounded the corner into the kitchen, I sniffled an apology, my chin and cheeks still dripping with tears.

She turned around and let out a sharp cry. *"Trời đất ơi! Trời đất ơi!"* I thought I was in trouble again and flinched, but she cupped my face and she herself began crying. *She* was crying? Her hands were covered in blood. A lot of blood—my blood. I didn't know that I was bleeding.

The rolled-up magazine had split my temple, next to my left eye, and there gaped a large, two-inch gash. My mother sobbed. "I'm so sorry! Oh, Phúc, I'm so sorry!" I winced as she wiped a cold washcloth over the cut. Wiping. More wiping. Still more wiping.

Then some quick triage. A Band-Aid was applied to my head, brief and tender.

My father was still working second shift at the factory, so my mother and I shared our meal in silence as Lou babbled on. The side of my head pulsed under the Band-Aid.

Later that night, as she tucked me into bed, my mother inspected the gash once more and stroked my cheek. "I'm so sorry, Phúc. I'll never hit you again. Never."

It was, in fact, the last time that my mother ever struck me. The first time? The first time is lost in the fuzziness of a child's recall and the blur of so many other assailants. As my mother now tells this story, the scar along my left eye is a constant reminder, an ever-present censure, of the lasting harm that a moment's anger could inflict. She tells this story as her own cautionary tale.

But it's not the scar, whose small crease is still visible decades later, that I remember the most. It's her apology—the only apology that I ever received from someone for striking me.

The only apology ever.

1980

Do kids know whether they're rich or poor? Do rich kids know that they grow up without any wants or needs? That they get everything they desire? What about poor kids?

I can tell you that I knew we were poor early on. I knew that I was wearing discarded clothing that someone had donated to us. I knew what *no* meant when I asked for a two-dollar Han Solo action figure at the store—it meant we didn't have enough money for it. Like the violence I lived in, our poverty had no context. Adults like to say that kids are resilient, and that's true, but it's because they don't know anything different. Kids are kids, and their ignorance allows them to accept things as they are. That's their resilience.

Bà Ngoại and I were at Willow Street Variety, a small, locally owned grocery store in town that carried a limited selection of produce. I had tagged along because the grocer had a spinning rack of comic books, which I perused while my grandmother basketed milk, sugar, and butter. By the comic books fluttered magazines, newspapers, and small cardboard boxes of trading cards. I chose to look at an issue of *Captain America*, skipping over the trading cards, which feted players whose names I didn't know, excelling in games whose rules I didn't understand.

But then, looking up from *Captain America*, I saw the unmistakable image of Darth Vader emblazoned on a waxy yellow Topps package among the trading cards. *See ya later, Cap'n. The dark side is calling me.* I picked up two packages and felt the rectangular silhouette of gum on the obverse side. I held them to my nose to inhale the powdery sweetness. *Star Wars* trading cards—surely we could afford them.

"Bà Ngoại, can we buy this?" It was twenty-five cents per pack.

"No, we can't. We have just enough money to buy butter and cooking oil." I didn't realize that we were buying groceries with food stamps nor did I know what food stamps were.

"What about just one pack?" I begged, stunned that we didn't have even twenty-five cents.

"No, put them back. We have to go home now."

I walked back to the rack of mustachioed sports heroes, and as I approached the cards, I cast aside my caution and morality. I slid the two *Star Wars* packets into the waistband of my shorts. If I'd known the expression "fuck it" at that age, I would have said it. My magnetic love of *Star Wars* redirected my spinning moral compass, forcing the arrow to point toward Darth Vader. I continued to walk casually past the Topps display and met my grandmother at the counter where she was finishing her transaction.

"Are you ready to go, Phúc?"

"Yup!" We held hands on the walk home as I felt the waxy packets rubbing against my sides under my shorts. I harbored no remorse for the theft, looking forward only to opening up the cards as soon as I could.

When we got to my grandparents' apartment, my grandmother went to the kitchen to make lunch. I sat behind the couch (because hiding behind the couch was the extent of my criminal master plan) and opened the trading cards. Grand Moff Tarkin! C-3PO! Sand People! I examined the cards and flipped them over. Some cards had trivia on the back, others were parts of a larger jigsaw puzzle, while others had behind-the-scenes details. I popped both pieces of trading-card gum into my mouth, chewing them into stiff, saccharine shards.

I fanned the cards out to look at them further, any guilt that I might have felt about stealing them being quickly detruded by my delight of having twenty-four trading cards. *I would be the envy of my class*, I thought as I looked over my booty.

The gum and salivation made me thirsty, and I went to the kitchen to get water.

My grandmother heard me chewing loudly. "What are you eating?" she asked, her high brows raised as high as they could go. Not good.

"What? Oh . . . uh, gum." I could see things were going to end badly.

"Where did you get gum?!"

"From the, uh . . . the . . . uh . . ." Oh boy.

She barreled into the living room and saw the trading cards strewn across the floor behind the couch. I winced, their discovery heralded by yelling and screaming; I didn't know most of the words she was saying in Vietnamese, a harbinger of worse things to come. Her high brows twitched. I remembered Uncle Thái, and I braced myself for her trademark right hook across the face.

"YOU STOLE THE CARDS?! YOU STOLE THEM?! DO YOU KNOW WHAT WILL HAPPEN IF YOU GET CAUGHT?! THEY'LL SEND US ALL BACK TO VIỆT NAM! THAT'S WHAT THEY WILL DO!"

This made no sense to me, so I started to speak. "For stealing trading cards? *Really?*" Apparently, I had forgotten the grave motto of not interrupting Bà Ngoại. My impudent retort hurled my grandmother over reason's edge. She grabbed my ear in the sharp pincers of her index finger and thumb and pulled me into the kitchen, my whole body stuck in the tractor beam of her grip. We had stopped at the kitchen counter, and I heard the drawers clanging open and jangling shut until she released my ear.

"PUT OUT YOUR HANDS!" she demanded.

"What?"

"I SAID PUT OUT YOUR HANDS! IN FRONT OF YOU! PALMS DOWN!"

I didn't want to get slapped in the face, so I complied. Hands out in front of me. Palms down. What was she going to . . . *CRACK!*

A blinding pain shot through my fingers and knuckles as my grandmother shrieked in Vietnamese, "ONE!" She struck my outstretched hands with the handle end of heavy garment scissors. I started screaming immediately in alarm and pain. (At least she held the scissors safely with the pointed end in her fist.)

"BE QUIET AND KEEP YOUR HANDS OUT! I'M COUNTING TO TEN!"

I put my hands behind myself, but she grabbed me by the ear again. "DO YOU WANT ME TO COUNT TO *TWENTY*?"

"Nooooo . . ." Tears cascading, hands slowly stretching out. My diminutive grandmother, high brows on high alert, scissors in hand, counted from two to ten, each number punctuated by a hard rap on my knuckles, which reddened and split. In between each number, she yelled variations of "THEY'LL SEND US ALL BACK TO VIỆT NAM IF THEY CATCH YOU!!!" It was a searing eternity until the number ten arrived, snapping with one last, hard rap on my bleeding knuckles, the scissors and the number clacking in a painful two-part harmony.

"Now go kneel in the corner." Kneeling in the corner was Vietnamese time-out, and I had knelt in every corner of the apartment. You knelt on the floor with your hands crossed in front of yourself, facing inward in the corner, sometimes for minutes, sometimes closer to an hour. If, however, you were especially naughty or deserved a time-out deluxe, you would kneel on uncooked grains of rice. Yes—*hard grains of rice.* In the first few minutes of kneeling on them, the rice would feel sharp and uncomfortable, but after ten or fifteen minutes, they needled into your kneecaps, growing keener the longer you knelt. If you got kneeling-in-the-corner-on-rice, your knees would have tiny, painful divots in them for hours after.

My grandmother walked past the corner and threw a handful of rice on the floor just as I stepped into the angle. "KNEEL THERE UNTIL I TELL YOU TO GET UP." I didn't look at her, but I could sense how elevated her high brows were. Not a word from me.

I knelt, arms crossed, surreptitiously massaging my lacerated knuckles, which throbbed and distracted me from the rice that was boring into my bare knees. Maybe I was supposed to think about the morality of stealing, the crime of it. Maybe I was supposed to fear the punishment so much that I would never steal again. The truth, though, is that I ended up thinking about why we couldn't spare twenty-five cents for the trading cards and how to avoid getting caught if or when I stole something again.

If I doubted whether we were poor, I knew it now, beaten sore by the reality of it. I didn't think about the abstractions of crime and punishment. I thought about the concrete realities of cause and effect: I got caught, and I got punished. I stole cards because we didn't have the money to buy the cards. I had asked to buy something often enough to know that the answer was always no. Poverty—was *that* the crime?

Poverty is no crime—Dostoevsky writes this phrase twice in *Crime and Punishment.* Crime is a symptom of poverty; poverty is the real evil. I'd like to think that our poverty was what precipitated my crime. Maybe it did, but maybe it was the feeble morality of a six-year-old—because what six-year-old can do the right thing when faced with *Star Wars* trading cards?

I knelt for an hour in the corner, grains of rice stabbing into my knees, knuckles bloodied, wishing that we had had the money to buy the trading cards. I didn't hate Bà Ngoại and I didn't hate being caught for stealing. I hated the crime of being poor.

MAY 1980

Tim, Helen, Lorie, and my cousins Ann and Tiên gathered with me, spellbound in a circle. Speechless. Awestruck. Lou came running to see what all the excitement was about.

In the middle of our assembly, a majestic black crow stood, its left wing hanging open and limp. The rest of its sleek sylph-like body sharply contrasted the jagged angle of its broken wing, and its stray feathers, jutting out like black claws, scraped on the pavement. The crow cawed intermittently, keeping us at bay as though this mob of small humans intended to kill it. In fact, we were delighted to see such a large bird up close. Amid cries of *what should we do?* and *give it some room* and *don't scare it,* we kept the crow penned in as it hopped around in an elliptical orbit. After a few minutes, it wearied, sat motionless, and squawked weakly.

My cousin Tiên suggested that she get her dad, Chú Hữu, and we all agreed that this was a good idea. Tiên's dad could help the crow, and they lived just four doors down from us in the Colonial Square complex. Chú Hữu. Small, sinewy, muscular. Always with a joke and jaunty step, a smile as wide as his teeth were irregular, a glint in his eye, and a plan for something better. If we made a snow fort, he made it bigger. If we were riding bikes, he'd show us how to power-slide. Chú Hữu took everything to the next level.

He came outside, his flip-flops clapping as he padded over to the scene with a wide smile and a cocksure stride, Tiên bouncing alongside him. More neighborhood kids had come out, and a few other kids who had passed by stopped to admire the crow. "What's going on over here?" He rubbed his forearms as if he were about to wrench something loose.

"The crow's hurt. Look at its wing!" Different kids called out various ideas, a geyser of the good, the bad, and the ridiculous. *Take it to the doctor's! Someone get a bandage! Let's take it inside—we can keep it as a pet!* None of us thought past our initial suggestions. The crow was hurt, and we wanted to help it, wanted to do *something*—something seemed better than nothing.

Walking slowly toward it, Chú Hữu sidled through our perimeter. He bent himself at the waist, and the crow, which now cawed and croaked more loudly, hopped around but remained corralled by us kids, who stood fast. Chú Hữu made a soothing *shush* as he knelt even lower—and closer—to the crow. It stopped flapping and made a few small croaks as he picked it up gingerly. In the hands of an adult, the crow seemed even more magnificent and mysterious. Its body stretched the length of Chú's forearm, striking a regal profile with its deep black and purple against his white tank top. It hardly struggled as it was cradled in his arms.

Shssssssssssssh. Shssssssssssssh. It settled with his soothing susurrations.

Lou was particularly agitated. "What's he going to do with the bird?"

"He'll help it—don't worry. Maybe he'll take it to the doctor?" I assured Lou even as I privately questioned my own confidence in Chú Hữu.

Chú gently held the crow out in front of him and tipped it lovingly from side to side, eyeing it. Was the other wing broken? Was it just the left wing? How could he fix it? We had seen Chú repair all things mechanical, and we believed that he would find a way to do the same for the crow. The tenderness with which he cradled it affirmed our hopes.

"He's definitely going to help it!" we chattered to one another.

He started walking away with the crow, and our circle parted for him and the bird as we fell in line behind them. He led the way, holding it in front of his body, both hands extended. The ensemble painted a peculiar scene: a diminutive Vietnamese man in flip-flops and cutoff jeans walking slowly up a grassy hill, holding a shadowy crow in his hands, while a dozen kids paraded slowly behind him, excitedly calling out different remedies. It was a beautiful day in the neighborhood. Our optimism floated in the air around us as we promenaded behind him. A few kids were trying to name it. Humanize it. Empathize with it. *His name is Mr. Feathers!*

We followed Chú to the dumpsters of the apartment complex.

"Why are we at the dumpsters?" Lou wondered aloud. The dumpsters were closed in by weathered stockade fencing, marking off a square area that hid six large metal garbage bins.

Chú Hữu, silent other than the soft clapping of his flip-flops, stepped up to the dumpster area and asked one of us to open the gate. Tim, still my best friend in the neighborhood, hurried over and clacked it open.

We stood around the yawning gate in a wide half circle, wondering how Chú Hữu was going to fix the crow in the dumpsters. Maybe the dumpster was a quieter place for the crow? Maybe it would feel less agitated with fewer people around? It definitely seemed less agitated.

Chú Hữu lowered the crow over the edge of the nearest green dumpster. It flapped its right wing as it slid down. I could see the quick good-byes of a black wing, and I saw nothing more. Its squawks and caws echoed from the bottom, and we could all hear the rustling of trash as the crow hopped from bag to bag.

Among the semicircle, we stopped talking and looked on, mute with curiosity. None of us knew how to help a crow, and we wouldn't have chosen the dumpster as a place to do it, but what did we know? Nothing, apparently. What did we expect? Something, apparently.

Chú Hữu picked up a yard-long metal pipe, about two inches in diameter, that was propped up against the dumpster, detritus from a plumbing repair job in one of the apartment units.

The edge of the dumpster was as high as his shoulders, so he stood on his tiptoes to leverage his arms over the edge, his flip-flops drawn away from his heels. His hands gripped the top of the pipe, holding it vertically over his head as though he were operating a giant invisible butter churn. His arms formed a sharp triangle over his shoulders. Someone shushed the chatter in the back.

Stillness. What did we expect?

Chú Hữu stabbed the pipe straight down as hard as he could, and we heard the popping of garbage bags as the pipe pounded the bottom of the dumpster. Why was he popping the garbage bags? *BANG! BANG! BANG!* Muffled in the banging and popping, a gurgling squawk was heard. The smell of putrid garbage and rot circulated, making some kids cover their noses and gag.

A few kids cried out in surprise at the first blows. "Oh no! No!" Chú Hữu raised his arms up and down several more times, whacking around the dumpster, knifing downward left and right. *BANG! BANG! BANG!* His toes shifted and his triceps flexed as he sidled quickly along the edge of the dumpster, shifting one way, then sliding another way along the edge. I saw by his movements that the crow was trying to dodge the pipe. We heard the crow, still thrashing atop the bags. *BANG! BANG! BANG! BANG!*

The squawking stopped after the third series of blows. The last caw sounded distant and wet.

He dropped the pipe in the bottom of the dumpster, and it clanged a hollow, final peal. He closed the gate, wiped his hands on his cutoff shorts, and plodded down the hill toward the parking lot, silent. In his wake, half of the kids were crying because of what they saw, and the other half still were trying to figure out what they had just seen. I was in the latter, lingering behind.

Some kids ran home in tears as others stood around, bewildered. No one wanted to play tag or kickball, not after what we had witnessed. Our afternoon had spiraled from our idealistic pipe dream of saving the crow to its blunt bludgeoning in the dumpster. We were the witnesses to the murder. Powerless to stop it. Victims of the spectacle.

I meandered with Lou down the hill. What had I expected?

Chú Hữu had done what he thought was the right thing, and in his estimation, killing the crow was the kindest act he could bestow upon it. Clapping his hands together, wiping off the grit of the pipe, he went inside his apartment. The door clicked shut. He'd killed the crow with the banal ease of taking out the trash.

As I got to the parking lot of our complex, I saw Bà Ngoại coming over for a visit. She waved to me and Lou, her high brows in good spirits. She smiled and called for us to come over, hugging us both. Her perfume wafted the scent of peonies. My knuckles were still healing from the scissors.

Bà Ngoại, my grandmother. Gentle one moment, violent in the next. Violence was sometimes kindness. Sometimes it was love. Sometimes it was rage. But it was everywhere, always.

3

THE SCARLET LETTER

OCTOBER 1980

"*Tag!* You're it!"

I fell forward, hard, from the unseen blow that struck me square between the shoulders.

"I'm not even playing!" I yelled. I picked the loose gravel out of my reddened palms as I looked up to see Derek Elkins running away.

"Doesn't matter if you're playing! You're it! Phuc's it, everybody! Phuc's it!" The kids who were playing tag flew in every direction.

"I'M NOT EVEN PLAYING!" I went to the swings to look for Craig Fleckman and our X-wing squadron. I hopped on board a swing, and we took flight as Derek intruded into our airspace. He stood in front of us as we swung inches from his nose.

"You're still it!" he mocked me from below, sticking his tongue out. Derek spearheaded the reassembling group of kids.

"I said I'm not playing!" I was too busy trying to destroy the Empire.

Derek made his eyes into slants, fingers in the outer corners. "Nyah, nyah, you can't even catch me." I ignored it. Big deal—my eyes were shaped different.

Words were meaningless. We were at a deadlock, but the group consensus declared that I was it. That was how democracy worked, how the mob ruled. Their game needed an *it*, and no one wanted to be *it*.

That language itself—being *it*—was our first exercise in dehumanization. *It* starts early. When you play tag, you're not a person. You're a thing, an *it*. In the English language we deploy that gender at an early age to create an *it*, an *other*, to dehumanize, to flee, to amuse.

"FIND SOMEONE ELSE!"

With his eyes still finger-creased, Derek tried to provoke me to catch him. "You can't even catch me! Can't catch me! Can't catch me! You're just a stupid gook! A *GOOK*!"

What was that? I didn't know what that word meant, but I knew enough to read the crowd. Grace, Katie, Jon—they all froze. Their eyes widened. Disbelief. Alarm. Liza Lyons upbraided Derek. "You can't say that, Derek! That's a really bad word!"

I didn't know any bad words besides various combinations of *stupid/dumb/poop* with the suffix *head*, but this word *gook* seemed like it needed a response based on Liza's reaction. If it were a truly bad word, it needed a truly strong retort.

Derek persisted. "Well, he's it! And he *is* a gook—that's what my parents said! So he's *it*!"

The game had changed—it wasn't tag anymore. I leapt off my X-swing and ran toward Derek. None of the kids scattered as Derek turned to run from me. I hammered him three times, and his nose immediately gushed crimson as he fell to the ground. His front teeth cut into my knuckles, and my hand stung from the blow. I stood, tears streaming down my face (why was I crying?) when I felt an iron hand clamp down around my arm. It was Mrs. Boose.

Mrs. Boose was our second-grade teacher. Sporting a short sandy bouffant that looked more helmet than hairstyle, Mrs. Boose was a brawny woman who was just as comfortable splitting logs as she was hewing second graders.

She pulled us asunder. "What's going on here?"

Derek whimpered, staring at the blood sprayed all over his yellow *Mork & Mindy* iron-on T-shirt. The game was over, and Derek, the shock wearing off, was furious. "PHUC HIT ME! HE HIT ME!"

Mrs. Boose glared at me as her vise tightened on my arm.

Per her schoolyard forensics, Mrs. Boose was asking questions of the who-hit-whom-first variety, reconstructing the crime scene. "Why did you hit him, Phuc?" Without the wisdom of legal counsel or the reading of my *Miranda* rights, I offered the provocation.

"Well, Derek called me a gook—a *gook!*" I said it twice, hoping that it would be grounds for my acquittal. To my own surprise, I started to cry again. Humiliated, I couldn't look at all the kids who were still standing around us. I fastened my gaze only on Mrs. Boose. She was silent, and a frown flickered across her face. Her wattles tightening, her glasses twitched as she focused on me.

"Well . . . well, you don't even know what that word means, do you? And besides, we don't hit other people. You know what we say: 'Sticks and stones will break my bones, but words will never hurt me.'" The playground bell gaveled our due process over with the end of recess. "Everyone line up to go inside. We'll get Derek cleaned up. And, Phuc, remember: 'Sticks and stones will break my bones, but words will never hurt me.'" She raised her voice so that everyone in the line could hear, a convenient PSA to us all.

To the astonishment of all involved, especially me, nothing came of the fight. I was not sent to the principal's office nor was I paddled by Mr. Van Zandt, and in the judicial system of second grade, Mrs. Boose sent an unspoken but resounding message: there were some transgressions for which you could punch someone with impunity.

Apparently calling someone a gook was one of them.

And apparently I was one of them. Whether I liked it or not, I was *it*—and I wasn't even playing, was I?

Do we want words to be powerful or powerless? We can't have it both ways. If we want them to be powerful, we have to act and speak accordingly, handling our words with the fastidious faith that they can do immeasurable good or irreparable harm. But if we want to say whatever we want—if we want to loose whatever words fly into our minds—then we render words powerless, ineffectual, and meaningless, like the playground bromide of "sticks and stones." That childhood logic leads you to believe that suffering corporal trauma is worse than verbal trauma.

Nathaniel Hawthorne would beg to differ.

When I read *The Scarlet Letter* for the first time, in high school, it dawned on me how ridiculous Hester Prynne's punishment is for having an extramarital affair and a child out of wedlock. "Oh, hey. We're gonna sew a giant RED LETTER *A* on you." The teenage snark in me said, "Yeah, right. Why not just tear the letter off? Wear a T-shirt over it? Or move to another town?" I couldn't fathom how one letter of the alphabet could destroy a person's existence.

But in the olden, golden days of colonial Massachusetts, it was a serious sentence. Public humiliation was tantamount to a death sentence because you were torn from the social fabric of the colony.

Nathaniel Hawthorne understood that language is a social contract. We all agree that *dog* means *dog* and *cat* means *cat*. In that simple agreement, we are bound together, and it's the currency of our transactions. Hester honors that contract by staying in the colony where everyone knows what her transgressions are and what the *A* stands for (spoiler alert: it's for *adultery*). She consents to being publicly shamed. She stays at the colony because it's where she has a powerful (albeit negative) identity, and from that robust identity comes her purpose and meaning. Hester chooses to stay where she is *Hester*.

Even without knowing what the word *gook* meant, I was binding myself to the social contract of language, and in doing so, I allowed myself to be harmed by it. I was giving the word power. I could have ignored it or allowed my ignorance to shield myself, but that very ignorance would have further isolated me, and ultimately, dehumanized me. And that was the game of *it*. Ostracize and dehumanize.

But if I allowed myself to be harmed by words, I was showing them that I belonged at least by virtue of understanding their language. And all I wanted was to belong.

My mother had left the apple orchard and gotten a better-paying job at McCoy Electronics, a circuit-board factory. She worked the day shift on the soldering line, and my father arranged to work third shift and be home during the day in the summertime. With the hope of connecting his children to Việt Nam, he decided to use that time to teach me to read Vietnamese as I was reading in English now (Lou was luckily still illiterate in both languages).

My father and I sat at the kitchen table, just the two of us. In front of us lay a primer for Vietnamese, a thin paperback booklet with simple line drawings of kids and animals and single words.

"Say it again. This mark means the downward tone. This mark means the upward tone. Read it again." The spelling didn't make sense to me. I kept pronouncing the *d* as it was pronounced in English (a voiced alveolar stop for you phonologists in the audience).

"NO! That's not how you say it. *D* is pronounced like *y*." Right then, I decided that Vietnamese was a stupid language, or at least its alphabet was stupid. *D* pronounced like *y*? No thank *dou*.

I heard Lou playing with Tim and other neighborhood kids outside. They were running around throwing rocks and digging holes, having adventures without me.

I shrunk low in my chair and scowled at the page. There weren't even sentences to read. Just the musical notations of the six different tones. Up tone. Down tone. Higher tone. No tone. Up-down tone. Question tone.

I said *dơ* wrong.

"NO! YOU'RE NOT TRYING! DO IT AGAIN!"

I said *dơ* wrong again.

"AGAIN!"

Wrong.

"AGAIN!"

Wrong.

My father struck the table with his fist. Tears streaked my face. "How are you going to read Vietnamese? Are you going to be a Vietnamese person who can't read their own language?!"

The rhetorical answer was yes, but my father's question implied a deeper logic: If I *chose* not to learn to read it, did that make me less Vietnamese? And if so, did that mean that I could be more of something else? If I read English better, did that mean that I could be more American? Already the answer seemed obvious to me: I wanted to be more American, to fit in. I didn't want to be more Vietnamese. Vietnamese got me teased. Vietnamese got me into fights. Vietnamese meant not-American. A gook.

My father limped through a few more weeks of instruction, but his efforts did not budge my tight-jawed recalcitrance. I had made up my mind that I was not going to learn to read Vietnamese, that it was a waste of my efforts, and so I sat saturnine at the table, willfully unteachable. No amount of spanking or punishment was going to sway me.

Kids covet things. They see something that other kids have, and they want that thing. They see a cool T-shirt with Darth Vader on it, and they want that shirt, too. Soon they want the house, the hair, the skin color.

I wanted to be Ethan Alder. Ethan was popular. Ethan was tall, blond, athletic, charismatic. He was the first kid who was cool, which meant that he didn't care. He didn't care that he was bad at reading or that he was being sent to Mr. Van Zandt's office. And he certainly didn't care that we all thought he was cool.

Ethan wore distinctive Björn Borg–style wristbands. White terry cloth, with red and blue stripes. With his insouciance, he looked perpetually ready to serve an ace shot. I wanted Ethan Alder's wristbands.

Ethan and I weren't friends. I was still playing *Star Wars* with Craig

Fleckman on the playground. However, I started to realize that Craig and I were the only ones who played with each other. Craig was tall and rangy. He laughed at the wrong time in story circle and would tease girls. But Ethan—Ethan, on the other hand, didn't participate in the imaginary heroics of recess. He was the Achilles of wallball. Boys lined up to challenge him, only to be vanquished. Girls flocked around him at the end of every recess. He was sweaty, but I swore he sparkled.

Being Ethan was an impossible aspiration, and I decided that the next best thing was to look like him. And to look like Ethan Alder, I had to have Björn Borg wristbands.

One Sunday afternoon at Woolco, as I wandered the department store aisles, I found wristbands. *Eureka*—I might as well have discovered solid gold bullions. I clutched the wristbands, triumphant, and ran to my mother. "Má! Má! Can I have these? I want these!"

My mother looked at them and flipped them over. She couldn't make sense of what they were possibly for. "What are they?"

"They're wristbands. They're for your wrists. You wear them."

"Risk bans? What for? Are they like gloves?"

"I don't know . . . but can I have them?"

"No, you can't. No risk bans."

I didn't ask why. I knew that my parents calculated the family's monthly budget weekly, if not daily. I pictured my father at the kitchen table. Bills in one pile, pencil and notebook in another. We had recently stopped taking hand-me-downs from our sponsors—a proud day for my parents. While rebuilding their lives, they were piecing together their pride, the blocks of their self-esteem mortared together with self-sufficiency and independence. We didn't need free clothes anymore, and even if we didn't wear the finest clothing, the clothes that we did wear we bought for ourselves.

There was no extra money for the wristbands. I didn't even know what wristbands were used for, but I knew *exactly* what I would use them for: to look like Ethan Alder. And being more like him meant being less like myself. But we went home with new socks and no wristbands.

That evening, I closed my bedroom door behind me as my brother watched television in the living room and my mother made dinner. Scissors in hand, I rummaged through my drawers and pulled out a pair of new athletic tube socks, pearly white, with striped scarlet bands at the top.

I flipped them inside out and saw that their fuzzy interior looked like loops of terry cloth. The scissors clacked the elastic tube tops from the footlets. If the boy couldn't have wristbands, then the boy would make wristbands out of athletic tube socks with scissors. See ya later, socks. Hello, wristbands.

I tucked my wristbands into my backpack, ready for their runway debut.

That Monday morning, amid the bustle and rustle of backpacks and lunchboxes, the squeaks of chairs and flip-up desktops, I reached into my backpack and slipped on my wristbands (aka my decapitated tube socks turned inside out). They looked *exactly* like Ethan Alder's. I eyed his Björn Borgs from across the room as he gesticulated wildly about something cool. I looked just like him now. It was a proud new day.

I played it cool, not drawing attention to myself, but looking around to see if anyone noticed my new accessories. Craig looked at them but didn't say anything. I didn't see this as a setback, because Craig didn't notice a lot of things—he was still sneaking paste under his desk and eating it, which he had been doing since kindergarten.

As we lined up for the first recess of the day, I positioned myself behind Ethan. No one had said anything all morning, and I realized that I was going to have to seize the day because the day was passing by without any acknowledgment.

"Hey, Ethan. Look." I held up my wrists. "Wristbands." I said it just in case it wasn't obvious to him that he and I were the same.

He eyed my wristbands suspiciously. "Those aren't wristbands. What *are* those?"

Grace Hazelwood, who stood behind me, butted into the conversation. "Are those socks? They *are* socks!" She and Ethan giggled as the recess line processed outside. "THOSE ARE SOCKS! Oh my God, Phuc is wearing socks on his wrists!"

As soon as we got outside, I distanced myself from them even as I heard them sniggering on their way to the wallball area. My mind began a furious debate. *Should I take them off?* I wondered. *Leave them on? Give them the satisfaction of humiliating me or persevere?* I decided that I would show them. The wristbands stayed on.

I kept the dismembered socks on all day, enduring taunts until the novelty of it wore off. Craig, in true-friend fashion, said nothing. That was the extent of his friendship—not participating in sock-mocking, a neutrality that was good enough for me.

After school, Lou and I played outside until my parents called us in for dinner by yelling out the window for us as they always did. We bolted in and up the stairs, sliding across our chairs to bowls of rice and stir-fried vegetables. A heap of rice was half in my mouth when my mother noticed my wristbands. I had forgotten to take them off.

"What are those? I didn't buy risk bans. Whose are those? Did you cut your socks up? DID YOU CUT UP PERFECTLY GOOD SOCKS?!" My mother kept yelling as she pulled me from my seat to confirm her suspicions, but my father didn't wait for the results of her inspection. The mere accusation that I had cut up brand-new socks was enough for him, and his hand struck my rear with several sharp blows. My mother provided the blistering soundtrack to my father's assault as I ran off to my room, mid-dinner. "We just spent money on those socks—brand-new socks!—and now you cut them up? Are you a fool? Do you think we're making so much money that you can do that? Why don't you just throw money away?!"

No more risk bans. No more scissors. Lesson learned: humiliated at school, beaten at home. The wristbands had not been worth the risk.

My father's rage would erupt in primal and unpredictable ways. Our spankings (beatings, in fact) were regular and, as I later realized, vicious. It was not until my adulthood that I understood his abusive behavior. As an adult, I can explain and even understand where his anger came from (PTSD as a refugee, his own abuse as a child, the cycle of abuse that can perpetuate itself in a culture that equated obedient children with great parenting). As a second grader, I knew this violence as my only reality. If I spilled something, disobeyed, did something too quickly or too slowly. The violence that pelted me bore no morality or judgment, amassing like storm clouds that darkened the sky only to disperse in vapors. My mother would warn me, "Wait until your father gets home," and I would go into my room so I could put on two pairs of underwear in preparation, in the hopes that two pairs of my favorite Spider-Man Underoos would deflect the blows and deafen the bellows.

But did my uncouth behavior merit beatings? I was a sassy, mouthy, overly energetic kid, always on the go, always talking. My report cards regularly said: "Talks too much." Infractions of all sorts precipitated a variety of punishments. Sometimes it was a slap on the ass, sometimes it was the ol' kneeling-in-a-corner-on-uncooked-rice, and other times it was being beaten by whatever my parents could get their hands on. Brutality bore ingenuity.

That fall of second grade, however, I received a beating that eclipsed all others, so savage that I don't remember what it was for. I could make something up, but to what end? Would the cause matter or somehow justify it?

My father had started using a metal rod that he brought home from the tire factory. He couldn't hit me as hard with his hand anymore (the manual spankings had stopped hurting me), and even a wooden spoon did not inflict enough pain: hence, the metal rod, dark gray and about the length of a yardstick, pitted with bits of ruddy corrosion. The rod was a piece of machinery that had been thrown away, and my father, eyeing it in the scrap heap, immediately saw its domestic potential. The rod was more efficient because it hurt more. And as a result, it required less effort while achieving maximum results. American efficiency, meet Vietnamese ingenuity. With the metal rod, two or three cracks across our buttocks or the back of our thighs sufficed. Message received, loud and clear.

In that particular incident, however, I was beaten with the rod across the rear end and legs with a dozen or so blows. I remember crying into the floral velour pattern of our brown couch and hearing my father counting off the blows. (He counted upward from one, so I never knew when he would stop.) *Một. Hai. Ba. Bốn. Năm. Sáu. Bảy. Tám. Chín. Mười.* Ten. I lost count after *mười.*

What I also remember vividly was that I was not able to sit down the next day. I could barely move my legs to get dressed the next morning, my hamstrings and butt were so ravaged. My aching thighs carried me to school slowly, and the neighborhood kids ran ahead while I trudged along, falling behind.

In class, when the Pledge of Allegiance ended, we pulled out our chairs to begin our schoolwork. The chairs and chair backs were hard plywood riveted to gray steel legs. Everyone assumed their positions, but I couldn't bear the touch of the seat on my rear, so I stood at my desk, leaning over my worksheet.

"Phuc, you need to sit," Mrs. Boose directed.

"Okay," I said as I put my feet on my chair and crouched with my butt hovering over the seat.

She walked around the room to check our spelling worksheets, circling back to my cluster of desks, and she saw me squatting in my chair. "You need to sit down," she said.

"I know, I'm sorry, Mrs. Boose." She walked away to another group of kids as I sat crossed-legged on my shins with my feet underneath me, but that still hurt too much.

I was still hovering on my knees, shifting from leg to leg, fidgeting. Mrs. Boose came back to my desk. "Phuc, do you need to go to Mr. Van Zandt's office?"

"No, Mrs. Boose. I'll try to sit. I'm sorry." I pretended to sit, floating over my seat, putting my weight on my forearms. My seat might as well have been a bed of nails given the way it needled my backside. The squat made my thighs burn, so I stood again. Mrs. Boose saw me and her thin lips quivered. Her voice had a tautness, trebled with aggravation.

"Okay, Phuc. You need to come up here and see me right now at my desk." I stood straight and pushed my chair in before limping toward the front of the room. The kids at my desk group had stopped their writing exercises and watched me walking toward Mrs. Boose. She smelled like old Christmas candy and sweat. My face smoldered flush and hot. I dreaded getting sent to the principal's office because my parents would find out and then there would be another beating. Or even worse: What if I got paddled at Mr. Van Zandt's office? I could barely walk as it was. And I would get spanked at home again. The thought of my father thrashing my already swollen backside was unbearable. I had been beaten as much as I could physically bear, and the prospect that I might get paddled, beaten, or spanked again cracked the fragile shell of my composure. When I was within arm's reach of her, Mrs. Boose sat in her chair and swiveled it so that we were square to each other.

"Phuc, why are you disobeying me? Why are you refusing to sit in your seat? I think you're going to need to go to Mr. Van Zandt's office."

My face burned even hotter, and I disintegrated. My pain, humiliation, and fear of further reprisal ruptured, exploding into sobs of agony and trepidation. I found myself weeping in the front of the classroom, telling Mrs. Boose why I couldn't sit, leaning forward and hiding my wet face in her stale hair. I blocked out my classmates while I cried, locking my attention on Mrs. Boose and the immediate consequences. I told her that my father had beaten me the night before and that my legs and back were too sore to sit. I told her about the metal rod. I blew my nose and wiped my face on my sleeve.

She listened intently, her face softened, and she leaned forward. "Go back to your seat and do the best you can. Thanks for telling me about what was hurting you."

I walked back to my desk, holding my eyes fast to the floor, stinging from the degradation of crying in front of my classmates. But I just wanted things to go back to normal, so I busied myself with my worksheet. The rest of the day was a blur while I stood at my desk awkwardly for the remainder of school, trying to focus and pretending that my class hadn't witnessed me sobbing. Recess was painful, as was the walk home.

It turned out that sticks and stones did hurt. So did words and metal rods. Everything hurt.

That night, my parents answered a phone call from Mrs. Boose. She wanted to visit us at home and talk to them.

I fretted over the intent and outcome of her visit, uncertain about what she might say or do. My father ruled our household with an iron rod. This was how he compelled order, discipline, compliance. In my childish logic, if my mother were stronger than my father, her will would have been the way of our home. If I were stronger than my father, I could have imposed my will upon him just as I physically prevailed upon my little brother with farts on his head, punches in the arm, shoves and noogies.

Might made right under our roof, and Mrs. Boose would not be able to assert herself physically. No good would come of her visit for me—I was sure of that. I anticipated a beating immediately after her visit since my father instantly asked me why she was coming over and if I had misbehaved at school. I told him that I didn't know and neglected to tell him about my confession to her.

The next day, after school, Mrs. Boose's yellow Mercury pulled into the parking lot of our apartment complex. I had been watching for it all afternoon since I had gotten home. In her mustard overcoat and a flowered scarf, she swayed back and forth, scanning for our apartment number before she headed toward our front door. She did not walk like a woman who was ready for a fight. She dressed as she did for school: wearing polyester floral, gold necklaces, helmet hair, and rogue lipstick that went a little farther than her lips actually were.

The doorbell rang, and my brother and I sat while my parents let her in. "Thank you for giving me a few minutes of your time, Mr. and Mrs. Tran. I won't be long." They offered her water or tea, which she declined. "It's nice to see you. Phuc, would you and your brother wait in your bedroom?"

Sequestered from the adults, Lou pushed a Matchbox car around on the carpet, but I didn't want to play with our toys. Huddled against the door, I parsed the muted murmuring of their adultspeak, noting the change in tone of different speakers. I didn't hear my mother and presumed that she yielded her minutes to my father. No yelling. No fighting. I didn't hear any sign of a match of physical strength. My father did not wield the iron rod, and their talk seemed to end amicably.

After several minutes, our bedroom door opened, and my brother and I came out to say goodbye to Mrs. Boose. "I'll see you tomorrow, Phuc. Thank you for your time, Mr. and Mrs. Tran." She lumbered out and into her car, leaving a faint smell of her candied perfume in the room. Her arrival and departure felt even more mysterious because of its calm.

I didn't want to ask but was unable to quell my interest. "What did Mrs. Boose talk with you about?" I interrupted my parents Vietnamesing with each other quietly. "Am I in trouble?" I anticipated another spanking.

"No, you're not in trouble," my father intoned flatly.

I was amazed to hear his reply. "So why was Mrs. Boose here?"

"She said that she learned that I was spanking you a lot. She said that you couldn't sit at school because your legs hurt so much. Mrs. Boose said that here, in America, parents can't hit their kids *as much* as they do in Việt Nam." He didn't go so far as to say that he *wouldn't* spank me.

I was surprised to hear Mrs. Boose's message to my parents, particularly since Mr. Van Zandt, our principal, paddled kids in his office all the time (and by paddling I mean beating kids with a wooden oar). What was the distinction between beating kids with a wooden oar and beating kids with a metal rod?

More frightened than relieved, I reiterated. "So I'm not in trouble?"

"No, you're not."

I nodded and went back to my room, unsure of what the ramifications of Mrs. Boose's intervention were. I didn't dare to hope for the beatings to cease—I had already hoped for that before, only to be sorely disappointed. I assumed that the worst outcome would be that nothing would change. That was the wildest hope that I allowed to flutter free in my mind: that things would stay the same.

But they didn't.

My father didn't beat me that week. Nor the next week. And he didn't beat me for the rest of that school year. It was a long reprieve for me, and I was thankful for it. Thankful for Mrs. Boose and for her words.

Maybe words *were* powerful—maybe even magical.

Derek hadn't called me a gook since we'd gotten into the fistfight, but I was still the bull's-eye of his schoolyard taunts. During recess, when we were free to fly, I escaped his focus, running as far and as fast as my X-wing legs carried me.

I was most exposed and vulnerable when we lined up for the beginning and end of recess, and in the line, I couldn't put enough distance between myself and Derek and his coffle of lunkheads.

One day Derek slithered up, two kids behind me. Caught in the line, I was trapped, wriggling and writhing, gasping to get away. "Hey, Phuc! Why is your nose so flat? Did you guys ever notice how flat his nose is?" Laughter. Humiliation. Words still hurt me, but at least he didn't call me a gook.

Even Craig was laughing, my Chewbacca. There's betrayal, and there's the stinging betrayal by your loyal Wookiee friend.

Karen Larkin, who had never participated in any taunting, was next to Derek and jumped in, too. I didn't blame her. The train of second-grade taunts was always on the express route, and if you didn't get on board, you got run over. "Yeah, why is your nose so flat?"

Immediately I fired back. "Oh, when I was a baby, I got run over by a bus in Việt Nam, and then—SQUISH—my nose got flattened!"

Karen's eyes saucered wide. "WHAT?!"

"Yup. A bus went right over my nose—just like this!" I smacked my hand against my face hard, mimicking Curly from The Three Stooges. And then the laughter pivoted. Grace was laughing with me. Craig laughed, too. My joke was the proverbial and metaphorical bus under which I had thrown myself. Just for emphasis, I had hit my own face for laughs, a gesture of things to come. At least everyone was laughing with me, and I didn't have to punch anyone. I preferred laughter *with me* more than *at me*. That was the power of prepositions.

As the line processed inside, Derek hissed from behind me. "You're still a *gook*. I don't care what you say. *Still. A. Gook.*"

And he was right. I couldn't change his mind about that. I wielded no control over how he saw me. I would always be a gook to him.

That I couldn't take off. *G* was my scarlet letter.

NOVEMBER 1980

The first week of November, as the Halloween skulls, hissing cats, and green-warted witches came down from the walls of the classroom, Mrs. Boose announced the Thanksgiving writing contest. The school-wide competition was to write and illustrate a sentence about what you were thankful for, and each grade would have one winner chosen.

The five winners would get to have lunch with Mr. Van Zandt, and the lunch was no ordinary lunch. Mr. Van Zandt took all the kids—in his own car—through the McDonald's drive-through for Happy Meals, and then they all returned to Mr. Van Zandt's office to eat their Happy Meals. This was an annual tradition, and we all knew other kids who had won and come back to tell the tale from the luncheon. The fabled Golden Arches. Hot french fries. A milkshake. For those of us whose parents seldom bought fast food, the McDonald's prize luncheon for the Thanksgiving contest was the gold standard of prizes.

On contest day, Mrs. Boose handed out beige composition paper. She was sweatier than usual as she circled the room, squawking out the instructions. "Okay, class—please write a sentence and draw a picture of what you are thankful for. Remember: the teachers will be getting together to look at all the drawings and will pick one winner from each grade. And as you remember, the winner will be having a McDonald's lunch with Mr. Van Zandt."

The class scribbled furiously for what felt like an hour. I spied elaborate compositions. Flourishes of loop-the-loop clouds, saltbox houses with lemon-yellow suns shining down. At the end of the allotted time, Mrs. Boose collected our papers and tacked them to the bulletin board at the front of the room. I handed in my drawing, and as I looked at my classmates' illustrations, I realized I had drawn the wrong thing. My classmates' pictures were idyllic and joyous: they were thankful for new puppies or a trip to Disney or skiing at Roundtop Mountain. My drawing did not herald any of this. As I looked at their gratitude for magic kingdoms, ski slopes, and puppies, I knew then that I had misunderstood the assignment. I hadn't drawn a vacation or a spectacular gift. I had drawn something so basic, so simple, and I knew that I stood no chance of winning.

After school, I didn't mention the contest or the drawing—I didn't bother my parents with it. Who cared about a second-grade Thanksgiving writing contest? It was 1980, and the Trần family was bustling and bursting with the arrival of my father's parents, his youngest sister, and younger brother in Carlisle.

The four of them—my paternal grandparents, Ông Bà Nội; Cô Bảy; and Chú Năm—had been left behind in Sài Gòn in 1975.* My grandfather, Ông Nội, planned their escape, and in 1978 he put their plan into motion. They acquired falsified documents which said that they were

---

* Ông Bà Nội means *paternal grandparents* (to be distinguished from Ông Bà Ngoại, my maternal grandparents). Cô Bảy and Chú Năm are the titles that my brother and I use to address my father's siblings (our aunts and uncles). Cô Bảy literally means "aunt on my father's side, sixth born." Chú Năm literally means "uncle on my father's side, fourth born." Vietnamese has a complex set of pronouns and titles that convey gender, status, paternal or maternal connection, relation by marriage or birth, and birth order among siblings.

Chinese nationals. My uncle Chú Năm had secretly installed a tractor engine onto a local river barge, and under cover of night, they stole the barge and chugged away from Sài Gòn across the Gulf of Thailand. My teenage aunt was disguised as a boy to avoid being raped in the event that they were boarded by pirates. Several days later they arrived in Malaysia and bribed local officials with ten gold bullions, and in Malaysia they languished at a refugee camp for six months while they tried to contact my father. They finally arrived in America in January 1979. Photographers met them at the Harrisburg airport. A grainy black-and-white photo appeared in the local Carlisle paper along with a story about their harrowing months-long odyssey. The front-page article read "Boat People Find Refuge in Carlisle." The arrival of more Trầns was headline news for our drowsy town.

My parents rented for Ông Bà Nội a vacant apartment across the parking lot in Colonial Square. My aunt Cô Bảy was enrolled in the high school immediately, for her a bewildering reentry into a routine that should have been banal. They had so much to learn about Carlisle, about America, about their new life. My parents didn't have time to pay attention to Lou, me, or Mooreland Elementary School's Thanksgiving writing contest—not when they were helping my grandparents adjust to their new life in Carlisle. Even I forgot about the writing contest.

Two weeks later Mr. Van Zandt came on the loudspeaker to announce the winners of the Thanksgiving contest. I heard clapping from the other classrooms as winners were announced. Oh right—the contest. The one that I had gotten wrong because I didn't write about puppies or ski vacations. I looked over at Grace, haloed with her radiant blond hair and rosy elven features, and assumed that she would win. She had written about a Florida vacation that she and her grandparents had taken: snorkeling, stingrays, sun-bleached sands.

". . . And from the second grade, Phuc Tran."

I was stunned. Hello, Happy Meal and an awkward lunch with Mr. Van Zandt.

Before I left school that afternoon, I strode down the hall by the library where all the drawings adorned the walls. I scanned the patch-work assemblage of art to look for the yellow winner ribbon pinned to the lower right corner of my drawing. I gazed upon my scribbly master-piece that had won me a Happy Meal.

My drawing was of a rudimentary airplane, and below it were my grandparents, my aunt, and uncle as stick figures, limbs akimbo, dots for eyes. My sentence was scrawled in block letters under the picture. "I AM THANKFUL THAT MY GRANDPARENTS ARE SAFE IN AMERICA."

To me, it was the most obvious thing that I could have been thankful for. My grandparents—who spoke no English, who had fled Việt Nam on a stolen boat—had bested my classmates' new puppies and Disney World vacations and ski weekends.

I hadn't misinterpreted the assignment. It was my words that got me a Happy Meal. Words *were* powerful. They could destroy you, and they could save you, too. And maybe earn you a hot Happy Meal—thankfully.

4

A CHRISTMAS CAROL

AUGUST 1981

"I'm *not* going to spank you." We heard him speak those words of mercy, but the tenor of his voice said, "But I want to spank you." In the rearview mirror, my father's eyes were narrowed, darkened pupils fixed on the road ahead. His voice ground thin and tight, as if in the wrong gear. My mother shifted noiselessly in the front seat (she was always silent under the grays of his forecasted anger), and Lou and I were relieved at his announcement. We hadn't been spanked since Mrs. Boose's visit.

Our car sped along a stretch of country road that led from Saint Patrick's newer church, erected in fields of whispering corn, folded in undulating meadows of wheat as if its spire sprouted up as part of the golden harvest. Pennsylvania farmers tilled the earth for corn, wheat, and faith.

Lou and I had found church that Sunday morning even more boring than usual, so he and I played Spider-Hand. I hummed the *Spider-Man* theme quietly to him, while my left hand, outstretched like an arachnid, crept glacially toward him, making small minatory movements as we tried to maintain a fragile bubble of Christian composure. The sacrosanct surroundings of Saint Patrick's demanded that we comport ourselves with the respect that was eternally due to our Lord and Savior. Jesus' effigy floated triumphantly above the altar and its proceedings, his statue's complexion painted the same beige color as JCPenney's mannequins, but instead of offering summer khakis and blazers, Jesus was presenting eternal salvation with his palms outstretched, revealing his wounds to us.

In the pew, my father glared at Lou and me, sensing that nincompoopery was afoot. My mother's attention, as always, tuned in faithfully to Father Fontanella's homily even if her listening comprehension was unreliable. Her chin raised up as if she were at a microphone too tall, the uptilt of her face allowing her to watch Father Fontanella and mannequin Jesus at the same time.

My left hand crept slowly toward Lou, who was awash in chortles as Spider-Hand inched closer and closer. I softly sang to him: *Spider-Hand, Spider-Hand, friendly neighborhood Spider-Hand.* My mother heard Lou laughing and elbowed me.

Lou snorted, covered his mouth with both hands, his face frozen with a look of both terror and hilarity. He and I sprung leaks of snickering, which in church sounded loud. And inappropriate. My father hissed at us to be quiet, and the white family in front of us did the looking-but-not-looking-over-the-shoulder glower of reproach. My mother's face turned scarlet with embarrassment, and my father grabbed Lou by the arm, sliding him over to the other side of the pew. Game over.

After mass, we piled into our red Ford LTD (which had replaced the green Pontiac), Lou and I anticipating some repercussions of our misbehavior in mass. My father's brow was creased, asymmetrically folded and ruddy, like angry origami. His chin, flecked with the weekend's stubble, bent an unmoving frown. Trouble was up ahead. Lou and I were relieved when, in the car ride home, my father announced, "I'm not going to spank you."

The cornfields whooshed by in the open window and then slowed. He pulled the car onto the shoulder. "Get out." He didn't turn around, and Lou and I weren't sure what he meant and whom he meant.

"What?" I looked at the rearview mirror to see that he was bankshotting a look at me. "What do you mean, *get out*?"

"Get out, I said! Phúc, get out of the car!"

"What are you doing? He can't get out!" My mother's voice was shrill and frantic while Lou and I remained frozen. No one was getting out of the car.

My father raised his voice to a full yell, "GET OUT OF THE CAR! GET OUT RIGHT NOW! *OUT OF THE CAR!*"

I got out. The smell of August's fresh manure stung my nose and eyes. I scanned the berm for a comfortable place to lie down. If he was going to beat me by the side of the road, at least we were out of public view, clear of humiliation. Was I going to lie in the grass? On some fallen cornstalks? I knew that he didn't travel with the metal rod, and the more I anticipated being spanked, the more I was oddly confident. I was confident that I could physically endure whatever he had to mete out since he didn't have the metal rod. My butt was ready for whatever—except for what happened next.

He closed the door behind me and peeled away in a crackle of gravel and acceleration. My butt was not expecting that. I heard my mother through its open window. "What are you doing?!"

Between the road and the cornfield, the dust drifted behind the car, settling down as my surprise rose up. What had just happened? Was this their version of leaving me in a basket of reeds by the Nile? I listened to the shushing of the tires until I heard nothing but the faraway gargling of a tractor and the rural fugue of crickets, birds, and distant dogs. The late-summer corn was taller than I was, and on both sides of the road arose rustling walls of green. This was a joke, right? They couldn't possibly have just left me on the side of the road. Did they?

I had a vague notion of which direction to walk and was surprisingly sure that someone would help me. I knew my address and my phone number.

I didn't believe that I was abandoned by the side of the road, and my seven-year-old brain calculated that getting kicked out of the car was better than getting beaten. No fear for what was going to happen next. No fear of the future.

Totally calm, I squatted in a small grassy strip, picking up a few flat rocks to toss. I pushed the roadside gravel into a small ziggurat and put a stalk of wheat at the top to crown my achievement.

For seven-year-old Phuc, the math on this one was easier to explain: Abandoned > Beaten = Calm. This was another theory of relativity. Not brilliant, but just as practical.

I had experienced so much dread by that point in my life that being forced out of the car on a beautiful August day was—well, it wasn't the worst thing that could happen to me. When a kid gets the tar beaten out of him for the first seven years of his life, what more will be an effective deterrent? My past wasn't a Dickensian horror show of Victorian orphanages and hard labor, but it did make my present predicament relatively benign. I decided that I would walk home in a few hours (or at least head in the general direction of what I thought was home), but for the moment, I figured that it was better to stay put in case my parents changed their minds about Moses-ing me, and came back around.

I hummed the Blondie song "The Tide Is High" that my uncle Thái played constantly on his 45-rpm single, as I picked up more rocks to toss by the side of the road.

After some time had passed, my stomach growled, and I grew restless. I stood up and found a stick to swat at the cornstalks for fun. In the most dire circumstance, I figured that I could walk to a nearby farmhouse for food. Pacing back and forth, I whacked the cornstalks with my stick as hard as I could. *Thwack! Thwack!* Maybe a half hour had passed? Maybe an hour? The August midday sun throbbed, and the manure in the air had a cloying smell as the breeze pushed it around; the odor hovered at the edges, but it wasn't going anywhere.

Two cars had passed by me since I had been roadside, neither of them stopping or even slowing. I had been so intent on busying myself with my stick and rocks that no alarm was indicated. Just a seven-year-old Vietnamese kid in the Pennsylvania countryside, whacking cornstalks with a stick. No big deal.

I heard another car drive up and slow down, eventually stopping next to me. It was our Ford. Without turning around, my father growled from the front seat. "Get in." I opened the door and slid across the vinyl. If I had guessed, I would have surmised that my mother had begged my father to come back to get me, but I didn't ask. I didn't want to risk being misinterpreted and getting kicked out of the car again. Silent as we drove home.

I was hot and thirsty and happy that I didn't have to walk home.

Did we have a meaningful discussion about why my father kicked me out of the car? We didn't. My father's one parenting tool—physical violence—seemed no longer to be an option, but his rage and spring-loaded temper remained flexed, ready to snap at any trigger. Without a physical recourse in his parenting, since he now feared the shame of having my teacher come to our home again, he resorted to yelling and the tyranny of fear. Fear would keep me and Lou in line, but what did Lou and I fear now that we didn't fear his beatings? Did he think that we feared our abusive, ill-tempered father would abandon us? Did we fear that someone else would have to care for us?

That didn't seem like a terrible proposition to me.

I know that I was not the first kid in the history of the world to wish that someone else were his father, to wish that his parents were anyone else. I would have settled for one of my aunts or uncles for my parents. They were nice. They could take care of us. My uncle Chú Thu took me and Lou swimming at Dickinson College all the time (he was a chef for the college's dining hall). Who else could be our parents? Maybe some white people? Maybe one of our sponsors would adopt me and Lou? That seemed fine to me. Their houses were grand multiroom castles. They always smiled and said things like "come on in" or "make yourselves at home" or "can I get you something to drink?" And even if they *did* beat their kids, maybe that was a price worth paying in order to have a home like they did. For what was I paying my price?

From the back seat of the Ford, looking out at the grand expanses of farm and country, I murmured a pagan prayer, not directing it to Jesus, God, or anyone in particular. It was to the universe. To everybody and nobody. A message in a bottle. The worst outcome would be that nothing would change. Was it a sin to pray for different parents? A dad who didn't beat you? A mom who protected you? Parents who understood the world that you lived in?

I didn't pray for my father to be different or kinder or more loving, because I couldn't imagine him that way. He never spoke to us with affection or tenderness. His anger and his violence shaped how I saw him, and I wasn't sure he would even be my father without the anger and violence. But I didn't want him as he was—"as is" was the terms of sale for parents and children.

The wish for different parents fuels the archetypal fairy tales about evil stepmothers and children left in the woods. These fairy tales pivot around the wish that our parents, irascible and imperfect, aren't even our real parents, that a fairy godmother will reveal to us our true royal bloodline or magical lineage. Whether you're Harry Potter or Luke Skywalker or Cinderella, the fantasy is that the adults who are raising you aren't even your real parents, that your real parents are kinder and magical. The fantasy is that you have a destiny that is greater and more splendid than your current fate's contours.

On that car ride home, I dismissed that unbridled fantasy with stiff, sobering logic: if this was the worst that could transpire, I would be okay—I would be okay because I had known worse. My father hadn't beaten me or Lou in months—that was already an improvement, and I could live through the punishment of getting kicked out of the car. My past was worse than my present, and if my present indicated my future, I could live with that.

DECEMBER 1981

My mother's footsteps clomped down the stairs.

"Turn off the scary movie! You guys are scaring the other kids!" my mother Vietnamesed at me. "Look at your cousin Thi! She's crying! She came upstairs crying!"

"What are you talking about? We're watching a Christmas movie on CBS! This is a Christmas movie—it's about *Jesus* . . . maybe." I implored her to keep the TV on. I had invoked the name of Jesus, not as expletive but as costar. I didn't know if Jesus was in it. I had heard on a commercial break that the movie was called *A Christmas Carol*, and I knew that Christmas was sometimes about Jesus. If anything stopped my mother in her tracks, it was Jesus and the invocation of Jesus.

My mother's two eldest brothers and two eldest sisters had married and added their own kids, so there multiplied a quorum of young cousins in the basement (among whom I was the alpha cousin). This meant that nearly a dozen kids were all shoved downstairs with a couch and TV while the adults gathered upstairs to prepare dinner. Cooking was an all-day affair for the grown-ups, which meant that, without real adult intervention, it was *Lord of the Flies* in the basement. TV was the common denominator and pacifier. TV offered a respite from noogies, wedgies, arm burns, and all other punishments that trickled down in the brutal basement economy.

"This is NOT a Christmas movie!" my mom pushed back. "Why is that old man screaming?"

"He's being haunted by ghosts."

"Why are there *ghosts* in a Christmas movie?"

"*I don't know.* But it is a Christmas movie. . . . It is! LOOK!" My mother assumed that I was lying until I presented Exhibit A: *The Evening*

Sentinel's TV guide, in black-and-white. "Look. *A CHRISTMAS CAROL.* See? I told you it was a Christmas movie!"

This was no comfort to my cousin Thi, who was still sniffling. On the small TV screen, the ghost of Christmas Present had just revealed two emaciated orphans beneath his cloak, and we were all transfixed. I was excited to see that it was sort of a horror movie *and* sort of a Christmas movie—a strange holiday film to be sure. There was no Santa, Claymation Rudolph, or jazzy Charlie Brown. Just ghosts and regrets and British people.

My mother looked resigned. "Well, it's too loud. Turn it down." I noted that she said *turn down*. Not *turn off*. Christmas won.

Triumphant, I lowered the volume on the TV, but my mother's question began to haunt me. Why *were* there ghosts in a Christmas movie?

When I first read *A Christmas Carol*, I wasn't scared of the ghosts. I was, however, captivated by the idea of being haunted by the past. And beyond the chokehold of regret, I loved Dickens's reflections on the past, on the present, and on the cautionary lessons for the future. It's one of the earliest time-bending stories, shuffling the time deck backward and forward. Ebenezer Scrooge is trying to save his future, but unlike the Terminator and Marty McFly, Scrooge seeks his salvation not by altering the past, which for Dickens is unalterable, but by changing the present—changing the present so that he can save the future. The future is what's at stake.

Marley's ghost tells Scrooge that he will be visited by three ghosts. Scrooge visits himself as a child, and in the next moment, he sees himself as a young man. Dickensian time is jumbled, relative, and malleable. At the end of *A Christmas Carol*, Scrooge awakens in the present day, realizing that he can still save himself, that he can indeed save the future. Scrooge is overjoyed and cries out twice, "I will live in the Past, Present, and the Future!"

For a long time, this passage in Dickens didn't make much sense to me, until I started to think about my parents, my grandparents, and me. We were the past, present, and future, each of us an element of that continuum, yet constantly shifting, depending on the other's perspective.

CHRISTMAS EVE 1981

Lou and I bounded into Ông Bà Ngoại's apartment ahead of our parents, where everyone had gathered. We made the rounds like good little Confucian Catholics, bowing to our elders as instructed by my parents, saying *chào*, the formal Vietnamese greeting. We bowed, moving from one elder to the next. Hugs and kisses showered us from our aunts and grandmother while our uncles and grandfather nodded at our greetings, waving us off. *Chào, Ông Ngoại.* Bow. *Chào, Bà Ngoại.* Bow. My great-grandmother Bà Cố, eighty-five years old, was seated at the head of the large table, holding court in the dining room. *Chào, Bà Cố.* Bow.

"Bà Cố, can you do *bà phù thủy*? Do *bà phù thủy*! Please!" Lou and I begged her to do her game of "old witch lady."

In the initial tide of Trầns in 1975, my great-grandmother Bà Cố, at seventy-nine, made the journey to America with us. With iron resolve, she'd endured a lifetime of wars, the escape from Sài Gòn, and various relocations from refugee camp to refugee camp. A force of nature, the spirit of our family incarnate, she was an unbreakable woman. A relic of the old country, a piece of the past.

While all the other women in our family wore Western-style clothing, Bà Cố always wore an *áo dài*, the traditional Vietnamese long dress that women wore. Because her hair grew far past her lower back, she braided and wrapped it in a piece of black velvet (which was like a giant sock or a woman's stocking) and then wrapped the braid around her head in a large black turban. As the eldest in our family, she was distinguished by and revered for her age, set apart by her status and her distinctive turban.

Bà Cố hugged us as Lou and I begged her to play *bà phù thủy*. Her tiny, thin hands—bones wrapped in skin—reached up behind her head and released her turban, which uncoiled to her left in a slow, serpentine stretch. The soft dark velvet of the turban wrap loosened to reveal silvery hair in a waist-length braid that Bà Cố unraveled with a high, shrill cackle.

Lou and I were giddy as her braid came apart into a gray sheet of hair. She pulled all her hair forward so that it shrouded her face completely. Her hair was so long that it pooled around her knees and hips as she sat, motionless, behind the white pall. We laughed and pushed each other at the macabre sight as Bà Cố reached under the folds of her hair. After a moment of stillness, we heard her remove her dentures with a wet sucking sound and a row of human teeth emerged from the hair. Lou and I were beside ourselves. She placed the dentures on the dining room table next to her, and with her face still hidden behind the curtain of her hair, she began to moan lowly.

"Oooooooh . . . oooooooh . . . OOOOOOOOOOH!" Her hair moved in and out, and she moaned louder. Lou and I were chattering in laughter and terror. She lurched out of her chair, both hands clawing out for us blindly in front of her. "OOOOOOOOOOH!" Lou and I both screamed and fell to the floor, but we didn't scurry away. She parted her hair just at her chin, revealing only her wrinkled mouth, shapeless and glistening from the absence of dentures. Her moans now became audible words. *"Bà phù thủy! Bà phù thủy!" I'm the witch! I'm the witch!*

We were writhing on the floor in mock terror as she huddled over us, her hair shrouding us. We smelled her Tiger Balm ointment, which she always wore as both a perfume and arthritic analgesic. Her toothless maw, warm and wet, slobbered on our cheeks and the nape of our necks as she pretended to eat but was really kissing us. More screaming and shrieking. *Bà phù thủy! Bà phù thủy!*

My mother interceded. "Okay, that's enough! You two go to the basement and leave Bà Cố alone! Go watch TV!" Bà Cố caught her breath and straightened up, brushing her hair back and plopping her teeth back in as she smiled. One last hug and wet kiss before we headed to the basement. Lou and I heard our cousins' laughter at the basement door, the clacking of a Ping-Pong game, the TV in the background as we clambered down the steps.

DECEMBER 30, 1981

Lou and I scanned *The Evening Sentinel*'s TV guide section: "Late-Night Movie."

"What movie are they showing?"

"It just says 'Late-Night Movie,'" I explained to Lou.

"Is it a good one? What movie is it?"

"Good grief, I don't know. 'Late-Night Movie.' That's all it says. We're just gonna have to see."

"Dad, can we sleep on the couch tonight?" My parents talked to each other for a minute. It was a Wednesday night, but during the week between Christmas and New Year's Eve, every night was an excuse to pull out the couch and stay up late.

On special occasions, my parents let me and my brother sleep on our pullout couch. The break from routine, the exceptionalism of sleeping on the pullout, was a huge joy for us even though our bedroom lay eight feet away.

"Okay, sure. You two can sleep out on the couch." My brother and I hopped up and down as if a piñata had burst overhead, and hugged our parents—they might as well have declared a second Christmas. Cushions off. Couch out. Blankets, pillows, and a few stuffed animals trailing us from the bedroom.

Carlisle's local ABC affiliate broadcasted old movies after the eleven-o'clock news, a random assortment of black-and-white films and seventies cinema: *The African Queen*, *The Maltese Falcon*, *Shane*, *The Dirty Dozen*. The highlight for us was when they had aired *King Kong* a few months back. That night—*King Kong* night—we stayed up until the national anthem played, an American flag glowing in the dark for a few minutes before the static signaled the end of TV, the thing that seemed to have no end.

We theorized about what the movie might be, but in truth we didn't care. We were nestled into the somnolent fortress of pillows and blankets, basking in the TV's blue light. Programming was irrelevant.

A made-for-TV drama came on after *The Fall Guy*, and our boredom led to inactivity, and our inactivity led to drowsiness. Lights on. TV blaring. Our parents covered us, turned off the TV, and retired to their bedroom because Lou and I had fallen asleep long before the start of the late-night movie.

At some point in the night, I jolted awake. I thought I heard something.

Sirens. Fire trucks. I saw the tail end of red and white lights fluttering on the curtains of the living room.

In the dark, I rubbed my eyes and glanced around at the scratchy silhouettes of the television, the lamps, the coffee table. I looked down the hallway toward the bedrooms, and I saw my great-grandmother standing in the hall. She stood right in front of the bathroom door, silent and unmoving, but I knew her immediately by her form, her tiny stature topped by the bulbous turban. *"Chào*, Bà Cố! *Chào!"* I greeted her and put my head down on my pillow, settling back to sleep.

I lay next to my brother, listening to the fading sirens. I thought for a moment about my great-grandmother being in our apartment. *Why was she there? Did my parents go get her? When did they do that?* Since Lou and I were in the living room, maybe she was having a sleepover in one of our beds. I'd find out in the morning. Too tired to continue, I drifted back to sleep.

Suddenly I was awake again. The lights were on. Was it morning? My mother nudged me and Lou. "Phúc and Lou, get up." She stood by with our coats in hand. "Put your coats on. We have to go."

My father came out from the kitchen. "There was a fire at the other apartment building where Ông Bà Ngoại live. A big fire."

Our coats went on wordlessly as we ventured outside. The cold December set our teeth rattling.

From the back seat of the Ford, Lou and I were knuckling the sleep from our eyes, trying to piece together what my parents were saying to each other. A fusillade of questions from us: *What happened? Who started the fire? Was anyone hurt? How big was the fire? Were there fire trucks? Is it still on fire?* They ignored us. I could see my father's brow clenched deeper than usual as we drove uninterrupted through the blinking traffic signals, as my mom cried in the passenger seat. Lou and I stopped talking as we felt the cold glaze of fear and dread frost over in the car.

Past the short six blocks we pulled up to Ông Bà Ngoại's apartment complex; the flashing of the fire engine lights illuminated the parking lot and onlookers. Dozens of neighbors stood around in the late-December air with hastily pulled on layers, bathrobes, coats, slippers, boots. Their warm exhalations puffed red and white as emergency lights pulsed. My grandmother, grandfather, my uncles and aunts, crowded together on the sidewalk, fire department blankets cloaked over their shoulders, disheveled and disbelieving. My parents parked near the fire engines and told me and Lou to stay in the car. We pivoted to our knees to look out the rear window as they headed over to the crowd, their profiles glowing with lights. Even from inside the car, the December air was smeared with smoke and the sickly sweet of burnt plastic. It looked like everyone was okay.

In spite of the army of fire trucks amassed, the building wasn't the ash heap I was expecting. From where we were parked, it looked normal, except for one blackened, broken window up to which a fire ladder extended. Around the window, a halo of soot and melted beige vinyl siding marred the otherwise mundane building face, a gouged and charred eye socket.

My parents stayed for a while, helping to arrange for everyone to stay at my uncle Châu's apartment, which was in the same complex, and we headed home exhausted.

Back inside at Walnut Bottom Road, still zipped up in our winter coats, our parents sat us in their laps and told us that Bà Cố was hurt badly in the fire. She had been taken away to the hospital and we would know more in the morning. As they told me this, I looked down the hall of our apartment where I had just seen her. I hadn't seen her in the group of survivors, but I assumed that she was sleeping over at our apartment. I saw her in our hallway that night. *I saw her.* And now my parents were telling me that she had been trapped in the fire.

Lou asked more questions that my parents couldn't answer while I sat, glancing occasionally down the hallway.

I started to doubt what I saw. Maybe I *didn't* see Bà Cố in the hallway? But I did. But she hadn't been here. She was in the other apartment building. We later learned from the fire department that the fire had started in her room, and no one was able to get past the flames to reach her. Unresponsive and badly burned, she had been taken in an ambulance to the ICU.

Bà Cố. She had survived all the wars, all the helicopters, boats, and planes, all the relocation camps in Guam, Wake Island, Fort Indiantown Gap; had lived to see snow for her first time as an octogenarian, only to be engulfed in flames in her apartment.

That weekend, the apartment management moved Ông Bà Ngoại, my aunt, and two uncles across the parking lot to another three-bedroom unit, and we helped them drag the smoky remnants of their possessions in plastic shopping bags into the new apartment.

My grandparents visited my great-grandmother in the ICU and reported what little news they could parse from the doctors, but we younger children didn't go to the hospital. We were planted in front of the television as the grown-ups began stoically piecing together their lives again. My parents helped Ông Bà Ngoại and everyone collect and sort more clothing and furnishings from our sponsors. If they suffered or were devastated by the fire, they didn't show us, shouldering the tragedy with a tacit steeliness.

Bà Cố never regained consciousness, and she died a few days later from her burns and smoke inhalation. She was eighty-five.

My grandmother, Bà Ngoại, as the new matriarch of the family,

insisted on an open casket at Bà Cố's funeral—her first unilateral decision, a decision that was roundly protested but dutifully obeyed. No one
wanted an open casket for a burn victim, but my grandmother insisted.

At the funeral (my first), Lou and I recoiled at the charred remains
of Bà Cố, the smooth polish of the casket a sharp counterpoint to her
blackened features, only vaguely human and distinctly not her. Great
care had been taken to wrap the turban around her head even though
all her hair had burned off. A pastiche of the past.

My father pushed me and Lou toward the casket as we protested,
but he insisted that we pay our respects. Confucian filial piety, laminated with third-world Catholicism, overrode any sensible restraint.
He gripped our arms as he marched us down to the prie-dieu to kneel.

I lowered myself in front of the casket, remembering the false terror
that Lou and I had felt in our game with Bà Cố, feeling the awful, *real*
terror of beholding her disfigured face and hands. Lou and I held hands
and cried together, shedding tears that she might wake up and be in
pain from the burns, tears for her death, tears for the horror of beholding what used to be her.

Nearly every book and film that has ever had a ghost in the plot will
tell you: a ghost doesn't randomly show up without being a crucial narrative element. When ghosts show up in literature or film, they expedite
or pivot the story. In *Hamlet*, a murdered father appears to demand his
revenge; in *Star Wars*, Obi-Wan Kenobi slips into the snowy vapors of
Hoth to tell Luke where to finish his Jedi training; in *The Odyssey*, our
hero, Odysseus, goes to Hades, the Grand Central Terminal of ghosts, to
get some advice and direction that, apparently, he couldn't get from the
living. And of course, Dickens's *A Christmas Carol* has the nightmare of
spooky visions of what would have been, what is, and what could be.
The ghosts create meaning and impetus.

In the aftermath of seeing Bà Cố's ghost, I didn't know what it meant.
Bà Cố didn't say anything—she just stood there. I saw her in the hall-

way, and I went back to sleep. And then she was burned in the fire. Was she a premonition of an unavoidable tragedy? If so, why did I see her? Was she a vision of the past, present, or future? Or was she just a ghost, an apparition, a phenomenon with no larger or deeper significance than what I wanted to make of it? Maybe she wanted to see me one last time. Maybe she wanted *me* to see her one last time. I believe that I did.

APRIL 1982

"Do you want to go to the movies next weekend?"

I was shocked. My father had asked me if I wanted to go to the movies. *The movies.*

Going to the movies had been a chore outsourced to my uncles and cousins. My cousins on Staten Island had taken me to witness Rocky Balboa defeat Apollo Creed in *Rocky II*. My uncles dragged me to see Cheech & Chong's weed-fueled adventures, which I distinctly remember not understanding nor enjoying. Some older cousins took me along to see *The Blues Brothers*, which I also didn't understand. Sometimes I was brought along at the insistence of Bà Ngoại. "Oh, you're going to the movies? Why don't you take Phúc, too?" Their eyeballs rolled their annoyance that their young tagalong was coming, too. Of course, no one gave a moment's thought to the movie's rating, and my frequent suggestions that we see an animated or kids film were quashed unilaterally. I wanted to see *Tron*, but we saw *Friday the 13th* instead. I wanted to see *The Last Unicorn*, but we saw *Conan the Barbarian* instead. And during the movies, I triggered a landslide of shushing from my cousins. *Who's that? What's this? Why's he smoking that? Why is he killing that guy? Who's that guy anyway?*

Shush. Shush! Jesus, you're so annoying. Shush!

My father, however, rarely took me to the movies. I immediately assented to his suggestion to see a movie and threw my arms around him. "A movie! Sure! What movie?"

"I read about the movie in the newspaper. It's the *best* movie in America—I think we should go see it." He was referring to the winner of the Oscar for Best Picture that year, not that it made a difference to me. Reading *The Evening Sentinel* was my father's daily, ongoing effort at gaining some cultural competency and improving his reading comprehension.

"The best movie in America? That sounds good! What's it called?"

"*Chariots of Fire.*"

"Whoa, that *does* sound good!" I had never heard of it, but with the logic of a third grader, I parsed the title *Chariots of Fire* literally and aggrandized my father's enthusiasm at seeing the best movie in America. I had seen *Clash of the Titans* at my grandparents' house. The Trầns were moving up in the world. My grandparents had premium cable television and a VCR, and with that, Ông Ngoại had begun a small collection of movies that he pirated from HBO and PRISM. *Clash of the Titans*, with its sword fights, skeleton armies, and a Kraken, reigned as a household favorite. How much more awesome could *Chariots of Fire* be than *Clash of the Titans*?

"Can I bring a friend to the movie?"

It was rare that my parents allowed us to invite friends to the apartment or on outings with our family. The idea of a sleepover was a foreign concept, and they didn't understand why we would want to invite other kids to our house to play as opposed to meeting outside and playing there.

My father's past history, built upon so many no's, tottered with an uncharacteristic yes. "Yes, you can bring one friend. We can get popcorn, too. Maybe that will be fun." He said *yes* and he said *fun*. I hardly recognized my father, the stern, domineering killjoy who reigned with an iron bar. I didn't want to push my luck with more questions. The date was set. *Chariots of Fire*. Next Saturday. There would be popcorn. I could bring a friend. It would be fun. This was not the father that I knew, not the Chánh Trần of the past, not the one whose replacement I had prayed for.

At recess that Monday, I ascended the monkey bars and surveyed my choices of whom to invite. This was *Chariots of Fire*, after all. From my perch, I considered my options. Craig Fleckman, my long-time friend since kindergarten, was in the other third-grade class. It was the first time that we were not in the same class together, which meant that we might as well have been on different planets. Our love of *Star Wars* was strong but not that strong. We were on hiatus. Lizzie Kenyon? She was sort of a friend but to invite a girl? Nope. I didn't want anyone to think that I was asking a girl to be my girlfriend, and especially not Lizzie Kenyon. No girls. That eliminated over half the class. I could invite the kids with whom I wanted to be friends, but that seemed like an overreach. With only one berth for moviegoing, I couldn't risk the humiliation of asking a series of kids only to have them refuse.

Eli Huey it was. Winner. He was my go-to friend at recess, and I his. Eli was new to our school that year, and he and I were seated near each other. He was a fast runner, laughed at my jokes, ate his boogers, liked *Star Wars*. He lived in a nearby apartment complex and was the only other kid I knew in my class who also lived in an apartment. The parallels of our housing situations allowed me to map my experience onto Eli, which I couldn't do with other kids. Maybe people banged on his apartment floor too, as they did at our apartment? Maybe he shared a room with his sibling? Maybe his mom said no to toys because they didn't have enough money?

I asked Eli if he wanted to go to the movies with me and my dad, and he, like me, was hooked by the title.

"*Chariots of Fire*? Yeah, definitely! I gotta ask my mom, but yeah, I definitely want to go." His mom said yes that night, and for the rest of the week during recess, Eli and I agreed to play *Chariots of Fire* in anticipation of the movie. Our imaginations ran unbridled. *What do the chariots look like? Do you think they're always on fire? Do you think they shoot fire too? What sorts of creatures do you think pull them? Horses? Maybe Pegasuses?* In our frenzy, we hoped that the movie was a sequel to *Clash of the Titans* or at least borrowed from Greek mythology. By Friday's last recess, Eli and I had unspooled a tangled plot about the heroes, villains, and monsters, all of whom rode chariots—chariots of fire.

Saturday afternoon we drove to the theater, Eli and I excitedly discussing the movie on the drive over. How could the movie not live up to the title? It was the *best* movie in America. And it had chariots (of fire) in it. And my father had suggested that we go. His involvement was thrilling for me. My father had not taken me to *Star Wars* or *The Empire Strikes Back*, but here we were together. Seated on red upholstered movie theater seats. Popcorn in our laps. My father on my left and Eli on my right.

The theater darkened, and trailers for upcoming releases of boring talky movies flickered on the screen. And then the movie began.

A church flickered onto the screen. Some sort of mass. Okay, this was weird. And then a bunch of men in white underwear were running on the beach. I thought maybe we were watching a trailer for another movie, but the title card came up. *Chariots of Fire.* Had we made a mistake? Maybe the chariots would come later? Patience. It had only been three minutes. I looked at Eli, who was munching away at his popcorn. He caught my eye and shrugged, happy to be eating an entire bag of popcorn by himself.

An eternity passed. Still more running on the beach and through town. There were long close-ups of faces and even more running. The time period was not a mythical era with Medusas or Krakens. It was twentieth-century England. There were no swords, sandals, or togas. It was just supercilious Englishmen, talking and running against the synthetic swelling *ch-ch-ch-ch-ch* of Vangelis's theme song. At least that sounded cool.

The movie ran on longer without any signs of a chariot or fire. My confusion was supplanted by embarrassment, thirty minutes into the movie. This was not the *Chariots of Fire* that we had made up in our heads. This was not what I had promised to Eli, and I couldn't bear to gaze upon the disappointment that he shared with me, the disbelief that this movie was actually about Englishmen talking and running.

I didn't want to look at Eli even there in the dark, but I did. I forced myself.

Eli was asleep. Asleep amid unpopped kernels and the collapsed rubble of his popcorn bag. He snored slightly. I had invited one friend to a movie, and that movie was so boring—so terrible—that he fell asleep.

My father nudged me. "Wake up. It's time to go—the movie's over." I didn't remember falling asleep. The credits were rolling, and my lips stung from the salt that had crusted the corners of my mouth for the last ninety minutes. My father seemed chipper. "That was a *pretty* good movie, huh? Very inspiring. Geez. It was very inspiring. Did you sleep through the whole thing?"

"Sorry." I didn't know what else to say.

Eli piped up. "I get so sleepy when I eat, and then in the theater it gets dark. . . ." He shrugged and picked his nose.

We were silent on the car ride home from the theater, fully awake and refreshed from our nap but bereft of the customary post-movie postmortem of *wasn't it cool when* and *what about the part when*.

We dropped Eli off at his apartment and headed home. Lou wanted to know right away about the movie. "How was *Chariots of Fire*?"

"It was okay, I guess."

"What? Just okay? What do you mean?"

"I mean, I fell asleep. And Eli fell asleep."

"But it was *Chariots of Fire*!"

"I know . . . but it's not what you think. I can't tell you what it was about, but it's not what you think it sounds like."

We kids lived in a world that was barely metaphorical, where titles for movies and TV shows were tantamount to the ingredient labels. *Fantasy Island* was a fantasy island. *The Love Boat* was a love boat. *The Dukes of Hazzard* were the Dukes of Hazzard.

But *Chariots of Fire*? No chariots. No fire.

"It was very inspiring! Good story!" My father put his arm around my shoulders, but having fallen asleep, I couldn't disagree. It was an optimistic appraisal. I was still deflated and cranky from the movie not living up to my expectations, and I squirmed in his embrace. I placed all the blame squarely upon my father. He had said that it was a great movie, but it was actually terrible. He had failed me. Again. I heaped *Chariots of Fire* on top of *Wookiee* and *colonel*, and countless other misunderstandings and errors. Another instance of his inability to navigate the world with competency.

My embarrassment from the *Chariots of Fire* fiasco was acute, but in retrospect I'm able to see more clearly that he tried. It was, after all, the best movie of 1982. It had a cool title and we had popcorn. I can't remember many moments in my childhood where my father made a good-faith effort to do something fun, but I remember this one.

As an adult, I've been able to understand that my father was not as trapped by his past as I thought he was. He was often violent and angry, but now I can look back and see that he tried to do fun things from time to time, things that didn't fit into the narrow, cartoonish image that I formed of him. Fossil hunting on the shores of Pinchot Lake. Visits to the Indian Echo Caverns in Hummelstown. Impromptu trips to Washington, D.C., to see the Smithsonian because it was free. I had witnessed the tension of who he was and who he was trying to be. I wanted him to be loving and kind. But his old behavior, his temper, his rage, eclipsed his attempts at being a better father.

The past pulled us and the future pushed us. The tension of tenses.

We lived in the Past, the Present, and the Future. It wasn't only laid out in my grandparents, my parents, and me. It was in our relationships, it was in how we treated one another and how we looked at one another, heedless of who we actually were. My adult uncles were still slapped as if they were children. We could never grow up in our parents' eyes, but they could not grow or change in ours, either. Our past behaviors, our present needs, our future goals—all of them snares.

But even if the past is unchangeable, maybe our perspective of the past can change. And maybe the way we see past events can change, and if *that* can change, maybe the past event itself does change—not in action or outcome but in purpose and intent.

I couldn't see it in the moment, but through the years, with the interplay of memories, experience, and perspective, I've come to see our trip to the movies not as another failure by my father, but rather as an attempt to connect to his son. But in that present moment, I couldn't see it for what it was. I was unable to see past our past.

5

MAN AND HIS SYMBOLS

AUGUST 1983

"Where are you people from?"

We were shopping at Giant, pushing our cart slowly. Lou and I took turns dangling from the cart, making impassioned pleas to our parents to buy Count Chocula.

An older gentleman stepped into our path, intercepting us with his question—THE question that, as I grew up in Carlisle, I would sustain regularly, a query angled with varying degrees of inflection, from curious to neutral to cutting. "Where are you people from?"

Even at nine years old, I heard the nuances of *you people*. I caught his drift. His drift was sharp and edgy. It was pointed. His drift didn't sound like a friendly game of catch.

My parents hadn't heard him because they were Vietnamesing with each other about their shopping list, and they weren't expecting anyone to speak to them. No one knew us in that informal, neighborly way, and my parents weren't part of the small-town colloquium that burbled and babbled around us. I saw other people, friends and neighbors, stopping and talking to one another. *How's Little League? Donna doing okay? D'ja see the game last night?* We weren't in Little League. No one asked about my mother's health. We didn't watch sports on TV.

The man spoke up louder with the kind of volume that inferred lack of Englishing. "Where are you people from?"

I nudged my father, who broke off from his conversation with my mother to acknowledge the man. "Yes, sir?" Always publicly polite.

"Where are you people from?" The man had yellow-tinted aviators and a graying mustache—reminding me of *Magnum P.I.* from TV. His belly overhung a large buckle, pressing taut against his plaid shirt. Maybe he was a private eye? Maybe he was working a case or was grocery store security?

"Oh, we are from Việt Nam." My father smiled widely, nervously. His default was always to smile in awkward or strange situations, but I felt his posture tense up. My father also caught the man's drift, and he moved protectively in between the man and us.

"Yeah. Thought so. Thought I recognized it. Viet*man*ese. I haven't heard it since I was . . . in country. Thought to myself: sounds like Viet*man*ese." Lou started to correct the man's pronunciation of Viet*nam*ese, but I kicked him from behind the cart. Lou caught my drift as well and he shut up. "In the Marines there. Stationed in DaH Nang, '68 to '69." He looked at us all as he spoke, eyes slinking from my father's rigid smile to my mother to us kids.

"Oh yes. Đà Nẵng is in the middle of Việt Nam. We're from Sài Gòn." My father continued to smile as we stood still, nervous prey whiffing a predatory scent. My eyes scanned the American flag pin and other buttons on his jacket lapel.

The gentleman looked at us, but his eyes were distant, their focus going far beyond where we were—right through us. I looked behind myself at the produce section, understanding that he wasn't looking at the broccoli or cabbage.

"Beautiful country there, Nam." He said *Nam* with a Southern lilt.

Naaaaaam. Carlisle, surprising to most outsiders, has a slight Southern drawl to its local dialect. "Beautiful country, Nam. Goddamn shame what happened there."

My father nodded.

"Goddamn shame," the man murmured.

We all nodded and stood there for a time, staring at Mr. Magnum P.I. as he stared at the broccoli behind us. We as a family, in turn, looked blankly around; my parents gazed farther down the aisle, Lou and I fidgeting wordlessly at the cart, everyone bobbling their heads. The man hadn't asked us a question, so we had no answer to give.

"Well, you people have a good day."

"Thank you. You too, sir." My father and mother smiled and waved.

Lou had used the distraction to sneak a box of Count Chocula into the cart. He nudged me. "Why did that man ask us where we were from?"

My parents had already wandered farther down the aisle, sorting through the different cooking oils on the shelves. I was pushing the cart, so I answered Lou. "Because that man fought in the Vietnam War." The metal grocery cart resumed its screechy circuit in between the aisles.

"So?"

"Well, we're from Vietnam." I said *Việt Nam* the way the man had said it.

"Not me. I was born here in Carlisle." Lou had a point.

"Well, that *is* true. But people are always going to ask you where you're from."

"But I'm from Pennsylvania." Spoken like the future lawyer he would be.

"It's true, you were born here, but it won't make sense to people. They'll still ask you where you're from. They mean Mom and Dad. And me. Your family—where we're from."

"How did that man know that we weren't from here?"

"It's complicated. . . ." I chose not to explain bigotry to Lou, though he probably already knew it. He had experienced being the "only one" in his classes too, but at least the "other one" at school was his brother.

I was blindly hoping that he wasn't aware of the prejudice, but who was I kidding? Whose innocence was I trying to preserve?

"Why did he say that it was a shame what happened?" Lou persisted.

"I don't know. . . . He didn't really say, did he?" I was pained to tell Lou to get used to being asked where he was from, but he had to. And eventually he would, whether I warned him or not. Get used to it or get crushed by it.

We all learned quickly to smile and nod whenever veterans would see us and tell us that they were in 'Nam. They named their branch of service, told us what years they were there, where they were stationed, and how they found the people or the weather. Later, when I was older and a little savvier, I would round out my exchange by saying something like "Thanks for your service" or "My grandparents worked for the US embassy"—volunteering something to identify myself as one of the good ones. But that was much later, when I realized that this wasn't about me or my family. It was about them and what we symbolized for them.

How could I explain to Lou that we were symbols? That some people would never be able to see us as just people? That we were symbols of a painful and confusing war? Symbols of the refugees they saw on TV? Symbols of what they were afraid of? Symbols of the people who had shot at them and killed their friends, brothers, and sons? Symbols of whatever they wanted to see?

That was what we were for Mr. Magnum P.I. In the middle of the Giant grocery store, we had to pause our shopping and be symbols for what he saw in the fuzzy, distant gaze of recollection and trauma.

The Tràns didn't choose to be symbolic or archetypal, but it wasn't our choice to make.

Our family was a symbol long before any of us could identify that feeling of being a symbol: symbols of the war, icons of America's foreign policy, representatives of a country that people had only seen on silver screens and the convex glass of TV sets. I felt my symbolism long before I knew it. When I was young and people hated me, called me a gook or a chink, asked me where I was from, I thought: *Why isn't this happening to other kids? How is it happening to me even when people don't know me?*

Kids (and later, adults) were treating me as if they had already met me, and as a result, they treated me with a brisk familiarity. By being Vietnamese, I was tapping into a powerful and activating energy that compelled them to say something to me, to look at me and my family in a way that they didn't look at others.

In high school, I first read about the psychoanalyst C. G. Jung and his study of archetypes in his dream analysis. Jung had planted the seeds for groundbreaking ideas that would eventually find their way into psychology, anthropology, and pop culture, but in his pursuit of understanding his patients' dreams, Jung was asking questions that no one dared to answer: Why do so many people have similar, recurring motifs in their dreams? And why do so many cultures share similar, mythic symbols? Jung shaped what we now know as the archetype and archetypal characters. He proposed that humans all share a collective unconscious, that our shared experience as *homines sapientes* laid the bedrock for our dreams and myths. Jung said that we lived in a world of symbolism, internal and external.

According to his theories of dream analysis, images and concepts move beneath the surface of our awareness, leviathans of nameless fears and hopes that can evoke a powerful response. Jung writes that "a word or an image is symbolic when it implies something more than its obvious and immediate meaning. It has a wider 'unconscious' aspect that is never precisely defined or fully explained."

By those Jungian threads, could people connect us, the Tràns, to something more than our obvious and immediate meaning? Were there socially constructed images that provoked a stronger response than we could anticipate? Did our symbolism make people call us gooks, tell us to go back to our country, steal our bikes? Had we inadvertently stepped into a national conversation about refugees, patriotism, and *the* war, unaware of the acrimony and vitriol that preceded us?

We had, and we were unconscious of its symbolism.

OCTOBER 1983

Wednesday night. Ten o'clock. Long past our bedtime. Lou and I were jumping up and down on the beds, leaping from one bed to the next.

"Okay, your turn!" A flying leap from my bed to his, a stream of giggles fluttered behind Lou. "Okay, now me!" I pumped myself up and down a few times before hurling myself across to Lou, arms and legs pulled tight in cannonball position—great for a pool, not so great for a bed or your brother on the bed.

My full momentum landed on his ankle, and Lou unleashed a howl. "Oh my God, I'm so sor—" was immediately met by a barrage of his fists of fury. I deflected a few blows before returning fire. A full-on fistfight raged before my father stormed in.

"THAT'S IT! THIS IS THE LAST TIME I'M TELLING YOU TO GO TO BED! GO TO BED . . . OR ELSE!" He had already come into our room twice that night after banging on the adjoining wall and yelling at us *go-to-bed* multiple times. Part of my brain registered the dark circles under his eyes, his disheveled hair, and the sagging lines pulling at his youthful face, which was still boyish at thirty-three. But only part of my brain saw that. The other part of my brain, the reptilian amygdala nut, buried deep inside the cortex, thought, *He's not going to spank you. What's the "or else"? What's more fun than jumping?* Thanks, amygdala. This is why you're not on top and in charge.

But cerebellum was right. The last part of his declaration was tooth-less. Or else *what*? It had been two years since he had spanked or beaten me. I muttered a dubious *okay*.

Lights off (again).

Within minutes, lights back on. We were engaged in a frantic pillow fight, heaving our pillows.

If we were not archetypal boys, what were we? What function did we fulfill other than brothers who clobbered each other one moment only to dissolve into tender play the next?

I hit Lou with a pillow so hard that he flew off the bed and onto his back, and he burst into laughter.

We heard my parents' bedroom door open and close, and we stopped mid–pillow swing. We braced ourselves for more yelling. Maybe we had pushed my father past his breaking point. Maybe this is what it took to provoke Chánh Trần into a rage monster.

Frozen in battle positions. Pillows at the ready. We dropped everything and lunged into the nearest bed together, pulling the covers up over our shoulders, creating an absurd tableau of angelic boys even if the ruckus belied the mise-en-scène. We waited for our door to open, waited for some yelling. We waited and waited. But nothing happened.

We heard talking in the hallway and the jingle of keys.

"What do you think they're doing?" Lou sat up and pushed the covers off.

"I don't know—let's go see." I cracked the door open to see my parents, each with a suitcase. Coats on and shoes on.

"Where are you going?" I went into the living room, Lou trailing behind me.

"Are you going somewhere?" Lou saw my parents at the top of the stairs.

My father looked at us both. "We're leaving. You two are so bad. Naughty children. We don't know what to do, so we're leaving." Lou immediately began crying. My mother held her eyes fixed to the ground, her green suitcase firmly in her grip.

"WHAT?!" I pleaded as Lou's tears triggered my own crying. "NO! PLEASE! WE'LL BE GOOD! PLEASE!"

My father was expressionless, his dark eyes intense and focused. "It's too late. We're leaving now." They moved down the stairs. Lou and I grabbed our mother around the waist. My mother, always our solace and comfort, gently nudged us away. For the first time ever, she denied us, and my heart rent. We tried a few more times to clasp her waist, rebuffed each time, and my father pulled Lou off. "Maybe you'll be good next time." His parting salvo.

I sat down, defeated, at the top of the apartment stairs. "PLEASE DON'T LEAVE US! I'M SORRY! I'M SORRY I'M SO BAD!" My tears erupting with wails and deep sobbing as I leaned my head against the wall.

Lou was racked with grief. "I will be good! We will be! I'm so sorry! PLEASE DON'T LEAVE US! PLEASE!" He weakened with crying. We both sat at the top of the stairs as they left, hoping that they would change their minds, but the apartment door closed behind them.

We ran to the living room window. From the second floor we watched the Ford's lights turn on.

Were they going to do it? The brake lights flared at the end of the parking lot as the yellow turn signal flickered on the right. Maybe they would stop? The Ford pulled out onto Walnut Bottom Road and drove off.

They did it. Lou clung to the windowsill, crying into the pane as I turned around.

I didn't think they were going to do it, but they did. I stopped my own tears enough to talk to Lou.

"Come on, let's sit down." I put my arm around my brother and led him to the velour couch.

He sat, tears still falling. "What are we going to do?" Lou looked at me, and I felt an immediate burden. He needed me to be the big brother. He needed me to know what we were going to do.

I choked down a nauseating bolus of abandonment and fear. "I can take care of us." I pushed the words out calmly, even though I didn't actually know if I could, but I thought this declaration might comfort Lou.

"No, you can't!"

Jesus, really? Have some faith, Lou, I thought. I doubled down. "No, I can. Really."

"No, you can't! You don't have a job! You don't know how to drive! You don't know how to cook!" All good points.

"Well, we walk or ride our bikes everywhere anyway. And Ông Bà Ngoại don't live that far away. They can help us, too."

Lou started crying harder, which made me start to cry. "I'll take care of us. I promise."

"We're going to starve!"

"No, we won't."

"We are! We're going to starve! Mom and Dad left us!"

Jesus Christ, were we *already* arguing just moments after our parents had packed their bags and left? We were.

"Will you shut up?! We are *not* going to starve! We aren't! I'll show you." I marched into the kitchen. "Sit down—I'll show you. We can do it."

Lou sat at the kitchen table. Eyes puffy. Face wet. From his seat, he glanced out the window behind him, every passing car giving him the false hope that our parents had returned. They hadn't.

I grabbed bread and put two slices in the toaster. When they were done, I opened a lower cabinet door and found soy sauce. I sprinkled soy sauce on the toast and clacked the plate in front of Lou.

He was incredulous. "What's this? Bread with soy sauce?"

"Obviously. See? I told you I could take care of us." Lou cried harder, his face distorting. "Stop crying! Just eat it and don't be a baby!" I was breaking inside and huffed. "Just eat the toast. Eat the toast." I had done my best.

I picked up my slice and took a bite. Still warm. Crusty and salty. Lou immediately took the other piece, years of fraternal training and instinct kicking in. He knew that if he didn't claim his toast, I would take it.

I watched him force the toast into his mouth, eyeing it with suspicion. His crying stopped as he chewed, slowly and then faster. His countenance unknotted itself as he munched away. "This . . . this is pretty good." He ate the whole slice.

Lou seemed comforted. We wouldn't starve now provided that we had a steady supply of bread and soy sauce and a toaster. I put the plate into the sink and cleared the table after I got him some water. Our dinner plates that my mother had saved for the morning were heaped up in the sink. I decided I would do the dishes even though I'd never washed dishes before. Lou watched me as I put on a show, a parody of domestic confidence. *Look at me! I can make toast and do the dishes! We'll be fine!* I seemed to be saying. In his red-and-blue Spider-Man pajamas, Lou looked out the window, still monitoring the traffic as I rinsed the dishes.

I dried my hands on a towel. "Let's go to sleep. I'm tired." Keeping your little brother alive was exhausting work. "We still have to go to school tomorrow."

Lou insisted on sleeping in my bed even though we were too big to fit comfortably in the twin, and fatigue blanketed whatever discomfort I felt, whatever anxiety weighed on me.

This was not a typical Wednesday night, even by the Trần family's nonstandard standards. It wasn't every Wednesday night that your parents were so exasperated that they left.

In the dark, I awoke. I didn't know if it had been twenty minutes or three hours. I heard my parents come in, and I got up, letting Lou sleep. Good for him.

I saw my mother first. My father was in the kitchen; I could hear the water running as he got a glass of water. "You came back." I didn't know what else to say, standing by the bathroom.

"Thanks for doing the dishes." My mother had noticed the empty sink.

"We'll try to be good. I'm so sorry. . . ." I started to cry again, but this time from relief. She held my head against her chest.

"I know you will."

Their suitcases were still at the top of the stairs. "Let me help you." I picked up a suitcase, leaning into its weight, but it flew up in my hands, and I lost my balance. The suitcase was unexpectedly light. It was empty, in fact. My father came around the kitchen and saw me picking up the empty luggage. They hadn't actually packed their bags. They hadn't planned to leave us. He and I looked at each other as I realized their bluff.

My father eyed the suitcases. "I hope you learned your lesson."

I didn't reply. Instead I placed both empty suitcases by their door, and went back to our room, closing the door behind me. I pushed Lou, snoring lightly, to make room in my bed.

In the dark, I weighed my father's words. *Learned my lesson*? I did learn a lesson.

I had a grand and rosy notion of parents from television: unconditionally nurturing, kind, loving. The Bradys. The Cunninghams. The Waltons. Television had a Jungian archetype of perfect parenthood that was the yardstick for my parents. And in reality, I had a father and mother from *Grimms' Fairy Tales*: parents willing to beat, forsake, and terrorize children. My parents pretended to abandon us. I believed that they had left. And then I discovered that they had lied. Which was more monstrous?

This painful experience was, in fact, part of the Jungian arc of maturity: the separation from one's parents to become our own individuals. Jung writes: "But in making this break with the childhood world, the original parent archetype will be injured." My image of my parents was injured. I accepted that Chánh and Chi couldn't meet the symbolism of idealized TV parents, but at night, in my bed, I still held tight the flint of what I thought good parents were supposed to be. In our family's dark moments, I still needed and wanted fairy-tale TV parents. I struck that parental ideal against whatever pebble of hope I had, dreaming that the spark of my yearning would rekindle something in them, too. My idea of parents—my *ideal* of parents—was sputtering and barely alight, but it still smoldered, and I fanned a hope that they could be good parents, that they could be the parents I needed them to be.

Learned your lesson. My father's words struck a plangent chord.

I did learn a lesson that night. In the void of their departure, I learned to appear greater than I was. My brother needed me to be more than his nine-year-old brother. I learned that even if I didn't have a clue about driving or having a job or being a parent, the symbolism of being a parent—the basic act of making toast and washing plates—was enough for Lou. That was the power of the symbol.

NOVEMBER 1983

My uncle Chú Thu was not my real uncle. At least, not in the state that we saw him.

In the coffin, Chú Thu looked grayish, and even though his mustache and hair looked real, his cheeks and eyes were sunken. The effect of his deep-set eye sockets created a face that was my uncle's face, but its features were exaggerated and drawn. Long before I learned about the uncanny valley, I felt the apprehension of seeing something that looked almost exactly like my uncle but was not my uncle. I shuddered.

"Is that Chú Thu?" Lou was as unsure as I was. We were both dressed in button-down shirts and clip-on ties, ill-fitting blazers, and whatever dress pants we had—we wore the same outfits to Christmas mass and Easter Sunday, though our uncle's funeral was the antithesis of those occasions. Our dress clothes seemed to inaugurate the apices and nadirs of formal gatherings, celebrations, and mournings. "Is it really him?"

"Yeah, of course it's him."

"It doesn't *look* like him." I flashed a passing annoyance that he had called Chú Thu *it*, but *it* was exactly the right word. *It* did not deserve the pronoun *he*.

I nodded. My mother's second eldest brother was dead, and in the midst of the grieving, witnesses to our aunts' tears and Bà Ngoại's steely poise, Lou and I were debating the quality of the embalming and makeup, the verisimilitude of the corpse.

I was thankful that he hadn't died in a fire. At least we were looking at a relatively normal-looking corpse. It was the second funeral I'd been to, the second dead body I'd seen (third, if you count Saint John Neumann). I was ten years old, already able to determine the qualitative differences in open-casket funerals, and declared that this affair was not as gruesome as Bà Cố's funeral, but it unsettled me nonetheless.

"Why did he kill himself?" Lou asked the seemingly unanswerable, but his question exhumed a grim truth. My parents had gone over this already.

My exasperation with Lou's relentless questioning made me whisper-shout, "HE KILLED HIMSELF BECAUSE HE KILLED AUNT CINDY. Remember?" And in the pews, my father gnarred at me and Lou.

My uncle Thu had married Cindy a few years earlier, an American woman—a first for the Trầns—and they had a daughter, Heather, who was exactly Lou's age.

Lou didn't bother to ask my parents, whispering to me. "Why did he kill her?"

My uncle Thái (Thu's younger brother) had told me why, and I didn't hesitate to tell Lou. "Chú Thu found her with a boyfriend in bed. . . . I guess he got angry and stabbed and killed her. He stabbed her boyfriend, too, but the boyfriend ran away and lived. And then Chú Thu killed himself."

"But why did he kill *himself*? And Aunt Cindy had a boyfriend?! I thought they were married." I couldn't explain that last part because I didn't know much about their relationship. In that actual moment, we were dumb, divorced from any perspective other than our elementary understanding of love, marriage, death, and murder.

I hazarded a guess. "Maybe he felt really bad after he killed her. Maybe he felt so bad that he killed himself."

Lou seemed to accept that as much as any seven-year-old could. "But it was Thanksgiving. He killed her on *Thanksgiving*."

I didn't dispute that point of emphasis. Lou was right. Without saying it, he was circling the horror of the event the way that kids do: name the facts and allow the facts, in all their jagged, incongruous angles, to grind and scrape against one another. Kids don't have a euphemistic or subtle way of speaking about life.

"You're right. It was Thanksgiving. But I don't know why he did it on Thanksgiving." I didn't want to remind Lou of the worst part: It was also Heather's birthday. It was Thanksgiving *and* our cousin's seventh birthday, and now both of her parents were dead. Heather wasn't at her father's funeral. Her American grandparents had planned Cindy's funeral on the same day, at the same time, at another funeral home across town. Heather had spent the entire previous summer with us, and celebrated family holidays and birthdays alongside us. The death of her parents was the beginning of her slow disappearance as her American grandparents withdrew from our family, eventually relocating to Florida. We never heard from her again.

And poor Aunt Cindy. Twenty-six years old. I thought about how kind she was, how she was always smiling, and how she and my mother would commute together to the electronics factory because my mother had gotten her a job there. My uncle had achieved the American dream: a pretty American wife, a muscle car, a child, a dog, a great job. Jackpot. It was textbook, blueprint Americana. And he demolished it. All of it. It didn't make any sense to me. Our most successful—most *American* family member—had thrown it all away. His success had symbolized everything we were striving for, and now it ended with an orphaning murder-suicide.

I mulled this over as the funeral mass danced with its choreography of standing, sitting, kneeling, praying. Lou leaned over to me every few minutes to share a new thought that he had.

"Chú Thu was . . . he was . . . he was really nice." Lou's ellipses were fraught with the concessive reality that, yes, he was nice, and in spite of that, he also killed his wife and himself. "Remember how he took us swimming last summer? At the pool?"

I did remember. That past summer, Chú Thu had offered to watch me and Lou because my parents couldn't find childcare two days a week. He'd make us lunch (along with Heather) and then we'd all go to the indoor pool at Dickinson College, where he worked. We jumped off the high dive, screaming all the way down, the water hitting us so hard that it would wedge our swimming trunks all the way up our butt cracks.

Chú Thu, without swimming trunks, wore cutoff jeans, which attracted brow-raising disapproval from the other swimmers, but he didn't care. Tossing his long hair over his shoulders, reeking of nicotine and nonchalance, Chú Thu cannonballed right into the deep end. Right off into the deep end.

And now he was dead. And the corpse, presented in a polished mahogany box with tufted white satin, was supposed to look like him—but in a coffin.

Symbolism in our waking Jungian dream was a two-way mirror. We were symbols for our American neighbors, but our neighbors—with their polished cars, grand homes, backyard swing sets—they symbolized something for us, too. They glittered as goals, mirages toward which we endlessly stumbled. That day I mourned my uncle as much as I did the American success he symbolized, and I shuddered that the symbolism of the Trầns was now tinged with blood.

MARCH 1984

"Can I change my name?" It was Sunday, after church.

My father shrugged. "Sure. What do you want to change it to?" Neither parent bothered to ask why, because they already knew why: to Americanize. To blend in. To molt a foreign name that was ill fitting or that made the process of fitting in ill fitting.

"What? Really? What's your name going to be?" Lou's surprise was laced with excitement.

"I was thinking I would change my name to Peter." I anticipated the obvious question of *why*. "You know, like Saint Peter, my patron saint." We all got patron saints for our baptisms. Lou had gotten Saint Luke, and I had gotten Saint Peter. I wasn't sure how my parents or grandparents allocated the patron saints, but I had always been envious that Lou had gotten Saint Luke because of *Star Wars*. Who could possibly be a better patron saint for me, Phuc? Our names even rhymed, and *Star Wars* was my religion. It would have been perfect, but alas, not to be.

"Peter? That sounds nice. I like it. And I like that it's because of Saint Peter." My mother approved. My father mumbled assent. My mother had, in the nine years that we'd been in Carlisle, changed her name three times, from Lucy (her patron saint name) to Kim (her middle name, which coincidentally had an Anglonym equivalent) and then to Chi (her Vietnamese name). As she rebranded, she hadn't bothered to update her acquaintances at work, parishioners at church, or our neighbors at Colonial Square, so she was called and replied to all three names. My father, Chánh, had not changed his name because Chánh was easy for Anglophones to pronounce.

Meanwhile, my father's youngest sister had recently taken the name Michelle (after the Beatles song) because Ngọc was too unwieldy for English speakers. And her boyfriend, Chiến, adopted the name Paul (as in McCartney). The Beatles had a hallowed place in our family, and after the Bible, the Fab Four were our first stop for nomenclature. It was divine intervention that we hadn't yet named anyone Sgt. Pepper or Eleanor Rigby.

I went biblical and opted for Peter, but truthfully, I had chosen it because of Peter Parker. The association with Spider-Man was cool, and it amplified an otherwise normal American name. The f-word had crept into the Mooreland Elementary School playground in fifth grade as middle school approached, and it was not lost on me that my name had an uncanny and unfortunate consonance to the f-word. This was no time for inaction. This was the time to make the change, before middle school started, before the f-word would become the shock currency of vulgarity.

Over lunch, my family talked about everything except my name change—that was fait accompli. My parents were so amenable to it, I got the impression that they wondered why I had persevered so long with the name Phuc. That afternoon, my mother and father ran an errand at the mall, and upon their return, my mother called me into the kitchen.

"Hey, Phúc! We got you something!"

"What is it, Má?" I went into the kitchen.

"Here you go. We found it at the card store. It says your name!"

"Seriously? Really? My *name*?" I was skeptical.

My mother handed me a light switch plate that had a little angel painted on it, and in the puffy cloud above the cherub, it said PETER. Oh. *That* name.

"Thanks, Má!"

"I'll show you how to put it up in your room later." My father was always happy to put a tool into our hands.

Lou immediately protested. "Wait, why does Phuc get a nameplate for our room? What about me? Where's my nameplate?!"

"I'm older! That's why!" Primogeniture for the win. And just like that: with a personalized nameplate and a fiat declaration, I was ready to be Peter.

The next day at school I approached my teacher, Mr. Burgess, and told him.

"Mr. Burgess, I'd like to change my name. I talked with my parents yesterday, and they're okay with it."

"Um, okay. What to?"

"Peter."

"That sounds good. Do you want to tell the class?"

"Actually, can you tell the class?"

"I can. Let's do it tomorrow—first thing after the Pledge of Allegiance. Sound okay?"

I nodded gratefully. The heft and authority of Mr. Burgess's announcement, a teacher's declaration, would give Peter momentum, power, and respect. Peter needed all the help he could get to sputter up off the ground.

The next morning we pledged allegiance to the flag and to the United States of America. The symbol of all symbols for which we stood.

Mr. Burgess waited until everyone was seated. "Class, before we get started, I have an announcement to make. Phuc is changing his name this year, and from now on, he's asking that we call him by his new name, Peter. So let's say hello to Peter!" A few kids clapped. A few giggled and said, "Hi, Peter!"

I smiled widely. I leaned over to Jon and said, "Like Peter PARKER." And in case he didn't get it, I elaborated. "Like SPIDER-MAN."

Jon nodded. "Yeah, cool. Peter. That's so different from Phuc, but it's cool."

Grace tapped me from behind. "But you look like a Phuc! We've known you since kindergarten as Phuc! You don't look like a Peter!" She grinned, joking, and we laughed as we got to our workbooks.

Peter was officially airborne, smoothly taking off. I was aloft, having thought that Peter's introduction would be a rickety, bumpy launch.

The bell rang for recess. A few kids took to calling me Peter right away. I forgot to respond a few times, and so it was both barrels for a while, with kids yelling, "PETER! PHUC!" I had to get used to it as much as they did. We were in the midst of a frenzied game of wallball when it happened. Of course, it was going to happen. Did I think that it would be so easy?

I was in line for wallball. Ready to challenge Ethan Alder, the wallball king. He served. I missed, and as I dove and fell for the ball, he grabbed his crotch and yelled, "You're out! SUCK MY PETER, Phuc! Oh wait, you changed your name! Suck my peter, Peter!"

The whole line exploded with laughter. I was still lying on the ground. Suck my . . . peter? I looked up at Ethan grabbing at his crotch in triumph.

Oh no.

I lifted myself up, brushing small stones from my knees. No scrapes or cuts. Karen was at the back of the wallball line, and I shuffled myself into the line behind her. "Um . . . is Peter another word for . . . a wiener?" I asked her.

Karen giggled. "Yeah, it is. . . . Isn't that funny?" But it wasn't funny.

My stomach turned, and I excused myself from the wallball line to avoid another one of Ethan's humiliating public service announcements of being sucked—sucked like a peter.

I found Mr. Burgess at four square with the other teachers. "Hey, Mr. Burgess?"

He smiled down at me. "Yes, Phuc . . . I mean, Peter? Sorry—I'll get it right. Yes, Peter?"

"Actually, I think I'm just going to stick with Phuc. Everyone is used to it. Is that okay? I know you just made the announcement, but I think I'll just keep my real name." Even then I was lying as I said my name *fook* in the Americanized way—it was real enough because it was what everyone else said it was.

"Are you sure?" he asked.

I wasn't sure, but I didn't know what else to do. I couldn't sit down with him or anyone else to ask: *What are all the names that I should avoid picking that have an association with genitalia? Oh, well, here's the list! I'm so glad you asked.*

I nodded. "Yeah, I'm sure. Can you make another announcement that I'm going to switch back to Phuc?"

"Sure. I can do it after the Pledge tomorrow morning, okay?"

"Okay." I had hoped that it would be today.

After the Wednesday morning Pledge, Mr. Burgess retracted Peter, reinstated Phuc, and school went on as normal. I sighed in relief, and I saw relief among my classmates too that they could go back to calling me Phuc, their habits and assumptions having worn deep, predictable grooves in our interactions. Did I think that I could upend their expectations without any resistance?

Of course, I was technically the same kid, but I had gotten the message: I couldn't try too hard to change or fit in, especially if it involved something as dramatic as changing my name. That was *too* much. Too symbolic. Too real.

I told my family over dinner that evening that I was going to keep Phuc as my name. They nodded and changed the conversation to something else. They didn't ask why I was reversing my decision, chalking it up to youthful caprice, and I didn't offer any reason.

Before bedtime, I got a flathead screwdriver, removed the PETER light switch plate, and put back the old, nameless beige one. Even Lou seemed happy to have things back to normal.

The light switch plate was the only object that I had ever had with the name Peter on it, a memento of those two days.

Maybe a person's name was something more than a name—maybe my classmates needed me to stay *Phuc*. I thought I could leave behind the aggregated discomfort, the misalignment, that the identity of *Phuc* had brought, that I could get a fresh start with *Peter*. I assumed that an American name (especially with superheroic associations) would heal my wounds. By Jung's analysis, my journey had already begun with the wounds. Jung says that the process of becoming an individual begins with a wounding of the ego, and mine was undeniably wounded.

| 6 |

MADAME BOVARY

7-Eleven glittered with its large glass panes, and through the windows, on the comic rack, I spotted a new issue of *Uncanny X-Men*.

Lou, Thuận (my older, teenage second cousin), and I walked into the store, with a collected eight dollars to spend and no adult to deny us as untethered consumers—the American dream. At the comic rack, we spun the stand slowly, scrutinizing the month's new shipments of Marvel and DC titles. *The Avengers. Hulk. Aquaman. The New Mutants. Green Lantern.* I picked two comics—*Spectacular Spider-Man* and *X-Men*—after skimming the new issue of *Firestorm, The Nuclear Man.*

In my reverie, Lou and Thuận wandered away, but I eventually found Lou at the Donkey Kong machine.

"Where's Thuận?"

He shrugged. "Don't know, but don't mess me up! I'm on the fireballs level!"

I left my brother furiously button mashing, fireball leaping, and princess saving as I walked past the wall freezers that hummed with Coke cans and Hungry-Man dinners.

Thuận stood in the back of the 7-Eleven at the wall of magazines, *Rolling Stone, Guns & Ammo, Newsweek, Car and Driver*, and *Time* looming over him. A wall of America.

"Hey—there aren't comics over here," I told him. "Well, except *Heavy Metal*, I guess . . . but those comics are weird."

"I know. I wasn't looking for comics. I wanted to look at *these*." He held a swimsuit catalog.

"Uh . . . really?"

"Yeah. Look at all these women. This is a good one. . . . Look at *this* lady." He flashed me the layout of a blond woman in a standard red one-piece bathing suit. There was nothing overtly erotic about her other than the fact that she was wearing a bathing suit in the middle of a Carlisle 7-Eleven, smiling warmly. "You can *almost* see her nipple." I grunted in agreement even though I did not espy the supposed, singular nipple, but I wasn't going to argue with him. I was nervous that he was so brazenly ogling these ladies, but he didn't seem to care. Emboldened, I looked over his arm, holding my *Spider-Man* and *X-Men* to my side, my childish trophies dimming in the glow of Thuận's beauties.

The women were all gorgeous, of course. Blondes, brunettes, red-heads, all shades of hair in between, purportedly modeling swimwear but in fact titillating teenage boys who had no interest in the latest season of ladies' beachwear. I stood next to Thuận, feeling flush and moving my comics in front of my shorts in case an ill-timed and unman-ageable erection decided to pitch a tent. My comics were a cover for my libido—maybe the most important thing Spider-Man could do for me right there. That was a superhero's work. I could have walked away, but the siren song of these maidens was stronger than the embarrassment of my sixth-grade boner.

Thuận paged through the catalog slowly, on the hunt for a nipple, singular or plural. Being only a swimsuit catalog, it yielded little else, but Thuận was undeterred, poring over the pages, a beachcomber des-perate for peekaboo pennies. Five yards away from us, the payload of real pornography splayed beyond the cashier's counter in plastic bags, behind a formidable fortress of moral and legal censures (the sign prominently said 18+ ONLY) and a less-than-formidable mustachioed clerk with a ratty mullet. From where we stood, we only peeked at the titles and the tops of cover girls, as if they were sawn in half, a lascivious magic show, the black plastic magazine panels shielding our friable innocence from the full-frontal nudity.

Lou was so good at Donkey Kong (and had at least three quarters) that he kept playing while Thuận and I looked through a second swimsuit catalog. We then picked up a copy of *Iron Horse*, a biker magazine, that brazenly bared women's breasts in grainy black-and-white amateur photos that readers had sent in of their wives and girlfriends. Thuận mumbled *gross* as he put the *Iron Horse* back quickly, repelled by the sagging biker tits, which, astride flaming choppers, were covered in blue tattoos.

"Hey," the clerk called to us. "This ain't a library." His declaration lacked conviction, the tired reading of a bad script. "Ain't a library. Y'all gotta either buy the magazines or leave."

"Okay." Thuận pried Lou from Donkey Kong while I laid my two comics on the counter and transacted the purchase. 7-Eleven Mullet Guy slid my comics into a paper bag as I not so subtly leered at the booty behind the counter. *Playboy. Penthouse. Hustler. Swank. Juggs* (why the extra *g*?). *Penthouse Forum.* I had no idea what differentiated one magazine from the other, noting only that their common denominator was the insurmountable barriers between me and their boobs.

The faint aroma of adolescent arousal evaporated in the harsh daylight outside the 7-Eleven, and on the way home, I refocused on my comics, walking with *Spider-Man* opened in front of me while Thuận flipped through the *X-Men*. Lou squeezed between us, reading both comics simultaneously over our elbows.

At our apartment, Thuận and I sat on the front step with the new comics while Lou hopped on his bike and rode a circuit around Colonial Square, looking for the neighborhood kids. We read our comics, stopping to show each other an ad for X-ray glasses or *Gremlins*. We debated

Wolverine's ability to slice through anything with adamantium claws versus Spider-Man's agility. They were our superheroes. Interwoven with their powers, deeply written into their narratives, were their tales as outsiders. Freaks. Exiles. Aliens. Were there ever two boys for whom comic books were more enchanting? If not us, for whom was intended the make-believe of so much power intertwined with the pain of being so outcast? I couldn't imagine.

Thuận said something that broke the spell of superheroes. "You know: I have a couple of *Playboy* and *Penthouse* magazines." He spoke without looking up from the comics.

"*REALLY?!*" I let the *X-Men* fall into my lap. "From where?"

"My older brother. Maybe I'll show you next time you're at our apartment."

"Seriously?"

"You can't have them, though. But you can definitely look at them."

And so it began. We didn't know it at the time, but in our own way, we were enacting the predictable teenage rite of bequeathing porn.

When he eventually did show me a *Playboy* and a *Penthouse*, we huddled in his room with the door closed; he explained to me all the subtleties of the pornos as we leafed slowly past glossy pages of Aqua Net and turquoise eye shadow, breasts and legs pulled in revelatory directions, tasteful props of neoclassical columns to elevate what was otherwise low and guttural.

Thuận was a fount of information as well as opinions disseminated as information. He was happy to pontificate, and I was eager to take notes. *Why was* Penthouse *better? Why was* Hustler *kind of gross? What exactly was* Penthouse Forum*? What was* Swank*?* Thuận knew (or at least had an opinion on) all of it even though he only had copies of *Playboy* and *Penthouse*. I marveled at how he had access to such verboten knowledge, but the porn pile under his bed did not lie.

And even though he couldn't tell me why *Juggs* magazine required the extra *g*, he was my first guide at the edge of a forbidden, primal wood. I lingered at its threshold, clinging to my comic books and

Saturday morning cartoons but feeling the visceral pull and tug of something fleshier and irresistible.

I carry a deep, and perhaps unlikely, connection to Flaubert's *Madame Bovary*. I don't have a past life as a disgruntled, quixotic nineteenth-century housewife, married to a second-rate doctor in rural France. But the first time I read *Madame Bovary*, I knew immediately that she and I had a shared passion.

In Flaubert's novel, Emma Bovary yearns for a life that is beyond her grasp. Her desire for a grander existence burns from her love of romance novels, and her devouring of these bodice-rippers enflames in her an unyielding desire. Nothing in life can satisfy Emma Bovary, and she tragically pursues affairs and extravagances until she has ruined her name and finances. Unable to fulfill her fantastical delusions, she commits suicide at the end of the novel—her escape from debt collectors, scandal, and the ennui of her marriage. Whence her fantasy? It swirled from her early love of trashy novels. Such is the power of art in Flaubert's world as he writes, "Emma tried to find out what one meant exactly in life by the words *bliss, passion, ecstasy*, that had seemed to her so beautiful in books."

But if literature moves you deeply, does it matter where it comes from? Does it matter that it's trashy or lowbrow? Isn't that emotional connection one of the purposes of art? To make you feel—*really* feel—emotions? To resonate with your life? And perhaps, in that connection, to introduce you to a world that lies beyond your own perspective, the utopia beyond your myopia?

My friends and I hunched over comic books with the passion of scholars, analyzing every panel, reading every issue, every word several times over. I looked up innumerable vocabulary words from the pages of my Marvel adventures in which the heroes cracked wise and the villains always had the time to lather logorrheic illuminations of their dastardly deeds. And beyond my comics, I slipped in between the covers of fantasy books, spiriting away to lands far from Carlisle's quiet corners: *A Wrinkle in Time*; *The Lion, the Witch and the Wardrobe*; *The Hitchhiker's Guide to the Galaxy*. I was transported to galaxies far away, times long ago, and between books, I always returned to my comics, my first loves.

In the realm of comics, I worshipped my heroes' powers and strengths, lamented their struggles and travails, and then—slowly—I noticed their physicality, their muscularity, their unitards that seemed to be painted on their nude bodies. Was that sexual world spread open by my cousin's initiation or by my own libidinous curiosity? My comics now stoked another fantasy beyond climbing walls and retractable claws, as the heroines' voluminous breasts and taut pelvises created Bermuda Triangles that my eyes could not evade.

Emma Bovary incinerated the tedium of her life with romance novels, and for myself, I had my comic books. And now I had my cousin's *Playboy* magazines. Fantasy novels, comic books, porn: I was afire and burning bright.

OCTOBER 1984

Max and I walked home from Lamberton Middle School together, having agreed to meet by the yellow lockers every day after the bell. We both walked the same route to and from school, and in the long parade of pedestrian kids, we bantered about *The Karate Kid*, *The Last Starfighter*, or why the thirteen-minute version of the "Thriller" video was better than the three-minute format. I had lent Max the Lloyd Alexander fantasy series, my favorite books, about a young hero, wizards, and a damsel in distress, and we debated whether it was a *Lord of the Rings* rip-off or not. Quintessential sixth-grade banter.

We cut in between buildings and houses, across parking lots and down tree-lined boulevards. As we neared my apartment, Max stopped and dropped his backpack.

"Oh my God—I almost forgot to tell you. I got the book from my house."

"Seriously?! You got it?"

"Yeah. But let me give it to you now and not near your house." He unzipped his backpack. I lowered my backpack too and, sensing the prurient nature of the transaction, nudged my backpack over behind a small tree (not that it provided much cover). I knelt down next to Max, who was fumbling in his backpack for the book.

A week earlier at lunch, Max had told a few of us about a book that he found on his parents' bookshelf. Initially we were unimpressed by his announcement of guys-I-found-a-book until he told us: it had *sex* in it. Descriptive, explicit, copious amounts of sex. This wasn't Judy Blume, skirting and flirting with your changing body, prepubescent, bowdlerized-for-Scholastic intimations of sex. This book was the real thing. This was *real* sex from an adult, by an adult, for an adult.

We all called bullshit on Max's report of the book, and in classic middle-school fashion we demanded that he bring the book into school. Max had no choice but to do it or forever be infernally branded as a liar, which was one level below the circle of snitches in the hell of middle school. We had unwittingly convened our first book club meeting, although we would only ever read and discuss this one book.

In the open air of the sidewalk, Max handed me THE BOOK. *The Happy Hooker* by Xaviera Hollander.

I read the spine to myself, not daring to say it aloud. "Whoa . . . you weren't lying."

Max was pleased with my awe. "Yeah, see? I wasn't lying. Give it to Jon after you're done. He's next."

"Okay. Will your parents know that it's missing?"

"No, I don't think so. It was on a bookshelf in the basement. No one ever goes down there." These were the delights of accidental porn. Max happened to go into his basement looking for who knows what, happened to know what a hooker was, and just happened to pick up the book and wade through the exposition long enough to get to the good parts.

We weren't literary critics, dissecting the authorial voice or insights into human sexuality or its commodification. We were looking for graphic descriptions of sex. We had graduated from our elementary giggling about girls menstruating to middle schoolers' inextinguishable, libido-fueled curiosity. Amid fusty boxes, Max had found an incendiary spark of a book.

I shoved the soft mustard-colored paperback in between red and blue Trapper Keepers and zipped it up quickly. "Thanks!" This was the real after-school special.

We parted ways at my apartment door, and I let myself in with my key. My parents were still at work, and Lou was at school, so I hopped on the couch and inspected the cover with its Farrah Fawcett–esque photo of Xaviera. She wasn't unattractive. Chapter One. Page one.

When Lou came home, I immediately hid the book. But after dinner, while the rest of my family watched television, I went back to reading, my parents misunderstanding my interest in reading as academic and not priapic.

Secluded in my room, I discovered that *The Happy Hooker* boiled with sexual activity of all varieties, and Ms. Hollander's escapades limned for me countless details and diagrams of coitus that I could not have fabricated. It was one thing to gawp at the glossy photos of my cousin's *Playboy*; it was another thing to be guided into the wilds of literary sex, lovely, dark, and deep. Passion, bliss, and ecstasy graced the pages of *The Happy Hooker*. Emma Bovary would have been proud. I read and masturbated furiously that week.

And then came the bad part. Chapter 11, page 196. It was after school. No one was home, and I was lying in my bed with my pants undone, one-handed reading. The happy hooker was giving a blow job to an Oriental (her words) businessman. This was still serviceable wank material. But then she described how his penis was, in fact, a FAKE

PENIS, because he was embarrassed by how small his actual penis was. After comforting the man, Hollander removed the prosthetic penis and sucked his real dick, which Hollander said was the size of her pinkie. She went on to make generalizations about how sex with "Orientals" was like washing her hands (clean and functional), and then—*then* she said that Orientals were "the smallest in dimensions."

WHAT? I immediately lost my erection as I read the ensuing description of the man's tiny dick and how it was even smaller than she had expected. If my penis could have shriveled from shame, it would have. I wasn't aware of this stereotype, and now, in the midst of a compelling after-school jerk-off session, Xaviera Hollander, a lady who had seen *thousands* of dicks, was informing me (and all her readers) that Oriental men had the smallest dicks. I zipped up my pants, not even wanting to see my supposed micro-penis.

I stopped reading that day and skipped the rest of the chapter.

Hoping to suffocate my impressions by piling on more sex scenes, I pressed on to finish the book the following week. Jon dunned me for the book, and I handed it over to him at school between two locker doors, flung open to conceal our exchange.

"How was it? Was it as good as Max said?" Jon delighted in his turn to have the book.

I nodded, feigning excitement. "Oh yeah, it's good."

Jon did read it. He passed it on to Ethan. Ethan passed it on to Stephen. Ms. Hollander's adventures made the rounds, and I had to assume that the entire group would read or had already read her observations about Oriental men's dicks being the smallest of all the dicks she had ever had the opportunity to suck—and sucking dicks was her job. I couldn't argue this point, and no one in our ad hoc book club would care enough to challenge any of her observations. And we didn't even talk about the seriously racist stuff in her book, in which she wrote authoritatively regarding stereotypes about Jewish men, black men, "Orientals," Irish, and more.

We boys had come for the jerk-off material, but I left scarred by and scared of her incontrovertible observations.

My only solace lay in my friends' being poor or slow or counterfeit readers. Maybe some of the kids at the lunch table didn't read that section or didn't read the book at all, but I wasn't going to give anyone a pop quiz about it.

The Happy Hooker was Madame Bovary in reverse. Instead of a book unleashing my fantasy, a book had circumcised my tumescent libido.

I wished I had never read it, but beyond that, I wished that my entire lunch table had not read it. I was the so-called small-cocked Oriental now because of a book, a shitty, terribly written, racist book. And without any recourse to discuss it (we were sixth-grade boys, after all), the book circulated and disappeared back into the hole of Max's backpack, safely sequestered in his parents' basement, never to be seen in our circle of jerks again.

JULY 1985, STATEN ISLAND, NEW YORK

Lou and I walked with our older cousins, Nhân and Huân, accompanying them on their paper route. Nhân and Huân took advantage of our eagerness to win their favor, and this meant that Lou and I did the bulk of the work, carrying and delivering the papers in the mid-summer swelter.

"You looking forward to the movie tonight? It looks good, right?" Nhân and Huân were going to take me and Lou to see The Goonies. Cyndi Lauper's radio hit had been on heavy rotation for the last month, and indeed, if the Goonies were good enough for her, they were good enough for me.

I was excited equally for the movie and for the occasion to hang out with my older cousins from the big city. "Yeah, the movie looks awesome! And it has the Oriental kid from Indiana Jones and the Temple *of Doom.*" I was referring to Jonathan Ke Quan, who had played Short Round in the *Raiders of the Lost Ark* sequel.

"*Oriental?*" Nhân repeated.

"Yeah . . . he's Oriental. I heard that he's even Vietnamese!"

"Dude, he's not *Oriental.*"

Lou and I were perplexed, and Lou jumped in. "Yes, he is! He's in *Temple of Doom*! Of course he's Oriental."

I backed Lou up. "Yeah, he's totally Oriental. Have you not seen *Temple of Doom*?"

"Christ's sake. That's not what we're *tawking about.*" Huân's Noo Yawk accent sounded thicker than usual as he became agitated. "*Oriental*? What the hell is that? He's Asian. He's from Asia. Asia is a continent. There's no continent called *Oriental*. Jesus. At least say he's Asian if you're not going to say that he's Vietnamese."

Nhân jumped in. "What the hell are you learning in Carlisle? Frickin' *Oriental*?!" He shook his head. That was the question for my lifetime, more loaded than Nhân's intent to insult small-town PA. What the hell were we learning in Carlisle?

With Lou at my elbows, it didn't seem like a good time to mention the frequent usage of *Oriental* in *The Happy Hooker*. What was wrong with the word *Oriental*? I wondered.

The adults and kids in Carlisle used the word *Oriental* interchangeably with *Asian* and *Vietnamese*, and by middle school, I avoided the word *Vietnamese* as much as possible as a self-descriptor. The media associations with the Vietnam War, the vets, the protests, and all the movies gave the word *Vietnamese* a swirling, psychedelic miasma of Huey choppers, hippies, and carnage. A prisoner executed in the streets, a naked girl screaming from napalm, Americans protesting a pointless war. Why would I want to associate myself with these things more than I already did?

Here, my urbane cousins nudged open the door of a different world for me to peer into. In Carlisle, the Trầns were indiscriminately Oriental, Asian, or Vietnamese, but in New York, a preference muscled itself in between the words *Oriental, Asian,* and *Vietnamese.* Was there a hierarchy of what was appropriate or accurate? Pejorative connotations for one and not the others? I knew none of this, and I shrugged, accepting the distinction as gospel, with my cousins as the evangelists crying out in the wildernesses of New Dorp, Staten Island. They were on the vanguard of something I had yet to understand, but I was willing to carry the good news back to Carlisle. Hallelujah! I was Asian, *not* Oriental.

I wanted to clarify. "So we're Asians or Vietnamese, but not Orientals?"

"Right—you're not *Oriental*. Rugs are oriental. Waddya, a rug?" Nhân's sharp sarcasm punctuated his question, and Lou and I nodded at his tutelage before going inside.

Asian had a grand, wider association—China and Japan. Saturday kung fu films. Bruce Lee. Chinese food. Indiana Jones's sidekick. *Asian* sounded cool.

We had family dinner with all the adults, and then we were off to the movies.

On the drive back from *The Goonies,* we rattled off the wasn't-it-cool-when moments of the movie while circling our delight in seeing an Asian/Vietnamese (but *not* Oriental) kid on the big screen. I immediately wanted to see it again.

This was not a movie about the war. We weren't antagonists or some faceless platoon of Charlie lurking in the jungle foliage. We were kids looking for adventure, and someone in Hollywood saw a place for us in the movies. We were exuberant to see a character who looked like us, cheering him on in his adventures and exploits.

But then when Lou said that he couldn't understand Data because of his thick accent, I winced because I knew that Lou was right. Even as Data stood there, twelve feet high on the screen, he was still part of Hollywood fiction. His bad English made him an obvious (and familiar) foreigner. He was the tech/math whiz, but he was a sidekick, a figure at the edges, bumbling and hamming it up for laughs. But at least he wasn't a Việt Cộng, and at least he kind of saved the day. I'd take it as a win, even if it was a pyrrhic victory for us.

Emma Bovary's books made her yearn for a dreamworld of emotional dramas and searing affairs. They seeded a delusion in her that grew quickly and blinded her, choking out the light except for the glow of fictitious hope. She was not ready for the quiet boredom of a married woman's life, and the yearning that flourished inside her made her own life repulsive to her. Could art do that? Could it make you long and loathe at the same time?

I know I did. I longed for power and acceptance and sex just as Emma did. I loathed a cultural landscape that had only a narrow, slant-eyed space for me. And in that loathing, I couldn't see changing that landscape.

A lumpy mass of American stereotypes was metastasizing inside me. It made me cringe when I heard Mr. Miyagi say, "Wax on, wax off, Daniel San." It made me pretend to laugh when I saw Long Duk Dong in *Sixteen Candles*. It made me sign up for tae kwon do that year because that was what Asians did. It would be decades before I diagnosed the lump of alienation, dual consciousness, and self-hatred, but it was already growing quickly, bilious and caustic. I only saw myself as the piece that did not fit in the puzzle.

At the end of our New York visit that week, we waved goodbye to my cousins from the rear window. I settled into the back seat and pulled out the third book from the Narnia series, settling in for a four-hour drive home to Carlisle. Lou was flipping through an Aquaman comic, and my parents Vietnamesed in the front seat.

Unable to read, I closed the book to watch Staten Island skitter by, to me so exotic and foreign. Bodegas, kosher delis, signs in Spanish and Chinese and Hindi. Carlisle had already stitched in me a provincial mind-set, and the dense tapestry of New York—the noise, the trash, the expanse—enthralled me. I held the realm of Narnia awaiting in my lap as I admired the lights from the Goethals Bridge into New Jersey, hoping to catch a glimpse of a New York landmark as the traffic slowed at the toll—the smudgy, glittering cityscape as alluring and fantastical as anything in C. S. Lewis's wardrobe.

In a long line of cars, we were suspended in the air, and Lou and I craned our necks now, looking down at the swirling gray waters, the blinking lights of planes arriving at Newark in the distance. All that adventure out there.

I played with the adjustable snaps on the back of one of the New York Mets baseball caps that my aunt and uncle had given to me and Lou. I put it on and noticed that Lou was already wearing his cap (that was the nature of siblings—we always got two of everything).

Lou looked at me. "Hey, you look like Short Round from *Temple of Doom*! He has the same hat!"

"Oh . . . yeah, I guess you're right." I looked at Lou and slid my hat off, feeling embarrassed that he immediately said that I looked like Short Round.

The truth, however, was that when I saw Lou with his hat on, *I* thought that *he* looked like the Asian kid from *Gremlins* in the Chinatown pawnshop.

I became saddened as I realized: It must have been a coincidence, right? Was it on purpose? Short Round *and* the nameless *Gremlins* kid—they weren't the same actor and the movies didn't happen in the same timeline. *Temple of Doom* took place in the thirties and *Gremlins* happened in '84, but I connected the dots: Both Asian kids wore New York baseball caps. Those kids looked the same in those two movies because *the audience* looked at *them* the same.

The movies were doing the work of America, ghettoizing us in our own minds, a slow and delicious poison, like Emma Bovary's novels. Our imaginations, our self-reflection, were circumscribed by what we saw, limited and funneled into someone else's view of who we were. We saw ourselves as others saw us, and when we *were* in the media (which was not frequent), our stereotypes were reinforced in the books we read, the movies we saw, the things our friends said to us.

In the back seat of our Ford LTD, Lou and I saw each other for a moment through the lenses of movies that we loved and movies that we yearned to see ourselves in even as we were squeezed into the box of not-belonging. My cousins may have deleted *Oriental* from my vocabulary but not *Orientalism* from my mind-set. Getting rid of the *O*-word was only a symbolic fight. The word was gone, but that didn't mean that the idea was vanquished.

I retired the hat into my pack and opened Narnia in the fading light of dusk. C. S. Lewis's world, the world of literature, seemed less specific, less explicit to me. I could see myself on a quest, unsheathing a sword, mounting a daring escape, the outlines of the book's heroes more opaque and far-fetched to me.

When we got home to Carlisle, I put my Mets hat in my closet, ignoring Lou's endearing request that we wear the hats to match. I didn't want to look exactly like Lou. Two more Asian kids in New York baseball caps. It's how they already saw us—we just had to look at the movies.

7

PYGMALION

1986

At Lamberton Middle School, I nervously noted the emergence of social spheres, their barriers rising up from the tectonic shifts of hormones, genders, and interests. In sixth and seventh grades, my friend group was a collection of comic book nerds. They were big-time nerds, and entering stage left, I was the Tolkien Asian of that nerd herd. For my seventh-grade home economics sewing project, I stitched for myself an *X-Men* throw pillow. I bought a four-pack of VHS tapes and recorded episodes of *Robotech* at my grandparents' apartment after school every day. Weekend after weekend in middle school, it was us boys hanging out, playing Dungeons & Dragons, debating comics, painting small lead figurines for our dungeon maps, or watching B-horror films like *The Return of the Living Dead*. At the edges of our consciousness swished the popular girls and the cool boys, demigods and mermaids at the borders of mythical maps. We were content to keep to ourselves and our twelve-sided die.

At Lamberton's spring dance, the cafeteria was transformed into a darkened, make-shift dance floor, with its folding tables pushed to the perimeter and sparse streamers strewn haphazardly over light fixtures. I stood with Craig and Derek in a tight circle, staring past their heads at the slow dance on the cafeteria-cum-dance floor. Madonna's "Crazy for You" gyrated over the PA speakers. In our coterie, I pretended to listen to Craig's tirade about the latest advanced D & D module while I stared at the dancers and gawked at the girls. I surveyed my geeky inner circle. My dissatisfaction struck me hard, there with the sparkling synthesizers cascading and Drakkar Noir oozing in the air: I wanted to break free from the Nerds of the Round Table. I wanted to take on this advanced module: girls and dating. I didn't know if I had enough experience points or charisma, but I had the hormonal drive and the naïveté to roll the dice. With my friends still more interested in slaying orcs, I needed a different alliance. But how? I'd spent so much time looking for and making friends, and I had them. And now I was apprehensive because I didn't know how to leave a friend group. Did people even do that? It seemed cruel, superficial, but necessary. Where was the blueprint for this conversation? Any compassion and kinship I felt for my friends was countered by a bubbling awareness of girls and their growing awareness of boys. *It's not you, it's me—actually, it's not me, either. It's girls. They're Yoko-ing our band, boys.*

That was how seventh grade ended, and over the summer of 1986, we moved across town. My parents had bought a house, and against my relatives' encouragement that my parents abandon Carlisle altogether for a more cultured environment, Chánh and Chi bought a house on the north side of town. Our new neighborhood meant that Lou and I would be enrolled in new schools.

My small worries about changing schools were eclipsed by my opportunism: I had hopes for my new school. At Wilson Middle School, I could break free from the chains of nerditude. Eighth grade in 1986 was the middle arc of adolescent Darwinism. We were amoebae in elementary school, gradually growing some spines when we entered middle school. But now it was going to be eighth grade. Everyone's genus and species in the natural pecking order was ossifying, evolving for high school's law of the jungle. Jocks. Preps. Freaks. Geeks. Rednecks. I was determined to make an evolutionary jump—if not into a cool kingdom, at least out from the nerd phylum.

In the summer of 1986, as eighth grade at Wilson Middle School loomed ahead, I saw my opening. I didn't have to be a nerd anymore, but I wasn't entirely sure how to join another group, either. I knew that I didn't want to attempt a name change again. I assumed that my new peers wouldn't allow it, and I didn't want to start off Wilson Middle School with a humiliating backpedaling. I was resigned to being Phuc. But in a new school, in a new context, could I change who Phuc was? Could I change who everyone *thought* Phuc was? I would try.

I just had to figure out who I wanted to be.

In George Bernard Shaw's play *Pygmalion*, Henry Higgins, professor of linguistics, takes in a common street girl, Eliza Doolittle, and makes a bet with a friend: he wagers that he can pass Eliza off as royalty by teaching her how to speak English properly. Higgins asserts that her low societal status is determined by her working-class dialect and her clothes.

Shaw's critique of the English class system propels the play, and bigger questions spin from the hub of the play's central question: Can you authentically move from one social group to another? Is your social status immovable or is it a matter of changing your speech and stripes? Or in my case, changing schools? And could changing schools allow me to change my social group? Would I need to change my clothes, too?

I was going to find out if I could be an Eliza Doolittle.

At the end of the first week of school, I brought my skateboard on the bus, intent on skating home. I had bought the skateboard from my new neighbor, Ritchie Johns (a high school kid who was happy to sell it for weed money), and he showed me a few tricks and handplants on curbs.

I couldn't ollie so well, but I could skate fast and carve along the road, and at the end of the first Friday of the school year, a warm fall day, skating home seemed more fun.

"Hey, cool deck. That's the Vision Gator deck—I've never seen that color before."

I looked up to see Liam Mahoney, a kid I had met the year before in tae kwon do. Liam wasn't in any of my classes, and we hadn't crossed paths in school yet, but nonetheless, I was relieved to see a face I knew in the week's endless tide of unfamiliar faces.

"Oh, hey, Liam! You skate?"

"Yeah, me and my older brother—you know Dylan? From tae kwon do? You should come over after school—we're all skating in front of my house. Meet me out front after the bell." He and I clasped hands, thumbs up to affirm. Blue eyes, big teeth, shaved head on one side and shaggy blond hair on the other. Liam would be my first friend who openly didn't give a shit about school and wasn't afraid to say so (an attitude that I found terrifying). His stride had a pronated wobble from a perennially ingrown toenail, but oddly, not when he skated. I was thrilled to be skating home from school and doubly so to be doing it with a friendly face.

At the end of the day, the bell rattled its last harangue-y clang, and Liam and I met at the bus loop and skated over to his house, a mile from school. We stopped at a ubiquitous 7-Eleven along the way and bought Slurpees before arriving at his house, huffing up a small hill, our hands flashing red and cold.

Liam's brother, Dylan (a tenth grader), was already skating in front of their house with four other high school kids. Backpacks were strewn around on the sidewalk, and everyone was taking turns at a stretch of chewed-up curb, loudly landing their ollies with a *CLACK*. At any other time, I would have crossed the street as a precaution or turned my skateboard around to steer clear of kids who looked like them. I knew enough to spot the uniform of high school miscreants. Ripped jeans. Black Converse sneakers. Flannel shirts tied around their waists. Two of them shirtless. All of them swearing. My heart's panicked bass line throbbed as I skated nonchalantly with Liam into their midst. No one asked me my name or said hi. I got a few nods of approval at my deck (which I didn't know needed approval, but I was happy to receive it regardless). That was the extent of my introduction, and I saw no need to walk around and shake anyone's hands or say my name like an idiot. *Hello, I'm Phuc Tran. How was your educational experience today?* I told myself to shut up and be cool.

On his skateboard, Liam tried to ollie and grind on the curb, but he missed and fell headlong. Dylan laughed.

"Way to go, you fuck-nut!" Dylan called out, slow-clapping ironically.

"Fuck off," Liam retorted. His two middle fingers punctuated his imperative.

"Let me show you how it's done." Dylan skated up to the curb to ollie to a grind (the same trick as Liam's), but before he did it, Liam fired his cherry Slurpee at Dylan. With a wet puking sound, the Styrofoam cup sluiced its contents all over Dylan's back.

"YOU MOTHERFUCKER!" Dylan picked up his board and tomahawked it at Liam as the rest of us abruptly cut our laughter and took cover. Dylan's deck whizzed over the group as some of us covered our heads and others covered our crotches, a revelation of everyone's varied priorities to protect either brains or balls. Liam was unscathed.

"I'M GONNA FUCKING KILL YOU!" Dylan, heavier and slower, chased Liam back and forth across the street. I would later find out that this was a typical afternoon in front of the Mahoneys' house.

Liam and Dylan were the stock, fighting Irish brothers. When they weren't punching the shit out of each other, they were best friends. If you picked a fight with one of them, you were sure to get a boot to the head from the other.

Dylan, pink and sticky, chased Liam, who left a vapor trail of soprano cackling in his wake. Dylan caught and wrestled Liam into a headlock on their front lawn, and I couldn't tell if their obscenities were playful or rancorous. No one had a bloody nose yet, so we sat back and enjoyed the bout of impromptu fisticuffs. *Fuck you. No, fuck you. Get the fuck off. Fuck you, you piece of shit. You got fucking cherry Slurpee all over me.*

A woman's head popped out from their screen door, a matronly cuckoo clock to announce the end of the round. Mrs. Mahoney. "KNOCK IT OFF, YOU TWO! KNOCK! IT! OFF! Oh, hello, boys!"

Liam and Dylan let each other go, and everyone waved to Mrs. Mahoney.

The boys went back to popping ollies, and I skated around, occasionally taking a shot at a homemade curb launch that rocketed me a stunted six inches into the air. Sometimes, I'd land with confidence; sometimes I fell. Everyone was practicing tricks with mixed success, and no one seemed to care who fell as long as you didn't bitch about it. The guys hurled the useless encouragement of "Don't be a pussy." I took in the whole spectacle with awe and realized that these were the boys who I wanted to hang out with. They were clearly the opposite of my erstwhile nerd friends.

Grouptalk (a natural extension of groupthink) moved on from skate tricks to who was a *poser* and wasn't a *poser*.

"Did you see that kid with that deck from Hills? What a poser!"

"Yeah, and that other kid? The one with the tail guard? That kid's a *total* poser. I saw him with a helmet on once . . . What a *fucking* poser!"

I didn't know anyone's name, so I kept quiet and listened. I inferred that a poser was someone who skated but was not a real skateboarder—they only *posed* with their board. Note to self: Don't put a tail guard on your deck. And definitely NO HELMET if I didn't want to look like a poser. But apparently, some accessories on your skateboard made you a poser while others didn't. The ballooning, philosophical question of authenticity had floated up, inflated with the hot air of its self-appointed wranglers. They were the ones who decided, the ones who steered it.

Was I a poser? I figured if I were, the group would have let me know with withering clarity and profanity. It seemed that I was allowed to skate with them on probationary status. Non-poser status until other-wise rescinded.

We skated along the block, popping up and down the curbs until the last of the warm September light stretched our shadows across the darkening pavement, the smell of the asphalt cooling with an autumn prelude in the air. I slung my backpack over my shoulders and clacked my board, wheels down, to head home. No one in the group had directly asked me my name, but it didn't matter. No one had told me to fuck off, either, and that was good enough for my first day with new friends.

About five yards off, Liam called out to me. "See you next time, dude!" I gave him a faux military salute.

Dylan and a few of the other kids gave their valedictions. "Yeah, see you next time!" One of them grabbed his balls and chortled. I gave him the middle finger, and from behind, I heard them all laughing in approval. I grinned out of view, having avoided the pothole of poser-status.

It didn't matter that they didn't know my name. They welcomed me into their midst with vile gestures and vulgar expressions. And they said, *See you next time.* That was the best thing I had heard that first week of school, and I was elated to have a potential group of friends who were . . . cool.

Real vs. poser. The amorphous idea of being a *real skater* was a hazy obstacle in my path. I hadn't consciously chosen to be a nerd but had somehow drawn those numbers in the social lottery of sixth and seventh grade. This never mattered to me until I cared, and the weight of this sudden awareness suffocated me. I cared about how people saw me, how people saw my group of friends, what they said about me, and I was now afraid and worried about it. I now knew that I *wanted* to be a skater, but wanting that was not good enough. The group could still deem me a poser based on its standards, thereby making me a wannabe. If a social group hated anything more than someone who didn't belong, it was someone who tried *too hard* to belong. Naked ambition was a form of nudity that was unwelcome to eighth-grade boys.

Being yourself was not good enough to move up in the world. Eliza Doolittle and I knew that much at least.

APRIL 1987, FRIDAY

I waited outside the hallway of the vice principal's office. The last time I was in the principal's office, I was at Mooreland Elementary School, triumphantly eating a McDonald's Happy Meal. This was not a Happy Meal scenario. I got a note that morning at the end of third period that said the vice principal wanted to see me. Crap. I knew exactly what it was about.

As I waited, I deliberated what I would say to him. Conjured from the pages of a Dickens novel, Wilson Middle School's vice principal was ironically named Mr. Friend. Mr. John Friend, a mustachioed middle-aged man who always wore a gray suit and red power tie. Mr. Friend, a Michael Douglas look-alike, his hair parted and his stride cock-of-the-walk confident.

I was summoned out of the waiting area and into his office, which was furnished with an obligatory and overly large fern and American flag in the corner. A placard that declared FRIEND on his desk signaled his name and status as good cop.

"Okay, sit down . . . uh . . . ." He looked at a legal pad, his auburn mustache twitching as he spoke. "Uh . . . Tran?" I nodded. "Okay, Tran. Listen to me." He didn't know which was my first or last name and had clearly flipped a mental coin. "Do you know why you're here, Tran?" Textbook first move in interrogation: ask your questionee what he thinks you know.

"No, Mr. Friend. I've never been in trouble or had detention or anything before at Lamberton." I mentioned my old school, hoping that I could emphasize that I was still too new a student to be involved in any nefariousness.

"Well, I heard reports that you're organizing a fight. A *big* fight. I don't know if it's true or not, but you need to call it off."

"But—" Faint denial.

"I don't care. The police have been notified, and they'll be around after school today. After the bell. If anything happens—*anything*—you're going to be back in my office, and we'll be talking with the police and your parents. Are we clear? No fight after school. Get the word out to your friends."

I nodded nervously and stood. *The police?* This was serious.

"You seem like a good kid, Tran. I don't want to see you back here." He put his hand on my shoulder, flashing a large class ring with a deep-set garnet the size of my biggest two knuckles. I felt the weight on my shoulder.

"Yes, sir. I won't be back in here."

"Good."

He had been right about the fight. We were preparing for a huge brawl after school that day, but I wouldn't have used the word *organizing*. I would have said *escalating*.

Here's what I hadn't told Mr. Friend:

On Monday that week, Travis—an eighth grader whose biological clock had already wound him forward with a beard and a smoking habit—had shoved me into the lockers. In my peripheral, I saw mullets and acid-washed denim hemming my way. I smelled hair spray, Old Spice, and Marlboros. I knew that I was going to have to fight someone. Travis and his two cronies had ducked into my locker row, and they decided I was their fodder that week. I squared up with him, and we exchanged some emasculating classics like *pussy*, *faggot*, and *bitch*. I got the standard tirade that began and ended with *gook*. Those were fighting words. They stepped forward and I didn't back down. Before any blows were thrown, I felt someone else sneak up next to me, and I pivoted to the side to avoid the ambush, ducking my head instinctively.

It was Liam Mahoney.

He spoke to them without even asking me what was happening. "You fuckin' hicks can fuck off now." Liam and I squared up, our union against their confederacy.

Travis and his droogs stopped because they didn't like the arithmetic: it wasn't three against one. Now it was three against two. "You skate fags ain't worth getting suspended for. After school. Friday. We'll finish this."

I didn't blink. "*Good.* Call *all* your fuckin' friends, you dicks." I was feeling emboldened by Liam's presence, my fear and adrenaline now replaced with arrogance and adrenaline. That was how it started. A few verbal snowballs thrown had triggered an avalanche of threats. And *skate fag?* Don't mind if I do. I was honored to be lumped in with the skaters.

How could I explain to Mr. Friend that this was the first time anyone had ever stood up for me in a fight? That in my short life of fistfights and pitched punches through elementary school, Liam Mahoney was the first person who was going to throw and take a punch next to me for no reason other than friendship. Liam had no personal stake in my fight, and his heroic overture bolstered me. I learned the most important lesson: friends were more than someone who shared your love of comic books or anime or skating. Friends could protect you, save you in a way that your parents could not.

I didn't mention to Mr. Friend that in the buildup to the showdown on Friday, we had brought to school various things as weapons: skateboards, baseball bats, hockey sticks. Someone brought his dad's pipe wrench. Travis said that he was bringing a tire iron. Some kids claimed that they were bringing their older brother or so-and-so's cousin from neighboring Boiling Springs. We were engaged in an arms race to see which side conscripted the most outlandishly rumored pugilist, a ringer who would be able to clinch a victory. I told someone that my uncle Thaí was going to come (he wasn't), and that he was a tae kwon do black belt (he was a blue belt).

And then I got a lucky break: the fight was canceled by Mr. Friend. Deus ex machina.

I never wanted to fight in the first place, but somehow fights always came to me. This one, however, had amassed a frightening potential of material and participants—real and alleged—and by the time Friday had arrived, the goddess of rumor was weaving wild yarns of who was coming with what for the bludgeoning of whom. In truth, I was terrified that someone was going to get really hurt, but I was more afraid of calling the fight off and looking weak. That would have put a target on my back for the rest of high school—every day would be an endless assault—so I pressed on with plans for a fight whose momentum I couldn't stop.

And in the grand fashion of untethered hyperbole that flies from the mouths of eighth graders, the teachers heard about it, then the vice principal. The next thing I knew, I was called into the office.

After English class I saw Liam and a few others in the hall and told them what had happened. "Dude, I just got called into Mr. Friend's office. He knows about the fight. Everyone knows. We gotta call it off. The cops are coming."

"The cops?! *Seriously?*" Liam seemed genuinely shocked and excited by the attention. "The fucking cops?"

"Yeah—they'll arrest anyone who shows up at the loading dock." I wasn't sure if they were actually going to arrest anyone, but it made sense to add that detail.

"Shit . . . I'll tell everyone." And Liam did tell *everyone*. By the end of the day everyone knew the fight was called off, and if anyone hadn't heard about it, then they first learned about the fight while also learning that it had been called off; and they learned that Phuc had been called into Friend's office as the organizer.

Whatever reputation or lack of reputation I had as a nerd was altered by that incident. A school-wide fight. A meeting with Mr. Friend. The cops waiting for us. I was on another level now.

A whirlwind of misinformation twisted through the school, and I embraced all of it (especially now that we didn't even actually have to go through with the fight). Part of me felt embarrassed—the part that knew that my parents would have been mortified, the part that felt as though I had brought shame upon the Trần name. But another part of me, a defiant part of me, felt proud and emboldened. We hadn't backed down from a fight, we got in trouble, and instead of ostracism, some of our classmates regarded us with an honored air. I could see how they looked at me and Liam. This non-fight was social cachet.

I fanned the embers to incinerate who kids thought I was (and who I thought I was). Per Travis's declaration, I was officially a skate fag now, and in the eyes of Mr. Friend, I was a ringleader. The word was out: from the rednecks, from the administration, from the rumor mill. My reputation was confirmed by three sources. This was my grand debut that year, but I was not unveiled by Henry Higgins as a duchess. I was ushered out of the vice principal's office, and I emerged a skater.

As the weather warmed that spring, we skaters gathered at Liam and Dylan's house to pop ollies and launch ourselves off rickety ramps after school and on the weekends. A boom box would come out, and buzzing from its tiny, tinny speakers was the soundtrack to our skating. I hadn't heard this kind of music before. It was angry. It shouted things with an urgency and authenticity that I had never heard. A bit out of tune but exactly right on time.

I bobbed my head to the music. "What *is* this?" Raw. Coarse.

Dylan landed a kick-flip. "Agent Orange. They're from California."

"Agent Orange?"

"Yeah. You know what that is, right?"

"No."

"Dude, seriously? Agent Orange? It was a chemical that they sprayed in Vietnam to kill the trees in the jungle so that they could fight the Viet Cong. Nasty stuff." It wasn't Dylan's intent, but I felt stupid not knowing the connection to Vietnam. "Yeah—that shit cleared out all the leaves and shrubs so they could see the enemy. I think it may have given people cancer, too. I dunno—think that was in the news."

"Huh . . . Agent Orange. Sounds rad—the band I mean. Not the cancer."

"You like it? I'll dub you a tape."

"Yeah, thanks. That'd be cool."

At school the next week, I got a dubbed copy. Liam handed me the cassette at our lockers. "Hey, Phuc! My brother said to give this to you."

"Ah, sweet . . ." I figured that the offer had been a casual nicety, but Dylan followed through. The tape case rattled in my hand as I flipped it over. Red-and-gray Memorex. Sixty minutes.

With monkish piety, Dylan's handwriting in blue Bic declared on side A: *Agent Orange–Living in Darkness*. I flipped the cassette over to side B: *Minor Threat–Out of Step*. Contrary to what I expected, he had also written out in careful minuscule on the J-card—the folded card inside a cassette cover—the song titles for each album. On the spine, there was a tiny doodle of a black sheep and the names of the two bands and their albums (I'd later learn that the sheep was from the cover of the Minor Threat album). My eyes widened at the care that had obviously been taken.

"Enjoy—Dylan said to tell him what your favorite song is." Liam tapped the clear case.

"Oh okay, definitely." I noted to myself that I now had listening to do.

That night in front of my algebra book, I sat at my desk in my bedroom and slid the tape into my Walkman, my headphones muffling my ears. I heard the click and hiss, and even as a third-generation copy, the music churned and chugged with the same urgency. In nineteen minutes, Agent Orange had burned through eight songs, and then it was over. I immediately hit rewind and play again. And again. And again. After an hour, I had only stared at the song titles and listened to the album three times, my homework still undone. This was *my* music, the music I didn't know I needed.

I felt a *click* inside me as the music and lyrics pressed my own internal button; a blinking red circle with FIRE stenciled on it. This firing sequence launched a Reaganized intercontinental ballistic missile of adolescent angst. My war began. Against a nearsighted conformity and a small-town narrow-mindedness. Agent Orange. Clearing out the undergrowth so that I could see the enemy, so I could fight them. A kid in a band was voicing things that I needed to hear. It made me feel angry, and angry felt good.

At our next meet-up to skate, Dylan asked me immediately about the tape. "How'd you like the albums?"

"They were awesome—thanks so much, dude." I squeezed a wide smile into a grin, hiding how much I delighted in both the cassette and the bequeathing of the cassette.

Dylan nodded and asked, "So what was your favorite song?"

I answered with confidence. "'Everything Turns Grey.' Definitely." It was a song that railed against mindless homogeneity with its descending guitar chords.

"Me too!"

"Yeah? I really like that opening guitar."

"Right?" Dylan affirmed my apparent good taste in guitar riffs. "And Minor Threat?"

"I loved that, too. So good." Dylan and I had connected, bonded over a shared favorite song. And that connection wasn't superficial—it felt a full five fathoms deep. There was no reason that Dylan and I, with little else in common, would have chosen the same song as our favorite. The tenuous and random connection made our shared bond fragile, and in its fragility, our crew all knew that the bond was something to protect and nurture.

The dubbed cassettes were the links of our friendship, and we forged them, one clacky plastic square at a time. One of us would buy a cassette or LP and dub it for someone else, and on we would pass the album, pooling our resources—our own teenage Marxist collective. Each person in passing on the album wrote the band name with care, the album name, and every song title. In one exchange, Sammy forgot to write the song titles to a Dag Nasty album (*Can I Say*), and he was roundly mocked. Dylan hurled the cassette back at him. "What the fuck,

Sammy?! How the fuck do I know what the songs are called?" Sammy knew better than to say that it didn't matter, because it did matter to us. For teenage boys, it was the only time that we all cared about legibility, spelling, and accuracy.

Among our group, tattered issues of *Thrasher* were passed back and forth, corners ragged, the covers reduced to vestigial staples with tufts of gnawed-up paper. For me, every page was illuminating, both the articles and the advertisements. In my comic books, ads for gag devices like whoopee cushions and X-ray glasses filled the back pages. In *Thrasher*, record stores listed new releases from bands (whose names were designed to make adults apoplectic), and grainy black-and-white photos captured young men, shirts off, screaming into microphones. It was my official guide to skateboarding, and I read every issue with anthropological care. In a shoebox, I put away my random collection of popular music that I now eyed with embarrassment: Billy Joel, the Beatles, Madonna, Culture Club. I swept away the glam and glitz for a new sound.

This was punk. I needed to know more about it, to be able to buy records, to contribute to our cassette tape communism.

And how did I learn more about punk rock in 1987? The library, of course.

SATURDAY MORNING

My dad was headed into the Bosler Library to borrow a Clymer repair manual for the Ford Fairmont, which had replaced our LTD. Say what I will about my dad, but he was willing to try to fix anything—emphasis on *try*. He was the original DIY innovator in our family, and it wasn't part of a cultural trend or punk revolt.

The DIY ethos flourished in our household because we couldn't pay someone else to do it. He did most repairs on the car himself, borrowing the repair manual from the library, making a list of what parts he needed, and going to junkyards to buy secondhand or refurbished parts.

All the repairs took place in our open carport, whether he was sweating in the August heat under the hood or freezing his knuckles around a ratchet and bolt. Lou or I were always conscripted to assist, standing next to the car, which was precariously jacked up on a stand of cinder blocks and two-by-fours.

That week, the Fairmont was running poorly, and my father suspected that it was the timing belt—which meant a trip to the library.

After his usual breakfast of a banana and a slice of hard cheese, I overheard my father talking to my mom about going into town. "Hey, Dad, can I come with you to the library? Are you going to be there awhile?"

"Sure. I'm leaving right now." I pulled on my Converse and jumped in the car. As we drove into town, my dad piped up. "Did I ever tell you . . ." This preamble usually meant that he had told me—multiple times. "Did I ever tell you that when we first came to Carlisle, one of the first things I did was get a library card?"

I stared out the window as the passing low hedges of ranch homes turned into the thoroughfares of downtown. The Woolworth's department store, the old courthouse, the town square, the Greek diner. "Yes, yes, you did."

My brother and I had heard this story many times, and each time my dad liked to show us the library card, the original dog-eared blue card, from more than a decade ago in case we doubted him.

He loved the library. My father's enthusiasm made him forget to swallow his saliva, and I heard the wetness of excitement accumulating in the corners of his mouth. He stopped at awkward moments in a sentence to swallow his spit. "I couldn't believe that it was *(swallow)* a free card—a *free* library card—that let you borrow any *(swallow)* book you wanted. Any book! I couldn't believe it. Geez. All that information and *(swallow)* knowledge! For free! Geez."

Geez was his English expletive of choice. Whenever he told us this story—which was often—his wonderment, his original awe, rippled in his wavering voice. His unshakable accent made the story feel even more proximate, as if he were talking about yesterday.

My father loved the library because it was a safe haven for him—no missed cultural cues, no bigoted insults from his coworkers, no glaring reminders of what was lost. All patrons of the library were pilgrims to the oracle, all seeking the same thing: knowledge. And in their pursuit of the same thing, they were all equals.

We owned few books in our house, since my father didn't see the point of buying books when he had his worn library card in hand. I was intimately familiar with the public library—growing up, we spent hours there weekly, reading books, checking out books, or accompanying my father as he checked out books. The stairwell to the kids' section was painted with a grand cast of literary characters: Winnie, Pinocchio, anthropomorphic mice, Charlotte and Wilbur. Suffused in the peppery scent of old oak, mildewed carpets, and yellowing pages, the library smelled to us like church, made from the same ingredients.

Frankly, I liked going to the library more than church. On our visits, Lou and I wandered off and thumbed through books about monsters or shipwreck adventures while my dad would look for a home-repair manual for the washing machine or a biography of a prominent American. He enjoyed biography and memoir, complaining about my reading fiction. "Why do you like reading books about people who never existed doing things that never happened? Geez!"

My mother rarely came with us, but she wasn't the bookish one in the family. She had barely finished high school in Việt Nam, and by their cultural standard, she was the paragon homemaker: cooking, cleaning, washing, loving. She labored under no expectation for an education beyond high school, and her marriage to my father, a young lawyer in 1973, cemented her pillars of motherhood and domestic affairs, pillars upon which she made a home with cheer and efficiency.

From time to time, as at that moment in the car, I was struck by what my parents' lives had been and what they themselves must have been like in Sài Gòn. My parents would sometimes tell us about the house in Sài Gòn—a noisy, nosy multigenerational household. My father never moved out of his parents' house. In Việt Nam, children stayed in the house, grandparents raised grandchildren while parents worked or took care of household chores. When my aunt got married, her husband moved in. When my father married, my mother moved in. My great-grandmother, grandparents, aunts, uncles, cousins, parents, and I lived in a white French colonial house. My father, the twenty-three-year-old lawyer, his twenty-two-year-old wife, and their firstborn son. Oh, and *twelve* other people. And as vivid and hot and crowded as that house on Phạm Ngũ Lão Street was—the only home they knew—it was gone, gone forever. Theirs was a life disrupted, a storyline unfinished, a song half sung.

The car idled at a red light, two blocks from the library. I took the opportunity to cross-examine my father, curious about whether he liked working at Carlisle Tire and Rubber. "How come you're not a lawyer anymore?"

My dad seemed stupefied at the question. "*Huh?* Geez, I have a family to support. That was in Việt Nam. I was a lawyer then."

Supporting a family *and* being a lawyer? The two things didn't seem to cancel each other out in my mind. I was still drowsy in the American dream, bleary-eyed with you-can-do-it-if-you-believe-it. "But you *could be* a lawyer again. I mean, do you like working at the tire factory? Who says you can't be a lawyer again?"

"I would have to go to college again. And law school. And learn the American laws. That would take a lot of time, and I couldn't work while I did that. We just moved out of the apartment. Me and Mom have bills. I have a job that pays well. It's better than my first job driving a truck." He didn't answer my question directly, but in a way he had answered it.

It felt like the opening line to life's little joke: an immigrant with a law degree walks into a tire factory to work a blue-collar job in a small town.

My dad's excitement about the library had put a vibrato and spit in his voice, but in our talk about his law career, his cheer deflated. At the library, however, as we pulled into the parking lot of the grand neoclassical edifice, he recovered his élan. My father turned and said to me slowly and reverently, "The library: it's an amazing thing."

Inside, my dad headed off to the home-repair/auto-repair section while I opened the card catalog. Music > Music History > Music History, Rock Music. 780s by Dewey decimal standards. I was on a punk rock mission. (Re)search and destroy.

Over in the 780s, I pulled down *The Rolling Stone History of Rock and Roll*, which seemed like a sufficient first step toward learning about punk. I flipped through pictures of familiar icons—Elvis, the Beatles, Chuck Berry, Jimi Hendrix, the Rolling Stones. The decades fluttered by under my thumb. In the late seventies, right in the midst of the disco inferno, punk reared its spiky head: a picture of the Sex Pistols. They were squeezed into a diner booth and sticking straws into one another's ears or pretending to snort cocaine off the table. They were teenagers, laughing and looking like a bunch of goofy kids. They looked like *my* friends. I didn't want to check the whole book out for just three pages of corporate reportage on punk rock, so I took it over to the photocopier, depositing thirty cents into the machine to Xerox the pages on punk.

"Did you find what you needed? What are you photocopying?" my dad asked from over my shoulder.

"Yup—all set. Just looking up some stuff about music."

We walked out of the library, my father with the Clymer repair manual under his arm, me with three pages of copied punk history folded up. We had our homework assignments. He needed to replace the timing belt on the Ford. I needed to upgrade Phuc the Nerd to Phuc the Punk with purpose and precision.

This summer of 1987, the summer before high school, I was formulating a plan as well as any thirteen-year-old could. High school lay before me, vast and parlous, as middle school receded in the rearview mirror. My new group of friends had stuck with me and was willing to fight for me. We had started sneaking beer on weekends, skating to abandoned parking lots where we shared filched forty ounces of malt liquor. If we couldn't find beer to drink, Sammy would walk into a drugstore with a trench coat and skate back to our group, victoriously clinking with bottles of Robitussin smuggled in the inside pockets. (The cough medicine made us woozy and itchy.) We were bound to one another by our shared love of skateboarding and general delinquency, and that fealty was further cemented by the bullying and ridicule that we received from the rednecks. I never flinched at a skate ramp or a beer or a joint—each one a test that I always took and passed.

When I got home from the library, I emptied out the contents of my health class's red Trapper Keeper and labeled the folder PUNK, drawing an anarchy *A* on the cover with scratchy blue pen. I inserted my inaugural three pages of research about seventies British punk.

The library: it was an amazing thing.

I was my father's son.

AUGUST 1987

My plan started with buying T-shirts from my skate friends who sold their old clothes for a new deck or a bag of weed. I had acquired half a dozen band shirts, which became the only shirts I wore: the Cramps, Social Distortion, the Clash, the Sex Pistols, T.S.O.L., GBH.

My father grimaced when he saw my Sex Pistols shirt, poking at it and asking me what it meant. "Sex . . . Pistols? Isn't a pistol a gun?"

I shrugged. "It's the name of a band . . . from England. *Pistols* isn't a bad word or anything."

"But the 'sex' part?" He shook his head and walked away, before warning me: "Don't wear that to church."

I nodded, and with that he seemed content to leave it alone. Soon thereafter, band buttons with Mohawked skulls and scribbly black sheep studded my backpack. Cutout *Thrasher* magazine pictures of kids with spiky dyed hair tendrilled up my bedroom wall. The rebellion of the punk ethos didn't seem any more foreign to my parents than anything else (all American teenagers seemed feral to them anyway), and they shrugged at my clothes, which were a uniform of band T-shirt, jeans, and a pair of black Converse sneakers with the occasional flannel thrown in. When I asked my mother to shave one side of my hair (we had never been to a barber shop), I told her that I wanted to look like the rest of my friends, and she agreed to lop the left side off, tacitly understanding the need to look like other kids. When I bleached part of my hair, my mother grumbled half-heartedly but didn't freak out. It was too late to stop me, and whom was my bleached hair hurting?

I needed money to buy records or maybe even a leather jacket, but my meager income from a newspaper delivery route was scarcely a trickle of cash at twenty-five dollars a week—barely enough money to spend on social events like movies or buying Slurpees from 7-Eleven. I knew that I could find record shops and punk boutiques on our next family trip to New York City, but shopping would be pointless without any money. I thought about other sources. My parents had no money to give. Christmas and my birthday were too far away. I surveyed my room and saw where all my money had been spent: my comic books. My stomach turned as logic murmured to me the grim answer to my predicament.

I had to sell my comic books.

I spent the next day rereading my favorite issues, trying to figure out if I could just sell half of my comics, but my favorite issues were either my most valuable or they broke the sequence in a numbered series, bringing down the overall value. I realized that it had to be all or nothing. I packed them up quickly and decided I needed to rip the Band-Aid off. Act now while supplies last. Sell, sell, sell. I had to sell them while my resolve was barely tipping the scales over to the SELL side.

My dad dropped me and all 220 of my comic books off downtown.

"I'm glad you're getting rid of them. That's a lot of money that you've wasted—geez, do the math. Seventy-five cents each? That's almost two hundred dollars!" He shook his head as he redid the math and said *geez* once more, looking for a spot to pull over. "Can you walk a few blocks? There's no parking near the store."

"Sure—thanks for the ride." I hefted the box out of the back seat. "I can walk home."

As I passed the large storefronts that lined Hanover Street, my reflection appeared and disappeared like an apparition, the ghost of High School Future carrying the baggage of Middle School Past. Rail thin, darkened from summer days of skating outside, my complexion contrasted with my white T-shirt, which declared SID VICIOUS DEAD. I wore a pair of secondhand red plaid golf pants which I had bought at the Salvation Army, cut up, and turned into shorts.

I took a right at the old courthouse and panted up to the comic shop. A narrow, railroaded retail space, bisected by rows of cardboard boxes crammed with comics sleeved in Mylar bags. I grunted open the door, the box in my hands. Extra-rare comics hung on the wall behind the counter, and sci-fi memorabilia adorned the shelves in various states of mint to good condition. Ultraman action figures. *Battle of the Planets* model kits. My excitement at seeing all the comics in the shop was a sweeping undertow to the surface of my intent: to sell the collection of comic books I had accumulated over my entire childhood.

The box thudded on the counter as I greeted the clerk, a thin bespectacled guy whose half-buttoned flannel shirt made shabby curtains, flanking the vista of his no-longer-white T-shirt.

I cracked every third word, honking *puberty* to all in earshot. "Are you guys buying any comics?"

"Sure—what do you have?" The clerk's tone rang indifferent, and I panicked at his lack of excitement. I was about to sell four years of collecting, four years of effort, four years of combing drugstores and 7-Elevens so I could get one missing issue in a story arc or in an artist's run.

"I have a bunch of great stuff. *X-Men*—John Byrne run. *Web of Spider-Man*—issue number one. *Daredevil*—Frank Miller run. *Secret Wars.* They're all in mint condition."

"What do you want for them?" The clerk didn't even look at my comics as he slid old issues of *The Avengers* into plastic sleeves and clicked a price on them.

"Well, I have a couple of issues in there worth five dollars or even ten dollars each alone—"

"What do you want for them *all*?"

"Well . . ." I stalled and did some desperate math in my head. "Two hundred and fifty dollars?" It was barely over a dollar per issue, hardly balancing out the high value of some rare issues.

"No way. We just opened. Don't have that much cash. I could give you two hundred dollars in store credit or a hundred and forty dollars cash."

Fuck. A hundred and forty dollars was a fleecing. "Shop credit or cash—that's all I can do." It was less than I had spent for them at face value, but what was I going to do? Carry the box all the way home? I sighed and agreed to the deal, avoiding looking at my comics as he paid me out. I was robbing Peter Parker to pay Paul Cook.

I left the shop both lightened and leadened. Peering into store windows, I walked slower than I had with the bulging box of comics. Two hundred and fifty dollars would have been a great start. A hundred and forty dollars was barely a start, and I immediately regretted my decision.

When I got back home, I found my dad under the car, mid–oil change, Lou helping him. Still plump with the innocence of elementary school, his adult teeth too big for his rounded brown face, Lou wore his slightly crooked Mom-ufactured haircut with the guileless confidence of an eleven-year-old. He shot me a look I knew well: *Where were you?! I'm stuck helping Dad, and you should be the one doing this. I wanted to ride my bike, and now I'm standing here holding this dirty oil filter. Jerk.*

I felt guilty for abandoning Lou to be the lone mechanic's assistant, so I took the oil filter from his greasy hands. "Go wash up—I'll take it from here. Oh, and change your shirt—it's gross. And make sure you're back for dinner." No matter what our schedule, my parents made sure that we had family dinner at least five nights a week.

My dad's black work shoes protruded from under the Fairmont. "Hey, Dad—I've got the filter here." My dad mumbled an acknowledgment.

Lou ran inside to clean up, and a few minutes later he ran back outside and climbed on my old ten-speed bike, tippy-toes on the pedals, flying down the driveway and yelling, "Thanks!" I had both hands on the filter and shrugged a weak "You're welcome."

I was again racked by a shudder of regret that I had sold all my comics for some cash to buy records and T-shirts. *What had I done? Could I go back and just return the money? Tell the comic store I had made a terrible mistake?* I pushed down my remorse, focusing on what I could buy with the money—new records and band T-shirts, things that I could have in common with my new group of friends, friends who didn't seem to give two shits about Spider-Man.

Holding the oil filter, I remembered that Lou, who had his own comic book collection, had recently bought a new issue of the *X-Men*. I turned my head and saw that he was still in earshot at the end of the block. I couldn't help myself and called out to him, "Hey, Lou! I'm gonna read your new issue of *X-Men*, okay?"

He nodded from the stop sign. "Yeah, just don't . . ."

"I know, I know—don't dimple the spine!" I scowled at the admonition because *I* had taught him that, and *never* in my life had I dimpled the spine on a comic book.

After the oil change, I cleaned up and went into Lou's room, picking up the new *X-Men*, issue 221. I examined the cover, which had Wolverine in agony, blasted by Havok's radiating white beams. I thumbed through the pages a bit and sighed. With a painful spasm of regret, I put it back down, unread, and went outside to practice my skate tricks. Comics were for kids.

The seriousness of entering ninth grade was lost on my parents. They didn't think about niceties like difficult school transitions or student-teacher ratios or bullying. They were happy for a free education for their kids. The passage into high school had no cultural or emotional significance for them. As such, I didn't confess to them my anxiety as we performed the great American tradition of back-to-school shopping the weekend before the first day of school.

I wanted a specific look as a punk and a skater, but how was I supposed to explain that to them? Say what you will about punk being an attitude—it was essential in the eighties to have the punk uniform, too. Punks looked for one another with the secret handshake of combat boots and band T-shirts.

Cultural historians will someday look back on the eighties and note that this was one of the summits of brand obsession, a decade marked by consumer culture and presented with an infinite array of must-have status-markers. Teen culture was a fertile furrow for the germination of trends and brands, and I was a youth of the eighties. The seeds were planted long ago in me, and my fully grown brand-consciousness was a thorny bramble that hemmed in my high school experience. And it was full of pricks.

As we walked through the parking lot of Boscov's, my mother asked me, "Why are you wearing Ritchie Johns's old boots? They don't fit you. We'll get you new shoes today, okay?" My mother still spoke Vietnamese to us all the time—it was easier for her, in her natural mode of communication.

I Vietnamesed quietly, embarrassed not to be speaking English in public. "No, that's okay. I bought these old boots from him. These *are* my new school shoes." My brother and I were in the habit of speaking in whatever language we were spoken to, and the larger the family gathering, the more mixed up our conversations were. In our nuclear family, my mother spoke Vietnamese with us, and my father, English.

Shaking his head in opposition to my explanation, my father Englished, "They're already worn-out—look at them." He pointed with his index finger at my boots, my first pair of Doc Martens. Two sizes too big and bright blue. Scuffed, balding soles, but my first pair of Docs. "How are you going to start high school in someone else's shoes?"

How, indeed? The metaphor of his question was lost on us.

As they complained about my boots, I noted the dramatic irony of how they themselves were attired. My mother was always overdressed, no matter the occasion, looking like she was ready for happy hour on the set of *Miami Vice*. Lou and I joked that she looked like a misplaced backup dancer for Sheila E. High heels, pancake makeup. Long permed black hair billowing like a cape while the front of her bangs was teased high into a stiff Aqua Net salute. Tight-fitting black slacks (never a dress or skirt) and a blazer with perfunctory eighties shoulder pads. It wasn't 1987's best look, but she made an effort, looking like a jungle lady CEO.

My dad limped along, sporting twill work slacks from JCPenney's, a white shirt, a light blue Members Only jacket, and two or three days of stubble. His short, straight black hair was forced into a part. My dad's look was always function over form.

The two of them stood there, pointing at my secondhand boots. I swallowed the aggravation of having to explain how cool my Doc Martens were to Members Only and Sheila E.

We entered the department store, blanketed by thick waves of perfume and cologne. The counters sparkled glassy and gilded, a gaudy cathedral of eighties capitalism.

Easy and abiding, Lou trailed my parents as they picked out new shirts and pants for him. His sense of autonomy was nascent, but he didn't know the difference between clothes that fit him and clothes that fit *in*. That was the hallmark of a child: to be dressed by your parents.

I intervened before my parents could pick out clothes for me. "Can I buy my own clothes? Could you guys give me the money?"

"Sure, you can buy your clothes."

"Okay—but not here. Can we go to Goodwill?"

"Is that a new store in the mall?"

"No, Goodwill. It's back in Carlisle. It's where you can buy used clothes." My mother looked confused, but it wasn't because she didn't know where Goodwill was. She knew *exactly* where Goodwill was.

She put her hand on my shoulder. "Honey, we're making good money now. We're living in a house—we don't live in an apartment anymore. You don't need to buy used clothes." She held up a polo shirt on its hanger and waved it in front of me. "What about this? Do you want this shirt?"

"No, Mom. It's just . . . it's not the kind of shirt I'm looking for." She didn't understand. I didn't know how to explain it to her, and she *didn't know*. That was the point.

There, in the middle of Boscov's, with 1987's pop hits filling in the cracks of our communication, my mom and I reached the limits of our language. How could I tell her that I was part of a group of cool kids? These kids were going to help me survive the odyssey of high school, past the harpies, sirens, and Cyclops of cheerleaders, hair-tech girls, and football players. How could she possibly understand my context? There were just some words in Vietnamese that I didn't know. Our communication had reached its threshold emotionally and linguistically. I looked at my mom; I saw her and she saw me, but we couldn't hear each other.

Point. Wave. Make sounds while exaggerating our hand gestures. Parental pantomime. Not knowing how to Vietnamese "style" or "punk" or "vintage," I looked at her as she waved the polo shirt in front of me.

"What's wrong? Don't you like this shirt?"

"No, I don't. . . . It's not that, Mom. They don't have the kind of shirt that I want here. I want a shirt that . . . uh"—how do you say *plaid* in Vietnamese?—"it has a lot of lines on it." I crisscrossed my fingers to make squares.

"Oh yes! I saw those! They're over here!" I wanted plaid flannel shirts, but she was pulling out preppy plaid *poplin* dress shirts. "Oh, and they're on sale! This is great!" My mother was jubilant with maternal victory, but I just needed her to stop.

"No, no, that's not it. . . ." Now I seemed like an asshole. Only assholes turn down shirts because they're poplin and not flannel.

Eliza Doolittle's first move to climb the English social ladder was to buy new posh clothes after disposing of her old ones. But I wasn't trying to climb *up* the social ladder. My friends were the punks and skate rats—they lived on the lower part of the ladder. My first move was to buy old clothes on my way down the rungs, wringing all I could from our econo-budget.

My mother grew quiet. "Okay . . . but isn't this the shirt you want?" She made her hands crisscross.

"It's what I said . . . but I just don't know how to tell you what I need. I'm sorry. Can I just have the money for Goodwill?"

The shadow of disappointment flickered across her face. My mother, always the optimist, didn't mask her defeat, and turned her gaze away from me. "Okay."

She knew that we had hit the ceiling, too.

My father, trailing Lou around the boys' section, had no opinion about any of it—he had fulfilled his duty of making most of the money and driving us to the mall where we spent it. We left Boscov's with several outfits for Lou and $120 for me to spend on clothes at a secondhand store.

At Goodwill, they browsed the housewares while I picked through racks of shirts for two dollars. I walked out with six plaid flannels, my mother still not understanding why I wanted to buy old clothes. "Geez— you got a lot of clothes for less than twenty dollars. That's great." Whenever my dad searched for something to say, he would comment on the relative price of something: its exorbitance, its bargain, its per-unit-price. He was pleased that I had managed to get so many shirts for under twenty dollars. Punk rock was alien to him, but its secondhand economy was a language that he understood and appreciated.

OCTOBER 1987

Kick. Push. Kick. Push. Coast.

My skateboard sped along. I was about three blocks from Liam's house, headphones on, a cassette of Stiff Little Fingers blaring away. *Gotta gettaway, gotta, gotta, gotta gettaway.* The chatter of my wheels over pavement clacked in between the songs.

As I passed the 7-Eleven, the driveway dip-and-rise popped up, and I launched myself into the air. Airborne! Ah nice . . . ah *fuck*. My wheels hit the ground hard, bucking me off my deck and sending me flying. An *almost* landed ollie. I overran my deck and turned around to get it.

I could hear laughter from the parking lot, and I knew immediately. Shit. Rednecks.

"Hey, nice trick, you *fag!*" More laughter. High fives. Spitting. *Don't look at them. Don't provoke them—you're outnumbered.*

I reoriented my board and skated quickly away. Kick. Push. Kick. Push. My haste sparked a predatory instinct in them, and before I got to the end of the block, I heard their truck coughing on as they turned onto the street behind me.

Skate *faster*. Shit.

"Hey!" they yelled from the truck. "HEY!"

I did the math. One-on-three. I made a plan to hit at least one of them with my skateboard if it came to that, but I was going to exhaust my flight instinct before the fight. I heard the truck stalking me, its low-speed tires making a *shurring* sound. Headphones on my ears, I clicked off my Walkman to be able to hear them.

"Hey! You fuckin' *faggot!* We're talking to you! With the fuckin' blue Smurf boots!" They flicked a half-smoked cigarette at me that flared across my path. Instinctively, I made a motion with my head that signaled that I saw them. Big mistake.

I skated harder. They'd have to knock me off my board, and then someone would eat a fucking mouthful of plywood. Kickpushkickpush-kickpushkickpush.

"Hey, we're talking to you, you fuckin' *nigger!*"

Jesus, you guys are idiots—did you seriously call a Vietnamese kid that?

"HEY! Stop! We want to tell you something!" That was a rhetorical request if I ever heard one.

I saw Liam's street ahead and skated hard for it, crossing in front of the truck, kicking furiously. The truck turned and sped up to keep pace, but I saw my salvation ahead: my friends.

Liam and a few guys looked up when they heard my skateboard

coming, and then they saw the truck in parallel pursuit. The crew fanned out across both sides of the street, heading toward me, some on their skateboards, some flanking the truck. They knew what was going on. We changed the odds from one-on-three to nine-on-three as we circled the truck, a small flock of overpowering Lilliputians.

Liam called out to me. "Hey, Phuc—you okay?" He spoke to me, but he was glowering directly at the driver, a stubbled kid maybe nineteen years old in a red baseball cap and a denim jacket. Liam's gaze was still locked on the driver as Liam extended his hand out to me. I was overjoyed to see him and clasped his hand.

"Yeah, I'm fine." I looked at one of the kids in the back seat and gave him the middle finger. "Fuck you, you fuckin' hicks." He immediately returned in kind. Middle finger still in the air as the truck drove past. The nine of us closed our ranks and stood next to one another in the street as the truck rattled down the block; Sammy grabbed his balls on the off chance the driver was looking for balls in the rearview. His signature move. And it was over. My pulse was still racing, and not from skating so hard.

"Sorry I'm late—did I miss anything?" I didn't need to linger on the rednecks—they harassed us regularly—and I was thankful that I had my friends to back me up, not that I would tell them that. We misfit boys had only two settings: cool or angry. We were trapped by our own scripts, unable to publicly show excitement or fear or sadness. The terror was still in my throat, but I had to play cool.

I moved on to the business of making plans for Halloween. We had all met up at Liam's house to plot out our night—*not* trick-or-treating. Candy was for little kids. Stealing decorations, smashing pumpkins, egging houses—that was our recipe for fun, and even if that fun was ephemeral and immaterial, we gripped it tight while the egg white slipped through our fingers. That was what fun felt like.

We sat on the curb, a few guys still pushing around on their boards while the rest of us legislated in punk rock assembly—our congress meant everyone talking all at once and at least a few of us insulting one another. *Whose house? Your mom's. Who was bringing eggs? Your mom. Where were we going? Your mom's.*

Our skateboard crew's face-off with the rednecks in eighth grade had welded the links of our friendship, and in high school, my introduction to the older punks was paved by Liam's brother, Dylan. Liam and Dylan presented me as the one who had organized the middle-school fight, and I got a chorus of *cools*. I was one of them now. We all loved skating, we loved going to punk shows, and most of all, we were corralled by our ostracism from the other social groups. And because I was the newest member to the group, I fretted over anything that wasn't vetted by someone else in the group. I had sold all my comic books. In the closing of that nerdy door, my focus was fixed on a portal wedged open by skate tricks and punk rock.

I had earned my social capital with my sarcasm, my willingness to jump off a loading dock to land a skate trick, and my readiness to fight for any one of them because they would do the same for me. They were hooligans, but they were my hooligans, and I was theirs.

HALLOWEEN 1987

I walked by Lou's room as he was unpackaging a tube of fake blood to smear in the corners of his mouth. He was trying on his hinged vampire fangs, a Transylvanian orthodontist inspecting his teeth in the mirror.

"Hey!" Lou lisped and spat, fangs popping in and out of place. "Are you goan shtrick-or-shtreating? Where are you guyssh goan? Issh there goan to be a lob ob candy?"

I lied. "Yeah, just me and my friends, though. You can't come." He couldn't come because he was still a kid. He wasn't a high school hoodlum. He didn't need to be like me or need to hang out with my friends—or did he? In fact, I didn't want Lou to come because I wanted to preserve just one more Halloween of candy for my brother before it turned to vandalism.

Lou took the Dracula teeth out to make sure I understood his earnestness. "Why can't I come? I can keep up with you guys! I can!" That might have been true if we weren't running from house to house, stealing pumpkins and throwing eggs.

"You can't come with us."

"Why not? Where are you going trick-or-treating? Maybe I'll just go to that neighborhood, too," threatened the dejected vampire.

"You know what? We're not even going trick-or-treating."

"What?!" It was unimaginable to him. "BUT IT'S *HALL-O-WEEN*."

"We're doing something *better* than trick-or-treating." Lou, de-fanged, was all ears now.

"What's *better* than trick-or-treating?" He eyed me skeptically. My parents weren't home, so I spoke brazenly.

"We're egging houses and stealing pumpkins. Don't tell Mom and Dad or I'll beat your ass. You'll *fucking* regret it." I didn't swear often at Lou, and it loaded my intent and purpose.

"Are you *serious*? Let me come! Please?" His entreaty was innocent and wholly sincere, and I couldn't ignore the half-applied vampire blood on his mouth as he was asking to be taken seriously. I was trying not to be a child anymore, and here was Lou asking the same thing. I looked at him and thought about myself in sixth grade. I would have appreciated a hint about what the rest of middle school and high school would be. Maybe it was time for him to see what high school was about. Maybe this would help him and make his sixth-grade year easier than it was for me. I was definitely NOT going to lend him *The Happy Hooker*.

"Okay. You can come."

"Really?! Okay!" He was beside himself with the prospect of hanging out with us. "Wait. Do we go trick-or-treating *after* we go egging?"

"No, we don't. Just egging."

"But what about the free candy?"

"You can buy candy anytime! Jesus—do you want to go with us or argue with me about candy?"

Lou persisted. "Well, I'm just saying that you can go egging anytime, too. But Halloween, you know, it's *free* candy. . . ."

"Look, there's no *free* candy tonight, so don't *fucking* complain tomorrow about not having any candy, okay?"

The second f-bomb I dropped ended the conversation. Lou surrendered. "Okay. Okay. I won't complain. Thanks for letting me come."

"Good. Wear dark clothes. We're leaving at five thirty p.m. on foot." As I turned around, he didn't see me smiling. My little brother was growing up, and I could help him. I felt important, needed, and patently paternal.

That night, we egged many houses, smashed many pumpkins. The crew was happy to let Lou tag along, and he cloaked himself in my black trench coat because he didn't own any clothing that was black. When we were chased by some remarkably vigilant homeowners, my brother won points for falling down with coat pockets full of eggs but scrambling away nevertheless. We all laughed at him and admired his heart. He became an honorary member of the crew that night, and my brother grinned as we gave him high fives. "Fucking Lou! You're a fucking nut just like your brother!"

Lou was tough—not a snitch and not a crybaby. He had a pocketful of broken eggs to show for it—better than a bagful of free candy from strangers. My brother didn't rat us out, even as his sixth-grade friends bragged the next day about their childish plunder of peanut butter cups, 3 Musketeers, and Kit Kats.

"Nice job tonight." I almost patted him on the shoulder. "I'll help you wash the egg out of the coat."

"Thanks. That was fun!" We picked and washed the shells and gooey yolks out of the coat together.

I had taken Lou egging and shepherded him into a wolf pack of high school boys. It was an education, and it felt as fundamental as his elementary reading, writing, and arithmetic, and if I could help my brother, smooth his way, I would. I couldn't tell him how I really felt—that silence was the prison of adolescence, wrapped in the chains of punk.

If teenage boys were unable to talk about their feelings, then teenage punks were doubly so, and Vietnamese teenage punks bore that burden by a factor of three because what Vietnamese male showed any tender feelings? But my actions spoke clearly: I cared for him, loved him, looked after him as well as I could; and I could show him love in my own adolescent punk rock way. The Henry Higgins to his Doolittle, I could show him what punk was all about, and maybe it would protect him, too. I had a foothold in the gutters of the social ladder, and I was glad to give Lou a hand down. He happily took it, and down we went together.

NOVEMBER 1987

I wasn't sure how it happened that fall, but Charlotte and I were hanging out, sometimes in large groups at the mall—sometimes by ourselves. Charlotte lived with just her mom, a single parent. Her mom was the cool mom. She dated a guy in a cover band and listened to underground records. ("Hey, check out this twelve-inch from this new band: They Might Be Giants. Oh, if you like this, you'll also like the Replacements.") She wore a black leather jacket, smoked cigarettes, and took trips to 21 + shows in the big cities like Philadelphia or Baltimore.

Charlotte and her friend Christine were known as the vampire chicks (popular culture would later call them goth girls, but that term hadn't gained currency yet in Carlisle). The vampire chicks read Anne Rice novels, wore black dresses with ripped fishnets, obsessed over Siouxsie and the Banshees, Bauhaus, and the Cure, and smeared black eyeliner on every morning. They were miserable, misanthropic, mysterious. We mocked them for their sad love of the Cure and the Smiths, even as I had secretly begun to listen to both bands at home.

Charlotte was older than me, and the first girl who (as far as I noticed) paid me any romantic attention, singling me out, separating me from the herd. Given my nonexistent track record for dating girls in middle school, her flirting swelled my acne-scarred self-esteem. She was taller than me and had, from what I could tell, voluptuous adult-sized breasts underneath her Robert Smith T-shirt and black cardigan.

On a Tuesday afternoon after the dismissal bell, Charlotte caught up with me in the parking lot.

"Want to come over after school? My mom's working second shift."

Charlotte and I had hung out a few times at her mom's place, an apartment downtown near the library. Conveniently, I had already told my dad that I was going to study at the library after school that day (which I did sometimes), so he planned to pick me up there at five p.m. As much as two teenagers, home alone, after school were the primary ingredients for teenage fantasy, I assumed that she and I would just listen to records and talk about music, as we had done the previous times. I didn't dare let my mind wander too far—the disappointment would have been crushing. Better to assume nothing.

We walked over to her apartment above the fire station. The hallway of the apartment building had the faint smell of hardwood, dust, and fuel from the fire station below.

Charlotte put music on as soon as we got inside, and she eased herself next to me on the couch. A boy, a girl, a Cure song playing on the turntable, parent not at home, golden autumn light glittering through the windows. Did she lean toward me? Did I lean in toward her? Did it matter? We kissed.

Her lips were soft, and we kissed slowly for a time before our tongues touched. My body tingled. And then we were lying on her couch, grinding, necking, tonguing.

I felt her pushing her chest against me, grinding her hips into my thigh. She pushed me back up and we paused. I was reading her cues as "Okay, we're done now." And in that moment that seemed good enough for me.

Panting slightly, I awkwardly obscured my erection with a casually placed hand. I moved to the edge of the couch to leave, when she pulled her Cure T-shirt off. My mind was on fire and my hard-on was forged in that fire.

Her bra clicked off.

This was not how I imagined my first kiss. She pulled me in, and we kissed longer. I caressed her tits. My mouth found her nipples. She was moaning, and I felt no indication that I was doing it wrong or that I was unwelcome. I felt the heat from between her legs against my jeans.

An hour earlier I had never kissed a girl, and now, here I was, staring at a topless girl whose tits I had been devouring. This was not how I had imagined things would go three months into high school. This was better. My limited imagination clearly needed to be more ambitious.

Charlotte pushed me up again. What did that mean? *Now* were we done? I didn't know how to read the situation, and with half her clothes off, my social-cue-reading radar short-circuited. I could only see exposed breasts gently swaying in front of me.

I moved to her side, and Charlotte stood up, pulling her skirt and underwear down in one push.

Holy fuck. I felt drunk, my head was spinning so hard. My erection deflated—a balloon blown up too quickly and with too much force. We had rocketed far past my expectations and were orbiting in the science fiction of a teenager's daydreams.

She lay down on the couch nude and spread her legs. I, on the other hand, was still fully clothed, out of embarrassment, because of all the zits on my back and chest.

But my inner nerd pushed my malfunctioning libido aside and took over the intercom. *Okay. Don't panic. You don't have a hard-on, so you're obviously not going to have sex now. Don't panic. You've watched your uncle's porn. You've read about this in* Penthouse Forum *and* The Happy Hooker. *What else do you need? That's pretty much the manual and the instructional video. Go for it. Don't be a pussy. Eat her out.* I couldn't argue with that logic. A tiny, internal dork was high-fiving me.

I knelt down between her thighs, her crotch exuding an acrid and primal heat that I had not read about in *Penthouse Forum*. I mimicked kissing her mouth on her mound—it's all I knew how to do—and she pushed into my face, quickening her pace and rhythm. Her hands were gripping the back of my head, and I thought I wouldn't be able to breathe, but I didn't want to surface for air. Charlotte bore down on my mouth as her body went rigid and shook. I thought she made some noises, but her thighs were holding too fast to my ears for me to hear.

My inner nerd had passed out from victory. My brain was deep-fried in its own heat.

After her thighs relaxed their grip, I sat up. "Was that okay?" I asked.

"Wow . . . yeah . . . that was," she said. I didn't have time for any of it to sink in because I glanced at the clock. *SHIT*.

The next thing I knew I was running down the sidewalk to the library. It was nearly five p.m., and my dad was about to pick me up in a few minutes. My face was still slick from Charlotte. I tasted her on my lips. My throat was tight and burning.

I hopped into the car in a no-I-wasn't-just-performing-cunnilingus kind of way and tried to relax. We had to get fast food for dinner because my mother had worked late at her new clerical job at the insurance office. On the drive over, my dad talked about a used riding lawn mower that he was thinking about buying to make the lawn care easier, but I couldn't hear him over the smell of Charlotte's crotch, which in my mind suffused the car and glazed my face. Did he know? How could he not know? I was a changed boy—no, not a boy. A man? No, not a man—I was still a virgin. Somewhere in between. I turned my head as far to my right as I could, pretending to look out the window. My deflated boner felt damp and triumphant and confused.

I had imagined that my first kiss would be more innocent, that it would be a lingering affair after a date of walking and talking, an evening of Friday-night flirting over fries. Its reality was jarring: an impromptu weekday grind-fest that went down faster and farther than I thought my first kiss would go. I also wanted to feel something for Charlotte, something like a crush or infatuation, but I didn't, and the physical part of our hookup felt shallow and meaningless. I thought that my teenage horniness would drive everything, but it didn't. I realized I'd actually wanted to connect with her in a real, emotional way before I ate her out, but I hadn't. The bitter aftertaste of the whole experience was real and metaphorical.

After we pulled through the McDonald's drive-through, I immediately opened my burger in the car, hoping to overpower the smell of oral sex and wash it away from my lips. I ate my cheeseburger slowly, and its steaming moisture reactivated Charlotte's pungency in my mouth.

During the car ride home, I had an innocent, childish urge to tell my dad *everything*. I didn't say anything, but the desire to share the most intimate moment of my life so far was evidence that my connection to him, no matter how threadbare, was still part of my fabric. As distant as he and I were—distanced by the violence and absence of common understanding—I recognized my indelible need to connect to him, to have him be my father. But in that need, I also knew he wouldn't understand. I was more afraid of his judgment and reprimand if I shared with him what I had done and how I felt, and in that fear, I was silent as he started talking to me about school and grades and honor roll.

With my mother, I lacked the words to tell her what I needed. With my father, I lacked the trust to tell him, the trust that he wouldn't respond with violence or disappointment, the trust that he could give me heartfelt advice, that he could see the olive branch I was extending to him if I shared an intimate and personal experience with him. I didn't believe that he would be anyone different from who he had been (no matter how much I wanted or needed him to be different).

This was my secret now, a real secret. It wasn't just an unsaid thought or unaired feeling but a real event that I would never tell him about, and in burying it, I was bricking over our relationship.

Underneath whatever my dad was saying in the car about the importance of grades and school, our relationship had been muted by its own history. We half listened to pop music on the radio. In between the notes of my own smell and McDonald's, I smelled my father's workday at the tire factory, pungent raw rubber and acetone—he was awash in it every day. He looked tired, and when he stopped talking, I didn't know if it was because he didn't have the energy or the audience.

When we arrived at home, I went straight to my room and closed my door, skipping our family sit-down in the kitchen since I had eaten in the car, declaring that I had too much homework to do. I did try to do homework, but I was distracted. I still smelled her all over me. When I brushed my teeth before bed that night, I skipped washing my face so I could smell her crotch as I jerked off in bed.

MAY 1988

"Anh! Anh!" my mother was screaming from the basement. *"Anh! Anh!"* She was calling my father in Vietnamese. "Come down here! There's water everywhere!" My father ran to the door, my brother and I closely behind. "There's water!"

We peered down the steps, and at the third step, we saw rippling and heard the lapping of water as my mother's strides sloshed around on the basement floor. She had hiked up her pants and was making her way to the laundry room. We had been in our new house less than two years, and with the pouring rain outside, there now slopped over two feet of water in the basement. With no previous signs of water in the basement, we had foolishly made the downstairs an entertainment room, fully furnishing it and putting the TV down there. My parents kept about two dozen boxes of things that they still hadn't unpacked from the move.

"Go outside and grab some buckets!" my father yelled as he squatted halfway down the stairs. Lou and I ran out and back inside with buckets in hand, dragging—and spilling—bucket after bucket of water from the basement, but my mother's cries stopped us all.

"OUR PICTURES! OH MY LORD, OUR PICTURES!" I was at the bottom of the stairs, closest to her, and moved in her direction. "OH MY LORD! OH MY!" My mother's grief—primal wailing—turned my stomach. I rounded the doorway into the laundry room, calf-deep in water, as random bits of paper and Lou's old plastic truck bobbed around my legs. A black-and-white photo of my parents, my parents on their wedding day, floated in the dark water next to me. My mother was sopping wet and, on her knees, scrambling to salvage what photos she could from waterlogged cardboard boxes, her face red, her mascara streaking. "Oh, our pictures . . ." She wept, scooping them up, soaking and crumpled, to her chest. My mother whimpered as she kept scooping up the photos; Lou, my father, and I joined in to help. I picked up dozens of photos, many of them crinkled, blurry, and stuck together.

Upstairs, in the kitchen, still in our dripping clothes, we tried to pull some of the photos apart, but they began to tear no matter how slowly or carefully we tried, and a new sob erupted from my mother with each tear. The photos were irreparably ruined. When she was distraught— which was not often—she would swat the air with both hands as if she were shooing away bugs. At the kitchen table, with the sound of the rain cascading outside, she swung at the air repeatedly, swatting with her hands.

I touched her shoulder. "Mom, I'm really sorry this happened." She cried and leaned into me.

"Yeah, me too, Mom." Lou joined in, embracing her from the other side. My father sat across the table, still trying to peel apart the sticky photos. Lou looked at the soggy few that were untorn and might be saved. "I didn't even know we had these photos."

"Wow, what's this one?" I pointed. My parents hadn't shown us these photos, and I was seeing them for the first time, rescued from the basement muck.

Wedding day (black-and-white): It's 1973, and neither of them is smiling as they cut the wedding cake—peculiar for a wedding photo. They look incredibly young and somber. My father is twenty-three; my mother is twenty-two. Dad wears a black suit, and Mom a white wedding gown. Dark ringlets of hair by her cheeks. Why aren't they smiling in the photo?

Because my mother is already six months pregnant with me, and my father *has* to marry her to avoid a full-blown family scandal, although I wouldn't learn this until a few years later.

Ugly baby in a baseball hat (color): The ugly baby is in a swing seat. I learn that it's me. I'm in Việt Nam, and I'm not sure why I'm rocking the baseball hat, but at least I have it cocked a little to the side like a gangsta, although it doesn't really offset how ugly I am.

Wedding party (black-and-white): My parents and their parents, flanking them. No one is smiling. My father and grandfathers look dashing in Western-style suits, my mother and grandmothers in traditional Vietnamese *áo dài*s and white culottes. Looks about right for a young man who had just married his pregnant girlfriend.

Old lady with ugly baby (color): It's a photo of my Bà Cố, my great-grandmother on my father's side, holding me in her lap. We left her behind with my father's parents because we couldn't get the paperwork for their evacuation. My mother tells me that when we left Việt Nam, Bà Cố was heartbroken and carried my baby shoes in her pockets as a memento. She's old in the photo (maybe in her eighties?) and I'm as ugly as I am in the baseball hat photo. While Bà Cố looks stoic, I look like I'm constipated or mid-poop. We're seated in front of a white Jeep.

Graduation day (color): It's a photo of my father and his father. My dad is in a black graduation gown and my grandfather Ông Nội is smiling in a suit—my father is graduating from law school in 1972 and is about to begin his law practice. His expression is a little flat and hard to read. It's the same expressionless look I see often—as stoic in victory as he is in defeat.

These photos, these moments, the quick flash of the cameras, froze single frames in my parents' stories. My brother and I didn't know what the rest of their story looked like before us—it was our youthful ignorance and solipsism that kept us from asking more, from wanting to know more. We didn't appreciate the pain that my mother—and maybe even my father—was feeling at the loss of the photos, photos never before seen, of stories never told. Our mild indifference amplified the tragedy, the last bits of their old life mangled and washed away.

My mom's face was red and brindled with makeup as she spoke. "When we left Việt Nam, we didn't take anything with us. We left everything behind, but we took these photos. Did you know that you didn't even have shoes when we left?" I did know that.

"Well, I think I had *one* shoe. . . ." I corrected her.

"*One* shoe! Okay, so you had *one* shoe!" my mother cried. "And we had a small valise of photos and clothes. It's all we had." Tears ran again. I couldn't tell if she was crying over the photos or Việt Nam or both. My father was trying to save more pictures while my brother and I comforted my mom as best as we could. He didn't show any discernible emotion, focused on what he could fix or try to fix.

"Who's this baby?" Lou gestured toward the Ugly Baby photo lying on the table.

"That's Phúc! Look at him!" my mother chirped. "Look at him! What a baby!"

"He looks *weird* . . . like he's angry or something," Lou joked, to which I responded with a short jab to his arm. "*OW!*" My mother ignored the punch as she looked at the photos spread out on the table, a dozen photos that had the likelihood of being salvaged.

"Did you know that Phúc was talking at one year old? He could count! It's true! So smart!"

I stuck my tongue out at my brother in mock triumph. "Sounds about right. I *am* a genius. You guys just don't recognize it," I said. "What about you, Lou? You're the one who Mom put in a dress! A girl's dress!" My brother hated that story, and I mentioned it to get a rise out of him.

"Shut up! That was when I was a baby!" Lou punched back.

My mom tried to deescalate our jostling. "Well, it was the only clothes people donated to us. We didn't have any other clothes that fit Lou except for girls' clothes when we came to this country. And it only happened a few times."

"Yeah, you stopped putting him in dresses when Lou showed his wiener!" He ignored me this time.

My father got up from the table, abandoning the photos. "Let's get back to the basement—we still have to clean up the water."

In Vietnamese, the word for *country* and the word for *water* are the same: *nước*. Context obviously makes it clear if you're talking about the former or the latter, but in Vietnamese, your country is not the terra firma or the nationality; it's the water. The waters that feed the soil. The waters that lap your shores. If you ask someone where they're from, you're asking literally from what waters do they come. The country of America is called, in Vietnamese, *nước mỹ*: the waters of America.

I've wondered why water was a synonym with *country*, but a quick look at Vietnam's geography seems to hint at its origin. Vietnam's two-thousand-mile-long coastline, thousands of islands, massive rivers and deltas, the waters that flow through Việt Nam, the monsoons that mark its seasons between rainy and dry: waters run its length, slice through it, define it. Its waters were so prominent to its primordial people that *water* defined where you came from. Water was your country.

Lou, my father, and I all carried buckets upon buckets of water up the steps and out the door, long past midnight, and we mopped up the rest of the basement. The kitchen clock blinked two a.m. when we finished. Our new home had ironically destroyed the mementos of our old life. Or maybe it wasn't ironic. Maybe our new home had to destroy the old things. Maybe that destruction had already begun, but we didn't know it.

Old water. New water. Old country. New country. Aqua vitae. Giver of life. Destroyer of memories.

At the end of *Pygmalion*, Eliza laments that she cannot go back to her old life, to her old ways, and she cannot find a place in her new world, either. In the currents of fitting in, in the push and pull of Americana that was sweeping me and my brother away, I could no longer communicate deeply with my parents. I had begun to forget my Vietnamese, and that act of forgetting was my Vietnamese forfeiture for my future in America. The slow erosion of our common language didn't happen with a cataclysmic flood—it was the gradual, imperceptible rise in the tides: one moment, I couldn't remember the word for *plaid*, then I began to forget words that I should have known, and then I didn't ask to learn them when I did forget. Sometimes, in annoyance, I chose to answer my mother in English, bypassing Vietnamese altogether. I didn't bother to consider what was lost in the undertow of the flood.

I was in the waters of America, and gasping, dying, I chose to survive.

I held my breath and dove deeper.

8

THE METAMORPHOSIS

Franz Kafka's *The Metamorphosis* is a simple story: Gregor Samsa awakes to find himself transformed into a giant bug. When he discovers that he's a giant bug, he immediately looks at the clock and thinks about which train he can still catch to get to work on time. By himself, he's not freaking out about being a giant roach *at all.*

His parents and sister, whom he's been supporting, freak out. His supervisor from work shows up and freaks out. Gregor has turned into a bug, but he does *not* freak out about his transformation until he has to navigate his relationships with his family and his work supervisor.

You read *The Metamorphosis* and you realize: it's his family's ugliness toward Gregor that moves the story. Gregor is now a giant roach, and he cannot do anything about it. His family, instead of acting with compassion and kindness, sends Gregor to his room and locks the door.

What's worse than turning into a giant bug? Turning into a giant bug *and* having your family act like a bunch of assholes.

And isn't that adolescence? A biological change over which we have no control? And then our family, like a bunch of assholes, treats us like an insect in the midst of a metamorphosis that we ourselves hardly understand. Suddenly, with a different focus, from the perspective of a bug, we see who they are.

SEPTEMBER 1988, PHILIP'S HOUSE

A bunch of us punks and skaters gathered on Sunday at Philip Lehmann's house to watch his band practice. Philip and three friends had formed the first punk band in our crew: Bündersplat. In his basement, the foursome churned out songs that were loud and angry with titles like "Prejudicial Prosecution," "Breakin' Down the Walls," and "Do You Wanna Fuck?"

Philip's dad, a wiry middle-aged man with glasses, greeted us with a warm hello when we arrived for band practice. After exchanging pleasantries about school, we retreated to the basement. Mr. Lehmann allowed smoking in the practice space, and in the murky, poorly lit, rumbling cellar, we gathered around Bündersplat, pushing one another, bobbing our heads, binding our tribe. The thudding music made the cellar concrete throb and hum.

Philip was a year ahead of me in eleventh grade, and he commanded everyone's respect in the punk scene. His older brother, Lucas, who had graduated four years earlier, was, according to Carlisle punk annals, the first punk rocker in our town.

The epic mythos surrounding Lucas Lehmann was hyperbolic. Lucas shaved and glued his hair into an eight-inch Mohawk—dyed it red, even. We referred to Lucas as if we were talking about Paul Bunyan or John Henry. And with his legendary Mohawk, he had gone to NYU. Fucking New York University. Our crew only had the dimmest gleanings about what our lives might look like after high school. We were too preoccupied with hooliganism, next week's party, or where to meet girls. We didn't know much about college. But there went Lucas to the city, *the* city, and he had moved there to go to college—no, not college—university. We'd see him home from New York, and Lucas would fire off stories about the Village or Alphabet City or Tompkins Square Park as we gathered around him, children in awe of big-city fireworks, oohing and aahing at his words bursting around us.

Band practice ended that Sunday, and several of us headed out to skate for the rest of the afternoon. We invited Philip to come along.

Still sweaty from rehearsal, Philip shook his head. "Nah, I have a shit-ton of homework already for AP US History." My antennae swiveled at this remark. Philip was turning down hangout time to do *homework*. We all heard what he said, and everyone else lobbed a "cool" before they took off. No one would give Philip shit for anything, even for choosing homework over hangout.

I lingered behind as the other guys left. "AP US History? What's AP?"

"Advanced Placement US History. Mrs. Romberger teaches it. She's amazing—fucking Pat Romberger!" Philip's face widened with a big grin and raised brows, using Mrs. Romberger's first name, Pat, as if they were old friends. "AP US is great." I was flabbergasted. This was Philip Lehmann, and he was glowing about high school—about AP US History. "Yeah, you should definitely take it next year. Plus, if you do well on the AP test, you can get college credit. Just do your work and study—you can't get shitty grades if you want to get into AP classes."

"Huh. Good to know." I had never heard of the AP, nor had I ever heard one of my friends express unequivocal love for school or a class.

"Hang on a sec. You like the Cure, right?" He wiped his sweaty forehead with the hem of his T-shirt.

"Yeah, the Cure? They're all right." I answered warily because I never knew with Philip if it would turn into an insult or not.

"Wait here." He bounded upstairs and came back down. "Read this." He handed me a black paperback, a copy of *The Stranger* by Albert

Camus. "This is the book that inspired their song 'Killing an Arab.' Give it back to me after you finish, okay?"

Philip lent me a book. Holy fuck. Not a record, not a cassette tape, not a movie. *A book.* I didn't even know that he liked reading. I looked at the back, skimming the blurb: *influential, terrifying, unrelenting grip.* "Yeah, cool. Kamm-uss," I said aloud, butchering the name.

"It's French, man. *Caw-moo.*" Philip snickered as I blushed with a searing embarrassment—the still present and perennial humiliation of pronouncing things incorrectly.

"Oh okay. *Caw-moo.* Got it. How do you say his first name?"

"How the fuck do I know? Probably just fucking Albert." It would be a while before I learned how to say *Owl-Bear Caw-Moo.*

I hopped on my skateboard to catch up to the other guys, calling out another thank-you as I skated away. Philip seemed different to me now, and our conversation sparked a revelation about both Philip and me. I had assumed that being punk and being good at school were antithetical to each other; that the first rule of rebellion was revolt against monolithic institutions like school. That part was right—our brand of punk was anti-school—but I had conflated *anti-school* with *anti-education.* Philip proved, in that moment, my assumptions were bullshit. I skated along, surprised at how excited I was to read *The Stranger.*

I had naïvely assumed that Philip's older brother, Lucas, had gone on to NYU because of natural ability and luck. Who knew? I had only the vaguest notions of how you got into college and figured most of us who could get in would go to one of the Penn State campuses. I was now beginning to realize that maybe Lucas had worked and studied hard to get into a good school rather than getting in by pure luck.

At school, I was doing well. My parents and I had negotiated an arrangement that allowed me to hang out late on weekends: stay on the honor roll, no curfew. I met my parents' expectations with ease, but I wasn't kicking or pushing myself particularly hard.

Regardless, I had kept my academic work to myself, hidden from my friends to better fit in with them—or with who I thought they were. Yet here Philip was, telling me not to be a dummy, to do my work and to study.

Could you love reading and still love punk? I had assumed that you couldn't be a skate punk and geek out on books, but Philip had changed that perspective. I had wanted to ensure that I would fit in, and suppressed my nerdiness as anathema to punk rock. But Philip had obliterated that premise in an instant with a copy of *The Stranger*. Maybe this was my opportunity to be regarded as someone different, more interesting and complicated than the Vietnamese kid or a skate punk.

It began here—a borrowed book because of a song. This was my invitation to be something more complex. This small, seedling moment would grow into my opportunity to change and flourish, to branch out with new ideas and shear away old assumptions.

OCTOBER 1988, THE MJ MALL

Conor and I had a shift together at the Coral Reef that Sunday. The Coral Reef was a tropical tiki-themed smoothie bar in the middle of the MJ Mall. Even on its busiest days, the mall's architectural expanse made it feel cavernous and half occupied.

Two kiosks squatted in the middle of the oversized concourse: a novelty T-shirt booth (where you could custom-order T-shirts with black-velvet bubble lettering that extolled your status as *World's #1 Grandpa*) and the Coral Reef. With fake plastic palm trees flanking its four corners, a thatched roof, and a dusty shellacked blowfish that hung dejectedly by the yellow sign, the Coral Reef was an incongruous vendor in the MJ Mall.

It was a typical Sunday at the mall. I didn't feel like doing chemistry homework, so I pulled out *The Myth of Sisyphus* by Camus while Conor cleaned the counters.

I had already finished *The Stranger*—amazing and horrifying in its nihilism—and went to the library to get another book. I looked up Camus in the encyclopedia. *French. Existentialist. Didn't believe in God. Died in a car crash.* The latter two items probably unrelated. The encyclopedia mentioned him in tandem with Sartre, and I decided that I wanted to read him or her, too. (What kind of a name was Jean-Paul, anyway?) Clueless, I picked the shortest book on the library shelves, a slim play called *No Exit.* The book jacket informed me that Jean-Paul Sartre was a man, but it didn't present me with a pronunciation guide for how to say *Sartre.* Shit. I would just have to avoid saying *Sartre* and only refer to the play title, *No Exit.* No way was I going to embarrass myself pronouncing *Sartre.* I piled *No Exit* on top of *The Myth of Sisyphus*—light reading for a fourteen-year-old—and tucked them both away in my backpack.

There I sat, at the Coral Reef on Sunday, reading *Sisyphus.* The hotdog cooker rolled the shriveled hot dogs in unison. They churned endlessly, cooked beyond recognition, dimpled with sweat and oil, yet with all their rolling, they went nowhere. Yup, that looked like existentialism, all right.

Conor nudged me. "What are you reading? Kamm-uss?"

"It's French. *Caw-moo.* Dude, you should read this book. It's about why you shouldn't kill yourself."

"Seriously? I don't need a book to tell me that." Laughter.

"Yeah—he says that life is absurd. It makes no sense. Has no meaning. Camus asks why we shouldn't just all kill ourselves. So crazy."

"Why shouldn't I then?"

"Um . . . I don't know yet—I'll tell you when I get to the end."

"Well, read faster. You're fuckin' bumming me out."

I read on as he straightened the condiments. Three o'clock. Shift over. Kevin, the manager, came and relieved us from Reef duty.

Conor and I hopped into the front seat of his parents' cobalt-blue Ford Escort station wagon. "Where are we going?"

"I don't know. Wanna just drive around? Roy got me a twelve-pack of National Bohemian."

"Seriously?!" I assumed he was joking, but he reached back behind my seat, nudging aside a blanket to reveal a tattered white cardboard box of warm beer. Presto.

"You already did your homework. What else do you have to do?" Conor's rhetoric was compelling.

Did I think twice about drinking in the middle of the afternoon? Did I consider what coming home a little drunk to my parents for Sunday dinner at six p.m. would look like? Of course I didn't. We didn't think far enough ahead to save the beer for a party, never mind the next weekend. "Are you kidding me? Yeah, let's do it!" Boredom short-circuited any forethought, and beer-in-hand did so, doubly.

The regularity of drinking had made us cavalier and careless. We had never been caught, and I assumed that whatever suspicions Conor's parents might have harbored were met with a blind eye—probably because he was the youngest of four siblings. It seemed they'd given up the cat-and-mouse routine of parent-and-teen pursuit.

My parents, on the other hand, didn't have even a sliver of a notion about American teenage culture and underage drinking. The idea that I might be drinking warm beer in a Ford Escort never crossed their minds.

"Fuck. Fuck. Fuck. Fuck. Fuck." Conor rattled off suddenly while pulling the car over. I figured we had a flat tire or he had forgotten something.

"What is it?" Then I saw in the rearview: police lights.

We pulled over and the police officer approached our window. License. Registration. Out of the car. *Problem, officer? Beer cans, son? Beer, what beer?*

We were in the back of the squad car, on our way to the police station. Our parents were also on their way, icebergs and ocean liners plotting their courses of intersection. In the interrogation room, when they asked me where we got the beer (*we found it, sir*), I felt oddly calm. No panic. I could only control my reaction to what was going to happen. They asked to go through the contents of my backpack—*no drugs in there, sir*—and I spread my belongings out on the table. Notebooks. A couple of pencils. Chemistry textbook. Camus. Sartre.

No exit.

From the police station, my family and I endured a wordless car ride home. Officially, I was given a warning, sealed records unless further violations were made, for which future violations I would be referred to juvenile court. *Keep my nose clean. Yes, sir. No, sir. I swear, we found the beer, sir. No one bought it for us, sir.* As I rode home in the back seat with my brother, the tranquility I had felt at the station gurgled into anxiety.

"What did you do?" Lou whispered.

"I got caught driving around with Conor and drinking beer." I didn't look at my brother.

"*Beer?!* Why were you drinking *beer*?!" Lou was dumbfounded. I stared out the car window, unable to twist any farther away from him. I didn't answer.

I was sent to my room when we got home, and my parents talked in the kitchen while my brother went into the living room and played Nintendo. I put on a dubbed tape of the Cure on my boom box and sat in my chair, staring blankly. *The Head on the Door* played on the A side.

I was fucked. How was I not? Whatever drunkenness I had felt dissipated; the beers were still in my gut but now congealed into a bezoar of unease and anticipation. I also kind of needed to take a shit.

I was going to get grounded. I was trying to guess for how long, maybe a few weeks. The Vegas odds: I was wagering several weeks—four? five? That seemed like a good punishment.

My parents called me into the kitchen. There was no yelling or screaming. They *both* spoke, so I knew it was serious because my mother never weighed in as a disciplinarian.

As they spoke, my father Englished, my mother Vietnamesed, and their dialogue diverged into two radio stations broadcasting simultaneously. I stared, downcast, into the dead air between them, the broken tuner, receiving English on the left channel and Vietnamese on the right.

"Honey, you know that you shouldn't drink beer *this is very bad that the police* you're too little *caught you and we are very lucky* you're just so young *that you did not have to go to jail* Some people drink beer when they're older *do you know how much shame this brings on the family* but not as a kid *it's terrible* Don't drink beer, okay? *was this Conor's idea?* I know that you just wanted to try it *you shouldn't be friends with him anymore* but don't drink beer, okay? *I think he's a bad influence.*"

"You're grounded for six months." My father's slender hands crossed on the table. My mother nodded, head wilting with a drawn expression, leaving the discipline to my father.

Short and sweet. No prelude, no long conversation about disappointment—just the sentencing. The grammar of justice in my parents' house was brief and declarative. Grounded for six months.

I didn't think this was the appropriate time to try to plea-bargain. "Okay."

I was grounded from October through April—*a lot* longer than the few weeks I'd been expecting.

I went back to my room, closed my door, and sat in my faded yellow corduroy reading chair. The Cure was playing the song "The Caterpillar" on my boom box.

I flopped onto my bed, staring out my window and thinking about my sentence when my perspective shifted. I looked at my bedroom window, but instead of a window, I saw a door. Was I trapped in my room like Gregor Samsa? No, I wasn't.

The next day at school Liam Mahoney caught up with me at my locker. "Dude, did you and Conor get arrested?"

"Yeah, it sucked. Rode in the back of the cop car and everything," I delivered it as lackadaisically as I could, glossing over any fear and panic that I had felt when I was waiting for my parents in the holding area. Our escapade already had its own momentum. I didn't need to sell my story with teenage histrionics. Nonchalance was my agent, and she sold it for me.

"Damn—that's crazy. I want to hear about it later. Hey, do you have your gym socks? I don't have white socks, and I'm gonna fail gym if I don't have them—it'll be the third time this marking period." Liam was referring to our school's mandatory gym uniform: a white T-shirt, green shorts, white socks, light-soled sneakers, and a jockstrap.

"Oh yeah—sure." I handed Liam white socks from the bottom of my locker, where my gym uniform lay unwashed and odorous.

"Hey, thanks—sorry about you and Conor getting busted. Later!" My white socks in hand, he was off to gym.

In geometry class later that day, Mr. O'Hara was in the midst of telling us a terrible joke about his friend who worked in Alaska, canning fish.

My friend was the cook for all the cannery guys, and all the workers slept in tents. While they were there, he had befriended some dolphins that would swim up to them on the coast for the leftovers. After this happened a few times, my buddy, the cook, woke up one morning, rang the bell, and yelled out, "Breakfast is being served for all in tents . . . and porpoises."

We groaned in mock disdain for the pun, but all our faces were wide with laughter. Mr. O'Hara's dark beard was covered in chalk and spittle as he laughed loudest and longest. Jim Taylor, who sat near me in most of my classes by virtue of the alphabetical seating chart, turned around. Word of our arrest was making its way through the school.

"Hey—are you grounded for six months?" The rumor mill worked fast at Carlisle High School.

"Yeah, Conor and I got busted for drinking." I tried not to sound like I was bragging, but I was bragging. Jim's eyes bulged with my affirmation.

I walked through the halls that week, thinking that, in my wake, kids were whispering and pointing. Maybe they weren't, but in my own mind I had moved up a peg in rebel status with an arrest and sealed police file. Maybe they saw me differently, but I certainly saw myself differently. I hadn't turned into a giant bug—this was a different kind of *revolting*. I was a full-blown teen rebel now.

Six months of being grounded could have been a crippling blow to my social life, but in fact, it amplified my social standing because I snuck out every weekend, which gave me even more social cachet and augmented my rebel status. Being grounded granted me confidence and credibility. My classmates asked me about it, and I was always poised to tell them; and when I showed up at punk shows or house parties, I was always met with a three-part-harmony of *I thought you were grounded?*

"I am grounded! Where's the beer?" Laughing and hand clasping. Beer cans in our fists, hissing open with quick fissures.

What had I learned from my arrest and subsequent grounding? Don't drink in a place that you can't run from, like a car, and be thankful that your bedroom is easy to sneak out of. If only Gregor had been able to see a life beyond his room, his home, and his family.

I flitted about in school, doing only slightly more than the minimum for my classes, though I now had more time at home than I had before. Philip's injunction about AP US History and school was planted in my mind, but it grew no firm roots and bore no fruits. My motivations at school were to maintain my grades so that when I was eventually paroled, I could go back to hanging with my crew, to skating, to going to shows without sneaking around in the underbrush of lies.

In English class, Mrs. Ferguson was dragging the class's discussion through third period, straining heroically against the inertia of kids who hadn't read *Great Expectations*. At some point in the discussion, Mrs. Ferguson mentioned something about the search for meaning in one's life. My ears perked up. Remembering what I had read about Camus, I raised my hand.

"It sounds like it's a common question, those big questions about meaning and life. It's a theme that shows up a lot, right? Like in the existentialist writers . . . like Camus . . . and uh, Sartre. Life is absurd. That's their take, at least, on the meaning of life." I overpronounced *Camus* and stumbled over Sartre's name, pronouncing it more like *tartar*. But I remembered a little about the existentialists, and I was cocksure that I had pronounced *Camus* correctly.

Mrs. Ferguson tilted her head. "Yes, I suppose that's true. It does have a connection with many other great books." She was gracious, given that I had anachronistically shoehorned an allusion about French existentialism into a Victorian English novel. I leaned forward at her observation that I had read a *great* book (on my own), and I felt the class's energy turn toward me. Even my listless peers stopped their doodling and looked up. "Phuc, have you read much Camus or Sartre?" Mrs. Ferguson asked with apparent intrigue.

"Uh . . . just *The Stranger*, *The Myth of Sisyphus*, and *No Exit*—so far. But I just borrowed *The Plague*." I added the *so far*, thinking that it sounded smart and hinted at an intent to read more, as vague and uncommitted as that intent was.

She nodded approvingly. "Well, thanks for making that connection, Phuc. See me after class, please—I can recommend some other books for you if you like existentialism." A teenage boy who liked existentialism? She might as well have said that chocolate was delicious or Freddie Mercury had a nice falsetto or Dickens was wordy.

Encouraged, I made a few more not-stupid remarks during our discussion, and after class she scratched out some titles on the back of an old mimeographed vocabulary quiz. "You should read some of these works, too, if you liked those other books you mentioned. It's a mix of novels and plays."

I nodded gratefully as I read the list. *Waiting for Godot* by Samuel Beckett. *Catch-22* by Joseph Heller. *Rosencrantz and Guildenstern Are Dead* by Tom Stoppard. *The Trial* by Franz Kafka. "Thanks—I'll definitely check these out. At the library. Pun intended, you know."

She laughed. "Well, good. Keep reading and making those connections. That's what it's all about—the connection."

I read the Beckett and Stoppard plays in quick succession and incorporated them into our class discussions when I could, my limited literary credentials of five and a half books on existentialism being more than anyone else's reading list of none. No matter. My classmates gave me wide berth and listened with a respect that I had never been afforded, and Mrs. Ferguson checked in with me about my extracurricular reading.

I was astounded and intoxicated by this shift in reality: what I read and what I said in the classroom mattered. It changed the way my classmates saw me (if they had seen me at all) and it changed the way my teacher saw me. And the truth was that I hadn't read that many books nor was I some sonnet-quoting super-genius of English literature—but I sounded like one because I could refer to other books that I had voluntarily read (which, apparently, no one else did).

Unsure of what else to read or what would sound impressive, I made certain to read our class's assigned books and whatever else Mrs. Ferguson recommended. I also figured that I could look up the authors in the library's encyclopedia just to be able to say something vaguely biographical about them in class discussions. My peers' esteem, which started bubbling in English class, boiled over into some of my other classes, and I happily rode the swells of admiration as my classmates realized that I wasn't some loser who was getting shit grades.

The feeling that I had with my punk crew—that feeling of being part of something, that feeling of respect—had crept up in a place I wasn't expecting: the classroom. The sensation was fleeting, hard to pin down, but it felt real and complemented my crew's safeguard on the streets of our town. My classmates' open regard was public recognition of me and my intellect. Some kids seemed intimidated, and in my immaturity, their intimidation felt like respect—or something close enough for me.

For the first time, I felt as though my peers were seeing another side of me, and this new side was earning their attention and esteem—it was a feeling that, at that moment, was completely unfamiliar to me. If I could command academic respect by reading six books, what would happen if I were to read twelve?

That fall and winter I read everything I could, filling my name-dropping arsenal with Orwell, Brontë, Woolf, Nietzsche, and whoever else was recommended. I savored the academic clout that reading a book gave me in school, and beyond that, I discovered that I actually liked the books my teachers recommended to me. My perceived *need to read* changed, slowly and surprisingly, into a *desire to read*—a desire that I didn't fight.

DECEMBER 1988, SAINT PATRICK'S CHURCH

For my mother, Christmas Eve mass was the culmination of her piety and devotion. All the Sundays, the extra masses we attended on Ash Wednesday and Good Friday—they all climaxed in December at midnight mass. My mind wandered as it usually did at the other masses, skipping from games of see-people-I-know to thinking about song lyrics. I played a game where I tried to turn everything into a Smiths lyric.

> *In the name of the father, and of the son, and the heir of a shyness*
>   *that is criminally vulgar . . .*
> *He will come again in glory to judge the living and the dead and in*
>   *the midst of life we are in debt, et cetera. . . .*

For us men and for our salvation he came down from heaven, and
heaven knows I'm miserable now. . . .

The chapel's lights dimmed as candles were fumbled in the dark. The liturgy ended as "Silent Night" swelled up from the choir and parishioners. The knot in my brow loosened. Usually, Sunday mass was a mixture of boring and embarrassing: boredom from the irrelevance that church and religion had for me; embarrassment because it was the most public space that I was in with my family, and it was when I was most acutely aware of how much we didn't fit in. But Christmas mass was different. It gave me a different lease on church and my family.

In the dark of the church, one candle was lit from the front of the pews, and as the meager flame passed itself on, one small glimmer of light spread itself across the pews, dipping, catching, lighting like twilight stars ascending. In the gloaming of the service, we were silhouettes, all of us, all our features and differences erased. In the darkness, everyone looked the same and I didn't think about being the only Vietnamese family in the congregational sea of white families. In the darkness of midnight mass, we were the same as everyone else. I breathed in the warm smell of wicks and wax and listened. *Silent Night.*

Barely awake when we got home, Lou and I gathered around the Christmas tree to open gifts before our drive the next day to Staten Island. My parents, ever the pragmatists, had given up on getting us actual presents a few years ago, per our request, and gave us money in envelopes to buy the gifts we wanted.

"Hey, fifty dollars!"

"Hey, me too! All right!" I had seen an ad in the *Village Voice* for a cool pair of boots, and Ulysses S. Grant was going to help me procure them.

"There's another present for you in your room." My mother patted me on the shoulder.

"Really? What?" I was well beyond bikes with ribbons, and given my current state of home incarceration, I wasn't sure what it could be. I padded down the hall in my socks, my parents behind me, and opened my bedroom door.

It was a stereo system.

Brand-new. Dual cassette decks. Turntable. I could play my records, dub cassettes for friends, make mixtapes with mixed messages for girls.

At the midpoint of my six-month sentence, my parents had gotten me a gift so specifically for me, I was astounded. I knelt down, and my hands glided over the faux wood paneling and the plate-glass door that enclosed the stereo components. I didn't understand why I deserved such a gift, and felt a searing wave of guilt and sadness. I recognized my parents' forethought in buying me a stereo. Among the components, between the dual-cassette decks and the receiver was something I hadn't seen before.

"Wow . . ." I mustered a few words together. "Is that a . . ."

"That's a CD player," my dad said from behind my crouched position. "Music is supposed to sound really good on a CD." None of my friends had CD players in 1988. I didn't own any CDs, but from working at the mall and seeing them in their giant, oblong cardboard boxes, I knew that they were more expensive than records and tapes. I skipped over the CD player to look at the record player and the remote control on top of it. "That's a remote control. Have you ever seen a stereo with a remote control?" I hadn't. I now had a nicer stereo for my bedroom than my parents had for our living room. I didn't know what to say.

Still lingering in the doorway, my dad continued with his showroom sales pitch. "I asked someone at work what kinds of speakers were good, and he told me that Advent speakers were very good." I was sold, but my silence sounded like indifference. I didn't say anything because I was too grateful. I didn't say anything because I, inmate Phuc Minh Tran, incarcerated at 1010 Harriet Street, couldn't believe that I got a brand-new stereo for Christmas in the midst of being grounded. "We can set it up when we get back from New York."

I was still silent, and the void of words created a space between us. My father retreated away from that gap, and as he walked down the hallway, the gap widened into a chasm. I didn't thank him, and his shuffles put a distance between us that gulfed too wide for words.

Muffled in the silken gauze of the ineffable, we lost an opportunity to connect with a kind word, with tenderness, as father and son. Maybe we would have failed anyway, but I didn't even try. We didn't talk about how he felt or how I felt or where our relationship was. We never did. I had never heard my father say "I love you" to me, and maybe this was his fumbling way of saying it. I didn't give him a chance to say anything, and I didn't acknowledge my suspicion that the magnanimity of the gift was my parents' attempt at mending our relationship.

We see you, they wanted to say. *We see you listening to music, we know that you love it, and this is for you because we love you.* Their kindness was confusing for me, and it was easier for me to play the simple role of a teenager being angry with his parents. It was easier for me to fixate on the cool new stereo and not to think about *why* I got a cool new stereo from my parents.

In the midst of my own changes, I wasn't able to change my perspective on my mom and dad, to consider that my parents might be changing. Maybe they *wanted* to change the story of parents being the antagonists in their children's lives. We didn't have the script for that scene. I missed the cues for the dialogue, and the curtain closed on another moment of disconnection.

MARCH 1989, CARLISLE HIGH SCHOOL

School was stomping along. On my way to gym class, I stopped at my locker to get my gym uniform, which was still unwashed (months later) and varying shades of off-white. No white socks. I couldn't find my gym socks.

Fuck.

Fucking Liam had borrowed them again earlier in the week and hadn't returned them. It was the third time this had happened, and our gym teacher strictly enforced the three-strikes policy: improper gym uniform three times in a marking period and you failed gym.

And this was my third gym class without the full uniform. I had everything except the socks, but that didn't matter to Coach Woods.

In the gymnasium, I walked past Coach and his clipboard, hoping he wouldn't notice or would give me a pass with some unheralded kindness. No chance. He called our names and rattled off the uniform as he checked them off. "Tran. White T-shirt. Green shorts. White socks. Light-soled sneakers. Athletic supporter. Tran, where're your white socks?"

"Sorry—I forgot them. I lent them to someone else so that he could wear them." Coach didn't acknowledge my explanation.

"You know this makes three, Tran? You'll get a fail for this marking period." Fucking fuck. I had *black* socks on, but I needed to have *white* socks. Fucking WHITE socks. I was going to fail gym class and not make honor roll. But I made honor roll with my academic grades, right? Would I really be denied honor roll because of a technicality?

In the days leading up to receiving my report card, I thought about trying to forge the honor roll stamp, but it was too mechanical, and I had never forged anything. It would be too much of a gamble. Besides, my parents *might* understand the absurdity of the policy. They bought me a stereo while I was grounded, right? They didn't yell at me when I got arrested, right? There was a chance they might be sympathetic, and I wagered on it. The chips were down.

The Monday that our report cards came out, I checked to see if, in the Byzantine bureaucracy of Carlisle High School, someone had forgotten about my failing gym. No such luck. The *U, Unsatisfactory*, for gym was clearly printed. The absence of honor roll also lingered there, striking in its absence. At least my other grades were good. Maybe my parents wouldn't notice. I thought about the stereo again, and the kindness behind it. It was genuinely benevolent. Maybe my father would surprise me again.

At dinnertime, my mother had made *gà xào* with rice (stir-fried chicken and broccoli). My brother and I sat opposite each other, and my parents flanked us at the ends of the table.

"Did you get your report cards today?" my father asked. My brother and I presented them. As my father reviewed Lou's grades, my vision tunneled and my mind raced. I was one month from finishing being grounded, and now this bullshit. I braced myself for further incarceration. Would they sentence me to another six months? That I could take, especially since I wasn't really trapped in my room anyway. But I started to wonder if he would ground me for a year. But still no matter. I felt confident that even that I could endure, whatever sentence he doled out.

My father perused my report card. "That's good—all *A*s. That's very good. Why is there a *U* for gym?" My brother passed the rice to me.

"I forgot white socks three times this marking period, so I was marked unprepared. I had everything else. *Can you believe that?* I had socks, but you need to have *white* socks. Crazy, right? Those gym rules . . ."

"But you do have white socks."

"I do—but I lent them to Liam . . . and he forgot to give them back to me. That happened three times." I couldn't explain to them the adolescent politics behind lending Liam my socks. Liam was the first person who had stood up for me. I owed him. If Liam needed something, I gave it up. We had each other's backs.

"Oh, Liam Mahoney. I like him," my mother chimed in. Well, that was a good sign. I lent socks to a kid whom my mother liked.

"Your grades are good, though. You still made honor roll, right?" my dad asked.

"Well, *technically*, no . . ." I hoped that I could misdirect him with further explanations. "But colleges won't look at honor roll anyway. As long as I have the grades and my SATs are good, this won't matter in the long run. It's just one marking period out of the six that we have, so in four weeks, I'll be back on the honor roll. It really is just a technicality. I'm just not on honor roll this marking period, but I will be again. No big deal." God, that was a fucking ramshackle defense.

A long pause hovered over the table after I finished my lawyering. "So no honor roll?" my dad asked.

"No."

He sat in silence, the bowl of rice wafting steam before him, holding the report card, unable to look at me. My mother and brother had begun eating, trying to ignore the situation and defuse the heavy silence by not chiming in. But my father continued to sit there expressionless as I tried to read his stubbled face, thinking that I was definitely going to get grounded for longer than I was anticipating. In my mind, I tried to guess how much longer, looking for a poker tell in his expression. I looked at his hands, flat and bone-thin on the table.

Suddenly, the end of the table snapped with a loud crack as the blue-and-white bowls and chopsticks went flying, the bowls breaking. Bits of blue-and-white ceramic dragons and bats scattered in shards on the floor. The chopsticks skittered with high, rim-shot clacks like a drumroll. My father pushed his chair back quickly. My report card flew onto the floor, covered in food.

My father had raised his arms and slammed them down so hard that the leaf at the end of the table had snapped. He had broken the table. His whole face twitched with rage.

He and I stood up simultaneously, and he lunged for me, trying to grab my arm. This was definitely not going to be a grounding.

I moved quickly to my right as he kept lunging for me, my brother and my mother still seated, though my mother was now Vietnamesing, "Honey, please stop! Dear, please stop!"

Years of playground instincts kicked in from avoiding the bigger kids and bullies—*don't let him grab you.* But this wasn't a game. My dad lunged for me again, and again I ran to the right, both of us sliding in our socks. Face-to-face, he lunged left and I moved left, sliding again on the linoleum.

What the fuck is going on? I thought.

He stopped chasing me and yanked a kitchen drawer open, brandishing a pair of scissors. Scissors? What the fuck was he going to do with . . . He lunged for me with the scissors.

Did he try to stab me? He swung at me again with a wide arc, scissors pointed forward. *Fucking shit, he's trying to stab me!*

We circled around the broken kitchen table three times, kicking shards of bowls and clumps of rice. "COME HERE! I SAID COME HERE!" He kept lunging at me with the scissors, missing. My mother's cries of *stop it!* and her sobbing were the background to my father's primal grunts as he lunged with the scissors. *Hnnh! Hnnh! Hnnh!* His face was crimson, his neck veins bulged against his collar, and his tousled hair lurched upward each time he jumped forward with the scissors. Lou had retreated silently to the perimeter of the kitchen and hid his body around the corner.

What the fuck is going on?

I ran out of the kitchen and into the nearest room—the bathroom—and locked the door. I backed away from the door, out of breath, and slouched on the toilet. I heard my dad standing outside the door, and he struck it a few times, rattling the flimsy wood. Jesus Christ.

He waited outside the bathroom door for a moment and stormed off down the hall. Doors slammed. Crashing. Splintering sounds. I opened the door and inched toward the noise, which was crackling from my bedroom at the end of the hall.

From the hall, I saw my dad, seething with fury. He was snapping my records in half. I felt sick. A small pile of records and their sleeves were accumulating at his feet, vinyl snapped unevenly in half, cardboard sleeves bent.

Hair disheveled. Panting. He knew how to hurt me. Everything that I had curated over the last two years lay strewn across my bedroom floor, broken and sliced into pieces.

After a few album dismemberments, he stopped taking the records out of their sleeves. He snapped them whole until he heard the vinyl crack inside. Some he threw against the wall. Posters and punk show flyers where fluttering down from the wall in large triangular slices, the confetti of destruction.

Siouxsie and the Banshees—gone. Public Image—torn. *Never Mind the Bollocks*—ripped.

My closet door yanked open, and the scissors clicked their edges together. My T-shirts began to tear and ribbon as the scissors did their work. My leather jacket was filleted. I was devastated.

I couldn't let him know. Don't show him. *Boys don't cry.* I didn't know whether he would try to attack me again with the scissors. There, in the moment, I felt the reverberations of my uncle stabbing his wife and himself to death. The last time our family was involved in a stabbing, it didn't end well for anyone. I wasn't going to wait around to see what would happen next.

I grabbed my skateboard, a flannel shirt, and sneakers by the front door. I was getting the fuck out of my house if I wanted to survive. My face was flush.

"Where are you going? Where are you going?" my mom asked, half crying. I didn't tell her because I didn't know. Lou wasn't in my periphery, and I guessed that he had gone into his room and closed his door.

Halfway out of the house, I remembered: I had a geometry quiz tomorrow. *Shit. Was I seriously thinking about that right now?* In the scariest moment of my life, in my most primal survival moment, I thought about school—like Gregor worrying about how to get to work on time.

I paused briefly at the door, stepped back inside to grab my backpack and books, and skated away.

It was dusk when I stopped at a pay phone on the other side of town.

I called Liam. He owed me one since he was the one who'd borrowed my socks. When he got on the line, I told him what happened.

"Jesus, yeah, of course. You can stay at my house tonight, but just tonight. Can you come to my window around eleven thirty?" We had a plan. Liam lived in a one-floor ranch house. Thank God for seventies architecture.

It was three hours until our rendezvous time. I had my skateboard and a backpack full of homework, so I skated a few blocks until I found a bench under a streetlight. This would do. I studied for geometry and read my English assignment.

At eleven thirty p.m. I tapped on Liam's window, and the pane creaked upward. I heaved my backpack and my skateboard up and over, and I pulled myself through his window. Liam and I spoke in a susurrous hush.

"I snuck you a sleeping bag—it's all set up in my closet," he whispered. The sleeping bag was unrolled across the bottom. It looked like a cocoon.

"Thanks, man."

"You can't stay here tomorrow, though. We should find another place for you to go. What about Grendl's place?" Grendl was an older punk in town, but he was rumored to be dealing from his apartment. I didn't know him that well, and staying in a drug den seemed like a bad idea even in my situation.

"Yeah, maybe I'll call Grendl." I lied. Into Liam's closet I went, where I tried to sleep but instead spent most of the night stifling my tears in the dark. Unlike the darkness of Christmas mass—I did not feel like everyone else. I didn't feel united by a common faith, real or feigned. In the worst moment of my life, I wanted to reach out to someone who could give me some insight, some solace, a hug. Anything. No one I knew had experienced anything remotely like this. I was alone, in the bottom of Liam's closet, riding the undulations of assorted emotions. My rage and despair opened up into a black chasm, swallowing any latent, childlike need for my father.

Fuck you, Dad. FUCK YOU. I can't believe you tried to stab me with scissors. What—the—living—fuck? Over a fucking report card? Over gym class? And you, Mom! You couldn't stop him? You couldn't say anything? My friends were the only ones who were there for me.

Gregor, was this what you felt like when you were a big fucking bug and your parents were total dicks? Was this what it felt like to be an insect? To feel small?

I put my head in my arms, and I cried.

I cried hard for everything. For nothing. For myself. For my parents. For the lives that we were supposed to have. For the stupid life that we did have. For the circumstances that made my father and mother who they were. I wanted to believe that they were better people. I cried for who they were and who they wanted to be. I cried for everything being so fucked up. I cried because I didn't see any future in front of me except for the bottom of Liam's closet. Whatever life I hoped to have was gone and irreversibly changed. I felt sure of that.

I pushed some clothes around to unpack space for myself, and I swore to God that if I found white gym socks in his closet, I was going to punch Liam in the face.

The next day in school, I told Conor what happened, and he let me sleep in his room on his floor the next two nights, but his parents began to get suspicious. "We gotta find you another place to go," he told me after school on Wednesday. I was resolved not to go home.

At the end of that school day, I intercepted my brother at his bus by the middle school. He was not allowed off the bus, so I tapped on the bus window in the parking lot and got his attention. He looked agitated as he pushed the window down, kneeling on his seat so that his face and fingers leaned over the pane.

"Phuc!"

"Hey, can you do me a favor?"

"Are you okay?! Where have you been?" Lou looked worried.

I spoke calmly not to alarm him. "I'm okay. Don't worry about me. Can you go in my closet and see if I have any clothes left? I don't have any clean clothes to change into."

"I don't know. Dad threw away most of your stuff. But yeah, okay—I'll look. How do I get you the clothes?"

"I'll meet you here tomorrow. You can drop them out of the bus window. Okay?"

"Okay."

I remembered that my uncle Thái had gotten an apartment in town and was living with his girlfriend. I called him from a school pay phone on Thursday.

"Yeah, of course you can stay with me. Just come over after I get home from work." Utter relief. No more couch surfing. No more closets and floors.

Lou came through for me that afternoon. I met him at his bus after classes, and he dropped a beige plastic shopping bag out of the bus window.

"I found two old shirts that were in the back of your closet, and I grabbed some other stuff that wasn't thrown away. . . ."

"Thanks." I opened the bag: shirts, boxers, black socks. Black socks? That was rich. "Thanks, Lou. I'll talk to you soon—when I have things figured out."

He muttered an unconvincing *okay* as I stuffed the bag into my backpack. The bus window clacked back up. I raised my hand in a half wave as I skated away to my uncle's apartment downtown.

My uncle Thái made dinner that night, and I didn't have a lot to say. "Do you have clothes?" He gave a quick flip to the frying pan. "You can wear some of my clothes, too. No worries, man."

"Thanks—Lou found me a few old T-shirts, but I'll need more than a few T-shirts. Thanks again for letting me stay."

"Of course—your dad is a prick—always has been. And your mom? She's never stood up to him. You know that story about your dad breaking his leg in the motorcycle accident?" I was half listening, but he didn't wait for my reply. "You know what *really* happened? He tried to run over a dog! On a motorcycle! That's why he broke his leg and ended up in the hospital for six months. What a dick, right? Who tries to run over a dog on a motorcycle?"

I hadn't ever heard that version of the story, but I didn't have the stomach to join in. I hated my father at that moment, for sure, but I was exhausted. Hatred required calories that I didn't have. Thái's girlfriend, Kerry—a zaftig, witchy brunette—was sitting at the counter that separated the kitchen from the rest of the apartment, making small talk about school and going to concerts, and after dinner, she laid out a blanket and a flat sheet on the couch for me.

"We're gonna watch a movie. Want to watch with us?" Thái lit a joint, and its cherry glowed with his deep inhale. He waved the joint in his hand toward me to punctuate "watch with us."

I nodded. "Sure, why not?" I don't even remember what movie he put on because I did my homework while the movie played, and I stayed up a little while longer after they went to bed.

The next morning, I awoke at six a.m., and as I was getting my schoolwork together, Thái shuffled out of his bedroom, shirtless and in boxers.

"What are you going to do with your day?"

"What do you mean?" It was Friday. I unfolded my school schedule to check it.

"No, you dumbshit. I don't mean what classes you're going to. You're not going to go to school, are you? I'm not your fucking dad. You don't have to go to school. Hang out. Do whatever you want."

I didn't pause. "I do. I do have to go to school. I have two quizzes to take." It reflexively came out of my mouth. "I'll see you later. Thanks for letting me stay here." I grabbed my skateboard and clattered off to school, the pavement whirring under my wheels like wings.

I went to my classes. I aced Mr. O'Hara's quiz, and I handed in a draft of a paper for Mrs. Ferguson. It felt easy. It felt like when I liked comic books—it felt authentic. My leather jacket, with all the studs and punk pins and painted band names, was gone. My brand-new boots that I had bought with Christmas money and my band T-shirts: gone. My Walk-man, my cassettes, my records: all gone. I had lost my protective shell of a leather jacket—no more punk pretenses. That was past tense. I was at school to learn, read books, and figure some shit out.

Was this the *real* me? Stripped of the ability to *look* like a punk—what defined me as one? Not my jacket. Not my clothes. My friends? My enemies? No. What I *did* determined who I was, not what I looked like or what I liked. My actions and reactions. Did I emerge from the shell? I felt naked and free. Was I now pupa or chrysalis? I felt like myself—and that was what punk was. The freedom to be who I was unapologetically, even if I hadn't chosen it.

I thought about my uncle's apartment: sparsely decorated with sec-ondhand furniture, the college dropout's hand-to-mouth existence of weed smoking and clock punching as he washed dishes at a restaurant. I thought about Grendl's drug-den apartment—even fewer prospects for him and his future. A few months ago, Conor told me that he was going to enlist in the army. That was his ticket out of Carlisle.

Enlisting was *not* going to be my ticket out of Carlisle. And smoking weed every day and punching a clock was not what I wanted for my life. Punk rock had paved a way for me through my first two years of high school, but I was beginning to realize that maybe anarchy and nihilism were not a blueprint for building a future. Punk rock was an explosive for detonating the present so that I could rebuild my future from the rubble.

I knew that only school could save me and would be my ticket out of Carlisle, my future's foundation. I would finish high school and dare to dream about college—anywhere that would take me. Get the fuck out of this town. Get me away from my parents. Maybe take Lou with me later when he was old enough or done with school. But I had to get out.

That's where you went wrong, Gregor. You didn't get out. You didn't take care of yourself. You kept thinking about your parents and your sister, thinking about how to take care of them. You couldn't see your family, your life, or yourself through a different lens. Your family didn't give a fuck about you, and you didn't see it coming, Gregor—and that blind spot killed you.

After two weeks, my mother tracked me down at my uncle's apartment. They never looked for me at school. I'm not sure why—maybe they assumed that I wouldn't have gone? Maybe my dad forbade it?—but I was at Thái's apartment when she called, and he didn't lie to her. He was making us dinner again. We had settled into a routine of making dinner, getting high, doing homework. Well, I did homework.

He handed me the receiver. "It's for you. It's your mom. She's crying. You should talk to her."

I held the receiver for a moment, thinking over and over: I was not going home. Fuck them. I was not going home. As soon as I heard my mother's crying and her flurry of Vietnamese entreaties, my heart broke. My father had tried to break me physically with his scissors, and I thought I had steeled myself in the intervening weeks. I thought that my parents couldn't hurt me anymore because I had escaped. I was ready to endure whatever fate inflicted upon me, but I wasn't ready for this phone call. I wasn't prepared to hear a mother's sorrow, *my* mother's sorrow. I wasn't ready to hear her voice, and beneath it, her love, undiminished and ever present. I wasn't able to bear my responsibility in her pain. The vessel of my heart couldn't hold both my rage for my father and my love for my mother. Like glass subjected to heat and cold, I cracked.

Whatever assemblage of myself that I had willfully pieced together fragmented under the tremble of her voice. I knew I had to go home again. I had told myself I wasn't going to cry anymore, yet there I was on the phone, eyes welling up.

I packed my schoolbag, skipped dinner, and skated home. The closer I got to my house—no, not my house—my parents' house, the more intensely I felt it in my stomach: rage. Pure rage. Rage at my father for not being reasonable. Rage at myself for not being stronger and resisting my mother's guilt trip. Rage at my mother for not sticking up for me. Not Lou, though—he was the only one for whom I had no bile. I figured that now that I was home, I would be the focus for my father's attention and irascibility. That was fine—I could take the grenade for Lou.

I kept both straps of my backpack on as I walked into the house, holding my skateboard, which could shield me from another scissor attack. My dad sat at the dining room table looking over some papers as my mother burst into tears. They had already eaten. He didn't look at me as I strained my ears. Not a word. I didn't hear anything. I didn't say anything. I didn't see a father anymore. I saw the man who had tried to stab me, who had abused me and my brother, who had destroyed my things. I ignored him and he ignored me—I could live with that.

"Phúc! Oh my God, you're home! Oh my God! Oh my God! Thank God! Phúc!" My mother cried inconsolably. I stood in the living room and let my mother cry into my shoulder. I wasn't going to give my father the satisfaction of seeing how shattered I felt—especially when I had come crawling home already like an insect. "You need to eat. I made you spaghetti and meatballs." The spaghetti and meatballs had a hint of *nước mắm*, the ubiquitous fish sauce that my mother used in everything.

I ate by myself in silence while my mother sat at the kitchen table with a hand on my arm, tears running down her face. She kept touching my face while I ate. Her proximity annoyed me, and her outpouring for me made me even more bitter. *Where the fuck were you when I was gone? Where the fuck were you when Dad was trying to kill me?* I knew she couldn't answer those questions, and I didn't want to ask them, not at that moment.

After dinner, I showered and went to my room. No, not my room. It wasn't my room anymore. It was their room. The records were gone, the closet was half empty. I nudged open the trash bag of all the broken and torn things in the middle of the room. I didn't know if my dad had left it there as a reminder or if my mother had left it there for me to salvage.

He hadn't destroyed one thing: the stereo.

It sat along the left wall, the wall pockmarked with staples and tape and tacks—telltale signs of posters and flyers now crumpled in the trash bag. The stereo stood untouched as an ironic reminder, a gesture of love that I didn't recall anymore.

Lou came to my room as I was getting out my binders to do homework. He sat down in my reading chair. "I'm glad you're home."

"Thanks." I wasn't glad to be home, but I didn't want to say *that* to my little brother. You were supposed to love your father, and he was supposed to love you back—that was the fairy tale I still wanted to believe, but I didn't. I couldn't forget what happened, and I couldn't ignore how I was feeling. I didn't want to hate my father, but I did. The reality of violence—the violence of my reality—pulled me in one direction even as I tried to make it all square up with what I wanted and needed.

Even though Lou had witnessed my father's outrage and my flight, I wanted things to seem normal for him. I was fifteen, but Lou was twelve. It was one thing to take him out on Halloween to egg houses; it was another thing to explain to him how much I hated our dad and how I didn't even want to be under the same roof. I loved my brother, and that love kept me from confiding in him. Maybe he could have a better relationship with my father than I did? Maybe I could keep my experience from tainting his? Maybe I didn't have to be a paternal figure to him? In my simplistic love for him, I hoped high school, our family, his life would be better for him, that I could somehow smooth a path for him or warn him in advance, so that he could just fall in behind me as I forged ahead. I just wanted it to be different for him even if all the elements were the same.

But maybe it was already too late.

There are a few moments in *Metamorphosis* in which Gregor can be described as happy, and they are moments when he embraces his newly found roach-ness, when he is not trying to pretend to be someone he no longer is. This joy is punctured by his mother's revulsion for him as her screams drive him back into his room. Finally, on an ill-advised attempt to leave his room, Gregor's father hurls an apple at him, badly wounding his bug body—and Gregor eventually dies from infection. Christ. At least *my father* had the decency to try to kill me with scissors.

During the two weeks that I was couch surfing, I went to school, dispossessed of all the things that meant anything to me, stripped of who I thought I was and of the things that I thought protected me. I kept going to school, because I knew where I was happiest. In geometry class. In art class. In English class. I went to my shifts at the mall. Things were surprisingly *normal*. None of my friends or teachers would have said that anything was different other than my limited wardrobe rotation.

My father and I never talked about what happened, and by that summer our silence with each other was bridged slowly by one-word replies and brief questions. The truce was easier than the truth. But the dynamic in our house had changed. My parents were my housemates. I didn't rely on them for understanding or support. If I needed that, I had an unruly tribe of friends who would do most anything for me. That was my family.

When the next report card came out, I felt a twinge of its secret history. It was the marking period during which I had slept in a closet, on a floor, and on a couch. It was the marking period during which my father had tried to stab me with a pair of scissors. It was the marking period when everything had been destroyed.

Even when I had nowhere to live, I went to school. For those weeks, school was all I had. School was the only way I was going to survive. School was the only *why* I survived. Homework. Quizzes. History. Chemistry. And here was the report card—the postmortem. At dinnertime, I silently slid the report card to my father across the new dining table with defiant confidence.

Painting I—A+

English II—A

Geometry—A

Algebra II—A
Chemistry—A
Western Civilization—A
Physical Education—Pass
Absence/Tardy: 0
Most important, across the bottom: honor roll.

9

THE IMPORTANCE OF
BEING EARNEST

Junior year of high school: it was the best of lies, it was the worst of lies. It was the age of truths and the epoch of lies. Things that I previously thought were true felt like lies, and the lies that I told myself ended up being true. Sounds confusing, right? It was to me, too, but then I read *The Importance of Being Earnest.*

From the moment I read it, I adored Oscar Wilde's play. I loved how it toyed with the conventional boy-must-overcome-obstacles-to-love-girl trope, balancing humor with tension. Wilde exposes the paradox of being true to yourself while wanting to be someone else (because who hasn't wanted to be someone else?). The protagonist, Jack, pretends to be someone named Ernest; his love interest is infatuated with him only because of the name Ernest. It's Wilde at his superficial and satirical best. Jack's best friend crashes his country home and also pretends to be Ernest. Hilarity ensues! Mistaken identities! Secret adoption! And in a Wildean twist, the play resolves the comedy by having the biggest lie become true. In the course of lying about his name being Ernest, Jack finds out that his real name is Ernest at the play's end. Marriage! Families reunited! Truths and lies are the same!

That was my junior year, and it was a bewildering one for me, too, but we should start at the beginning. It started out easily enough.

JUNE 1989, DICKINSON COLLEGE

This was the truth: I was an asshole punk.

"Dude—check 'em out. This one's yours, Phuc." Pauly opened up his backpack stuffed full of T-shirts.

I couldn't believe it. "No fucking way."

Liam was stunned. "You made these?! Holy shit, dude. I can't believe you made shirts. Is that . . . is that a *pig* on there?" Liam stripped off his Powell-Peralta skeleton-ripper T-shirt and put the new one on immediately.

We had convened, as many skaters as possible, at the Dickinson College library wall, and Pauly was handing out T-shirts that he had made. On the T-shirts he had drawn with permanent marker a crudely shaped pig and above the drawing, he wrote *THE RUNNING OF THE PIGS—1989*. The pig drawing, a grotesque slurry of Porky Pig, Elmer Fudd, with a dash of Garfield, doffed a policeman's hat.

"This year is going to be the best one yet. These shirts are fucking awesome, Pauly." Dylan was ready, his *Pigs* T-shirt pulled on over his clothes. Pauly beamed.

With stone benches, handrails, and high stairs, the Dickinson campus was a skater's dream, and in turn, we skaters were the campus's nightmare. We flouted all the posted signs that bellowed NO SKATEBOARDING. For the past three summers, we had convened on its campus daily to skate and conduct ourselves like the local louts. We would harass the nerds who went to the summertime enrichment camp, and try to pick up the ballerinas who went to ballet camp. We yelled at both groups from a distance, and the effect was equally fruitless to both. The nerds and the ballerinas thought we were townie assholes, and they were right.

The Running of the Pigs was our annual tradition, begun in the summer between eighth and ninth grade; 1989 was our third Running, and for us, it officially kicked off the summer. We would gather in the middle of the day on Dickinson's campus and skate around until the campus police gave chase. We would skate away, and they of course would pursue us. Police cars would pull up, and we would disperse in one direction as a whole unit, as preplanned by the group. Rather than scattering in all directions, the unity of the large group enticed the officers to follow, which they always did. Since we were on skateboards, at some point, we would cut off on foot over a patchy piece of lawn or leap over a stone wall where the patrol cars couldn't follow. At that point, the officers would stop their cars and continue their hot pursuit on foot, running after us, keys jangling, walkie-talkies squawking their locations, yelling and running and running and running until their personal resolve and/or cardiovascular health deadened their sprint to a trot, which was usually a ten- to fifteen-yard run.

If you could provoke a campus officer to get out of his car, the skate crew yawped with wild, boorish cheers because you had successfully *run the pig*. It was a stupid, intensely hilarious prank, and it lasted only about fifteen minutes before security gave up and we skated off to do other things of varying legality (hopping fences to skate a loading dock, figuring out who could buy beer, stealing snacks from the gas station). It would be a summer of lite malfeasance.

But first, we had to run the pigs.

1989's Running of the Pigs was off to a tremendous start. We brandished official T-shirts this year, an auspicious omen. We took turns at the handrail, and right on cue, campus security showed up. Squad cars—four of them this year! Running over the steps along the campus walkway toward a low wall, we jumped over the wall and had shaken the pigs. No one had run a pig yet, taunting them as we could. But then as Pauly and I rounded a corner, an extra security officer on foot grabbed Pauly in a bear hug.

Fuck.

I stopped to see what I could do, but he had grabbed Pauly's board, too.

And then I felt my right arm twist behind my back as a second officer lunged and caught me. The pigs were striking back this year. We were fucked.

Downstairs, in the campus security office, Pauly and I clanged into metal folding chairs. We had never seen this part of the Hub building, and if it were not for the red-faced security officer in front of us, it would have looked like any other Spartan windowless air-conditioned office.

"You two are going to be in a heap of trouble." The officer wielded a clipboard in front of him with some mystery paperwork, apparently the requisition for the aforementioned heap of trouble. "Are you kids the ones who have been stealing clothes from the dorm dryers, too?" We were.

"Of course not. What would I do with a pair of acid-washed girl's jeans?" Pauly was provoking the officer because he had, in fact, stolen acid-washed girl's jeans a few months earlier. I sat woodenly upright so that my Running of the Pigs shirt could be clearly seen. I had not been addressed yet, but I was eyeing both of our confiscated skateboards behind his desk.

"What are your names? We're going to call your parents and have them come pick you up. We'll discuss filing charges with the Carlisle Police Department for trespassing. Big trouble." This was not going to go well for me. What was I going to tell my parents? From the coarse straw of reality, my mind was spinning all the golden yarns for why I was arrested by campus police.

Thank God for Pauly, who spoke up. "You've caught me before, so you can save yourself the trouble of filling out that sheet. You guys already have a sheet for me."

"We do? What's your name?"

"Tony. Tony Hawk." I looked at Pauly. Did he just say *Tony* . . .

Fucking . . . Hawk? Tony Hawk was the most famous pro skater of all time. I pretended to rub my face in remorse but held my hand over my mouth to hide the grin, because I had the privilege of being arrested with Tony Hawk.

The security officer was relieved not to have to fill out more paperwork. "Hawk? Like the bird?"

"It might be under Anthony, I guess. Anthony Hawk." Pauly could not suppress being a wiseass.

The campus officer picked up the phone. In the muffled trill of the phone ring, cradling the receiver with his elbows on the table, the officer scribbled other notes on the arrest report.

No answer on the other line. "God damn it . . . I'll be back." He stood up and stormed out.

Pauly and I looked at each other, and we both swiveled our heads in disbelief. We were alone in the room, the student center's central-air vent making a frosty wheeze. We listened closely but didn't hear the officer in any adjoining room. The office door was open. *Wide*-open. Our skateboards lay there behind the desk. I knew what Pauly was thinking because I had the same plan.

RUN.

Our gazes connected with a desperate click before he leapt out of his seat, with me barely a breath behind. The metal folding chairs screeched as they skittered on the linoleum from the force of our leap, and I winced knowing that the noise had given us away. In two long steps we were behind the desk with our skateboards in hand, and without making another sound, we were shoulder to shoulder, sprinting out of the office, up the stairs, running as fast and as quietly as we could.

Outside the office, the vending machines blinked a blurring wall of COKEPEPSIDORITOSCHEETOS as we rocketed by them and up the stairs. The summer silence of the building amplified the panicked thudding of our Vans. Through the student commons, our sneakers yipped on newly waxed floors, and we strained for the door at the end of the hall that led to the outside. We thought we heard the jingle of security keys behind us. Fuck. It was a straight shot down the hall, and we were hurtling at top velocity.

For no good reason, I started yelling like a moron. "GOGOGOGO-GOGO!" I was laughing from terror and audacity, the sunlight outdoors in our view. The double doors throttled as we threw our bodies into the crash bars. The sunlight burned us as we squinted and stumbled, blind from the air-conditioned fluorescent bowels of the Hub building. I heard the loud clack of Pauly's board. We were wheels down. Across the campus. Behind the dumpsters. Down a walkway.

Furiously kicking up Louther Street, we skated and skated and skated. Pauly was making a strange whining giggle, which made me laugh even more as we both kicked away on our boards, hee-hawing like a couple of asses.

We wove an extra zigzag, cutting down alleys and up the wrong way of one-way streets until we got to Liam and Dylan's house, our rally point.

Shawn spied us a block away. "What happened? I thought you guys were right behind us?"

I was heaving from our biathlon of Sprinting and Skating, a goddamn Olympic effort. Gold medal. Pauly was still laughing, lips moving, no words coming.

"What happened to you two?" Everyone was pressing us for details, since we had missed the rendezvous at the 7-Eleven.

I was doubled over. "Dude . . . we got caught . . . by the pigs."

"What?!"

"Yeah . . . but we fucking escaped. . . ."

"What?!"

"Yeah . . . escaped . . . ask . . . ask . . . Anthony Hawk over there." I pointed at Pauly, who, upon hearing the name *Anthony Hawk*, hooted even harder, his tears glittering in the June sun.

We spilled the story of our detention and escape to the crew (Pauly and I dramatized various parts and dialogue in our midsummer's afternoon comedy), and they were speechless except for a series of punctuating profanities: "Are you fucking kidding?" and "No fucking way!"

Dylan confirmed that a few officers had, indeed, chased the crew on foot. Mission accomplished. The summer of 1989 was off to a spectacular start. We had run the pigs.

In June I quit my job at the Coral Reef in the mall and got a job at the Bosler Library as a library page. Kevin, the Coral Reef manager, had started limiting how much reading and homework I was doing at the Reef, and if I couldn't be paid to read or to do my homework, then I was inclined to get a job that seemed less servile and a little more dignified. My parents (my father especially), always aware of our perception among our family, were excited at the apparent prestige of working at a library as opposed to a Tiki-themed smoothie bar in a dying mall. They told all my relatives on the phone and at gatherings that I was working at the Bosler Library now. I thought it sounded impressive, too, but the truth was that I perused books and thumbed through all the magazines I wanted, and I got paid to do it. A few of my friends had landed jobs pumping gas, dishwashing, or landscaping, but the library was tailored for me and my goal to read more books and authors.

Through the summer, in the absence of assigned books for English, I read more works by authors we'd already read (including Dickens, Hawthorne, Emerson) or just randomly picked up novels that seemed to be in heavy circulation that summer of 1989 (Tom Robbins was a highlight).

With an official, engraved name tag that said *Phuc Tran, Library Page,* I filled the screechy steel book cart, reshelved returned books quickly for twenty minutes, and wandered the stacks for forty minutes, all out of the library marms' sight. It was glorious. The smell of oaken shelves. Well-thumbed hardbacks. The deep canyons of paperbacks. The solitude.

I strolled in the towers of tomes, walking in the stacks like Thoreau walked the woods, memorizing the Dewey decimal system, helping various library patrons find a book on plumbing, a guide to North American birds, the novels of Gay Talese (whose name always made me unexpectedly thankful that my name was Phuc). I wasn't the best or most diligent page, but I was certain that I loved working at the library more than the other two pages. Emotional investment counted for something, right?

In late June, I got a big assignment. Janet, one of the librarians, showed me to the basement. "We're having the annual discards sale at the end of the month, and we need to move all these onto the first floor." The basement bulged with cardboard boxes full of books. Hardcovers mostly. Heavy, heavy hardcover books. "We've been pulling books and records off the shelves for the past year to sell—these are books that have not been checked out in over three years. We need to make room for new acquisitions."

"Holy smokes! That's a lot of books."

"It's a good fund-raiser for the library and a nice way to send the books off with people who want them. We need these upstairs by the end of the month. Claire has a bad knee, and many of these boxes are too heavy for the staff to carry, so it's up to you." She didn't ask me— she declared that it was my task, skirting around the obvious statement that the all-female staff was asking me, the fifteen-year-old boy, to do the heavy lifting.

For the next two weeks, I spent my shifts panting and huffing the boxes from the basement, flipping every single box open to see what books weren't being checked out. *Gardner's Art Through the Ages*. Gibbon's *The History of the Decline and Fall of the Roman Empire*. *Introduction to Philosophy*. It seemed strange that the metric for the discard pile was public circulation, since they couldn't prove that people didn't just come to the library to read. My father certainly did that, and I did it, too, as a child—we'd come to the library to sit and read several books in an afternoon without checking anything out. But there I was now in Bosler's bowels: a book's circulation was its only vital statistic, the lifeblood of its relevance.

The discards were loosely organized by Dewey decimal, since a staff member had systematically gone down the aisles and pulled them. Mixed in were donations from library members. Families moved away, estates were liquidated, spring cleanings coughed up unread editions— all of this filled the bins in our alcove donation box.

And then I found the book. In an unmarked, random box, a yellowing spine caught my eye. *The Lifetime Reading Plan* by Clifton Fadiman.

Reading what? Plan for whom? I picked it up and looked over the cover, which claimed to be a guide to over one hundred of the greatest writers and thinkers of Western civilization's literature. Clearly Fadiman was a humble and modest man. I flipped to the table of contents. Homer. Aeschylus. Sophocles. Dante. Machiavelli. Montaigne. Shakespeare. Descartes. Milton. Hemingway. Melville. Dickens.

Some authors I recognized, others I had never heard of. I started to skim the introduction from Fadiman. He lamented the times, the customs: the iconoclasm of the sixties, the upheaval and overthrow of social institutions, the audacity to question the Western canon. Nothing was sacred anymore. This was the result of tuning in and turning off. He bemoaned that no one was interested in being an "all-American" boy or girl anymore but declared that these books were the foundation for being "all-American." He wrote with a zealot's fervor. Fadiman was not soft-pedaling or excusing himself. I trembled as I read the entire introduction in the basement. He was speaking to me. All I wanted was to be well-read *and* all-American, and now—*now* I had the book.

On my next ascent to the surface, I found Janet. "Hey, Janet. Am I allowed to buy any of the discards before the public sale?"

"Of course. Did Claire not say that? And as library staff, you get half off."

"Half off? Really?"

"Yup. For you, fifty cents for a hardback and twenty-five cents for paperback."

I had *The Reading Plan* in my hand. "Could I buy this now?"

"Sure thing. Fifty cents. You can pay Claire at the end of your shift."

I went home with *The Lifetime Reading Plan* jammed into my army surplus backpack.

That night, I reread Fadiman's introduction to his lifetime reading plan, his idea that any civilized person in the Western world should read these books, that these one hundred and four books were the foundation to any educated person's knowledge, a common touchstone with other cultured people. Fadiman's defense of the authors and titles was unapologetic. If people called him stodgy and old-fashioned? Fuck 'em. Well, that's not what he wrote, but that was the introduction's tenor. This was his well-informed, well-read opinion, and if people thought that he didn't include so-and-so author or this-and-that book or included too much of what's-his-name: well, fuck 'em. The introduction to *The Lifetime Reading Plan* was unflinching and steely. I thought it was so . . . *punk rock* (for an old white guy). I liked this Clifton Fadiman.

Reading over the list of authors and titles, I girded myself. My own reading was no longer an aimless expedition in a literary wilderness. I had a map. I had a goal. I was going to start reading *these* books. Fadiman said that I didn't have to read them in any particular order, that I could read what interested me or what I could get my hands on. Some of his descriptions sounded riveting and others sounded dull. Maybe I would understand a book or maybe I wouldn't, but Fadiman encouraged me to reread the books that I didn't grasp. Maybe they would make sense to me later in life. Good advice.

I read through the entire *Lifetime Reading Plan* that weekend, and at the end of the month, at our library's discard sale, I spent my month's aggregated paychecks (almost $150) on discarded books of all varieties: histories of art, guides to literary criticism, anthologies of poetry, Faulkner, Thurber, James, *The History of the Peloponnesian War*, and on and on.

By the end of the sale, I had over a dozen boxes full of books. When my father picked me up, he was simultaneously horrified and delighted. "This is *a lot* of books. Why did you spend your money on books that you can just check out from the library for free?"

I didn't have a reasonable answer, and since running away, I had been keeping my conversations with my father brief. "At least I'm not spending my money on records. These books are just getting thrown away. It seemed like a good idea to buy them."

"*Thrown away?!* Geez . . . who throws away books? I'm glad that you got them then." To my father, I was saving books from being euthanized, preserving humanity's accumulated wisdom and achievements from the trash heap of indifference. Back in circulation, back from the dead. He griped no more as we loaded the boxes into the car to take home.

From the driveway, Lou helped me lug all the boxes into my room.

"These are *a lot* of books. Are you going to read them all?" Lou thumbed through a few, intrigued by the cartoons on a Thurber cover.

"Not right away, but they're nice to have. It's good to be able to look things up, and I'll try to read them all someday. I can't possibly read all these books in one summer."

He pawed through a few other boxes. "What are they about?"

"All sorts of things. *Everything.* Literature. Poetry. Art."

"Everything?"

"Well, everything that's interesting to me."

Lou shrugged and went back to watching TV. I looked at my bedroom and surveyed my collection of books. I had the start of my own library. My bedroom now had a distinct, literary smell to it. I sank into my reading chair, and reread the introduction to *The Lifetime Reading Plan*, buoyed by Fadiman's passion for books and ideas. This was what it meant to be educated, to be American. *The Plan* allowed you to be part of an intellectual conversation that was hundreds of years old, and all you needed to do was read the books. Fadiman and his books didn't care where I was from or how much money my parents made or what language I spoke. The table was set and a seat was open for anyone willing to read the books—the books were both the invitation and the price of admission.

In between the lines of Fadiman's introduction glittered, for me, the promise of acceptance and connection and prestige. I'd be seen as an equal, as an intellectual—and as a well-read American. I felt certain of this given what was already happening in my classes. Kids were starting to refer to me as the book guy, the literature guy, in spite of how I looked or dressed. Courtesy of a newly opened vintage store, Classic Rags, my secondhand chic of plaid blazers, leopard-print creepers, and old-man shirts didn't connote literacy, but I was cracking their expectations (and mine) of who a so-called literature person was or looked like.

I rummaged through my books and picked one out. Up first to bat: Faulkner. First name? William. I didn't know who this person was. *As I Lay Dying*. What was this about? I was about to find out.

That weekend, Liam called to see if I wanted to go out. I lied and said that my parents wouldn't allow me, but in fact I hadn't even asked for permission to go. I knew that Liam just wanted to drink and get shit-faced at Scully's apartment, but I was starting to question what that would do for me anymore in the long term. We were about to enter eleventh grade, and then we were graduating the following year.

For the first time, I began to face the deflating and disappointing reality: my punk crew didn't have any real or reasonable aspirations for getting out of Carlisle. We all talked about leaving, but that refrain of "leaving Carlisle" was a broken chorus. Few of us were actually laying the foundation to get out, choosing instead to focus on getting laid or drunk.

My scholarly appearance was garnering more attention from other students and some teachers, but outside of school, my crew was still my crew. Going to shows. Getting wasted. Occasionally skating. Our cycle of skating, drinking, and going to shows was a plan for Saturday or for next week, but what about next year? And the year after that?

I realized that I needed a long-term farsighted plan, and I saw Fadiman as the knockout in my one-two combination. By reading through the books covered in *The Plan*, I'd hopefully gain some knowledge and, at the very least, sound smart, and maybe this might help me get into a good school after graduation. Then I could finally leave Carlisle and go to college. If reading a few dozen books made me the literature guy, being able to talk about all the lifetime reading plan books seemed to have endless potential. I'd be able to name-drop so many writers and their works without even actually reading them. Molière. Descartes. Marx. I read *The Lifetime Reading Plan* and its book synopses again.

Those two quarters for Fadiman's *Plan* were the best I ever spent.

OCTOBER 1989

Like many Smiths fans, I was introduced to Oscar Wilde through Morrissey's lyrics. I was also introduced to Keats and Yeats the same way. On the Smiths' magnum opus, *The Queen Is Dead*, Morrissey makes allusions to Keats, Yeats, and Wilde, and now that I had an anthology of English poetry, I could read the poems that Morrissey read, see what he saw, feel what stirred him. Our crew was divided on the Smiths, half of us declaring that they were horrible and sounded like suicidal Muppets and the other half of us loving them and Morrissey's misery.

I would never meet Morrissey, but at least we read and enjoyed the same things, connected by poetry and prose. Just as Fadiman promised, that was the power of literature, and beyond that promise of connection, I adored Wilde's writing—his plays, essays, novellas.

I savored his aphoristic precision, his ruthless satire, and irreverent humor, but above all, his courage to fuck with Victorian morality—he was punk rock in the same way that Thoreau, Emerson, and other intellectual renegades were punk rock. Victorians said *go right*. Wilde went left.

I bought and read Wilde's complete works and then devoured Richard Ellmann's biography of him. From there, I read other writers who had influenced him—Ruskin, Pater, and Huysmans. I referred to or quoted Wilde every chance I had in English class.

That October my English teacher, Mrs. Krebs, pulled me aside after class. "You like Wilde, right?" She had a sharp, toothy smirk and a breezy sarcasm.

"Yeah, just a little. I've only read everything he's written."

"Oh, so you probably don't care that Messiah College is putting on a production of *The Importance of Being Earnest*, right?"

"Really?" Sarcastic cease-fire. This was my favorite play by Wilde.

"Yes, really. You, of all people, should go." From her pine-green planner, she produced a small flyer with Messiah College's theater production schedule.

I looked it over. "Thanks, Jane." She shook her head when I said *Jane*.

"You're welcome. And for the umpteenth time, that's Mrs. Krebs to you."

A few weeks passed, and Mrs. Krebs checked in again about the play. "Are you going to see *Earnest* this week?"

"Oh, I can't. I don't have my driver's license yet, and I don't think any of my friends can take me." The first part was true, but the second part was a lie. The truth was, I didn't want to ask any of my friends to take me. The punk crew sitting through a production of *The Importance of Being Earnest* at Messiah College? No way. "But I did reread the play though. It would have been great to see it—thanks again for letting me know."

She frowned. "What if I took you?"

"Huh?" My heart fluttered both at the prospect of seeing the play and going with my favorite teacher.

"Would that be okay with your parents?"

"Yeah, I'm sure it would be. But, uh, you really wouldn't mind driving me?"

"No, of course not. It just seems wrong that you won't see this play after everything I've heard from you about Wilde this and Wilde that."

I laughed. "He's very quotable. I can't help it. 'The only thing more forgettable than a quotable person is an unquotable person.'"

"Did he say that?"

"No, I made that up."

Her eyes crinkled and we laughed.

Mrs. Krebs picked me up after dinner on Wednesday night. Under the impression that I had won an award or had been deemed worthy of some honor, my father insisted on accompanying me out of the house and thanked Mrs. Krebs for taking me to the play. "Oh, it's really my pleasure—I know how much Phuc loves Oscar Wilde." My father bowed dumbly.

The production was done in period costume, and the actors' theatrical accents varied from Scottish to bad British to a loud, accentless stage voice. The walls of the set swayed when the doors closed. The woman who played the elderly aunt was clearly in her early twenties. Was it amateurish and uneven? Yes. But was I disappointed? No. In fact, I was exhilarated.

Wilde's words thundered as they flew from actors' mouths. I laughed at every joke that I thought I had gotten and laughed even harder at the jokes that I had missed in my reading. I had been a starved boy who had filled himself by reading the menu, and now, at the play, I was feasting on the real experience.

When the cast bowed, Mrs. Krebs and I stood and clapped, long and loud.

On the ride home, Mrs. Krebs switched off the radio. "Wasn't that great?"

"That was . . . so amazing. Thank you so much for taking me." Could she see the tears in my eyes?

"What did you think of it? I haven't read *Earnest* in a while."

"Um . . . I thought it was great. I was surprised by how quickly the actors spoke—the dialogue sounded so much better than it did when I read it myself."

"It's great, right? When the production is different or better than what you imagined?"

"Yeah, especially when I had just read the play. It makes me think that only reading plays but not seeing them isn't really experiencing the play at all. At least, not as it was intended by the playwright."

"I think you're absolutely right—it's like reading the sheet music for

Beethoven but never hearing it played. I think you should see every play you can for that reason. Reading a play is only a half measure."

I nodded. "So how should you really teach Shakespeare? Are you doing it wrong?"

"Maybe I am doing it wrong!" She laughed at my contrived insolence.

"No, Jane—I think you're doing it perfectly. Seriously though. I'm being . . . earnest."

She needled me, chuckling. "Well, thanks for your approval. And I don't care if you're riding in the front seat of my car: it's still Mrs. Krebs to you." The short drive home was filled with *what was the significance of . . . ? What did you think of . . . ? Was that how you imagined . . . ?*

In the dark of the car, illuminated by the teal light of the digital clock, I looked out the front passenger window. Mrs. Krebs listened to what I had to say, and she replied with thoughtfulness and care as if she were speaking to an equal. In her tone and engagement with me, I was uplifted from the lowly caste of teenagers and felt for a moment like a valued, adult counterpart. I wasn't relegated to the back seat, as I often was in my parents' car.

She dropped me off, the ride too short.

As I got out, I thanked her. "Well, you know what Oscar Wilde says: 'The only thing worse than the final curtain is a vinyl curtain.'"

"I'm *sure* he didn't say that. See you tomorrow."

"Thanks again, Jane—I mean, Mrs. Krebs. It was *fantastic*." I waved through the passenger window.

I entered my house, jittery and excited, sparkling from my conversation with Mrs. Krebs. Was that what it felt like to connect with another person over a shared love of something? It felt similar to how I felt after seeing bands or slamming in the pit, but it was more . . . electric. Seeing punk bands and moshing with your friends felt dangerous, and afterward, the adrenaline rush was a slow downshift to your heart rate's baseline. But that was seeing a band. Having the bass line surge through you. Thrashing in unison with the audience. It was purely physical.

But seeing a play? I sat for two hours with my hands in my lap, and at the end of it, my heart raced just as breathlessly.

On top of that I felt connected and cared for by Mrs. Krebs. I felt known and seen, not for being Vietnamese but for my passions and ideas. For the first time in my life I felt deeply understood; the realness of that connection, of that brief exchange, ignited a thin, bright comet's tail in the dark horizon of my adolescence. This connection was what Fadiman was talking about. This was the power of sharing in great literature. I felt as euphoric as I had ever felt, and I didn't need to pound any beers or smoke any weed.

My parents asked me how the play was, and I mumbled a quick *okay* and made my way to my room, neglecting to share my excitement and enthusiasm with them. They hadn't been to a play, read any Wilde, nor known about Victorian England. What did my family really know about literature or theater? Ironically, the arts were connecting me to strangers, and yet they widened the already yawning gulf between me and my family.

I sat down at my desk, still giddy, to plow through my homework, when Lou interrupted me. "How was the play?"

"Oh, it was cool. Really cool."

"That's so weird that Mrs. Krebs took you."

"You think so?"

"Kind of—a teacher taking some student to a play?"

"I'm not just 'some student.'" I mocked Lou's dismissal.

He shrugged. "What was the play about?"

"*The Importance of Being Earnest*? Well . . ." How could I summarize the play for a thirteen-year-old? "Well, it's about these two British guys who pretend to be people they're not so that they can do what they want and marry who they want to marry. They're upper-class Englishmen. Everything is kind of backward and sarcastic, so they totally obsess over things like cucumber sandwiches but make fun of things like marriage and honesty. And there's a joke in it about being named Ernest. They both lie about being named Ernest. But at the end of the play, it turns out that one of the guys who's been lying about being named Ernest is *really* named Ernest."

"That sounds weird."

"I didn't do a good job of explaining. I have it here. You can read it, you know." Lou shrugged. "I guess you could say that it's a play about lying about who you are only to find out that the person you're pretending to be is who you really are."

"Still sounds weird."

I was annoyed that Lou's questions were sinking my buoyant mood. "I have to do homework now. Can you close the door?"

Lou lingered in the doorway. "How do you lie about who you are and then turn out to be the person you were pretending to be? That doesn't make any sense."

"Maybe it'll make sense when you're older." I turned back to my reading. Lying about who you are? It made a lot of sense to me.

I thought about the end of the play as Jack discovers that he is, in fact, Ernest: "It is a terrible thing for a man to find out suddenly that all his life he has been speaking nothing but the truth." The lie that he's been telling himself and everyone is true, and it felt as though my ruse to appear well-read was becoming a reality. I had started reading books last year to appear well-read to my classmates, and in the pursuit of appearing well-read, I had begun to love the classic books.

This revelation precipitated other questions: Could I still be a punk—an outsider—while yearning to be accepted in the classroom? Could I love reading and books while being part of the punk scene? My crew was unwaveringly punk and decidedly anti-school. I didn't know how to square my growing, bookish side with punk rock, and loving both felt like a lie, like a paradox, that only a plot twist could fix.

Authenticity was punk's most important tenet, and I contemplated what exactly was authentic for me, a Vietnamese teenager in small-town PA.

What part of me was the real me and what was the façade? In architecture, façades were the fronts of buildings, but they were no less a part of the building than the basement or the roof. Perhaps, like its architectural meaning, my façade was my exterior but still a real part of who I was, like any building whose front hid its inner chambers and their delicate treasures far from unfeeling passersby.

NOVEMBER 1989

In 1989, racism (and racists) came in all shades and colors. Some of it was of the red, white, and blue Confederate variety—the Rebel Stars and Bars were a regular sight in Carlisle—but other times, racism lingered in a gray area, its machinations not as easy to spot as a fluttering flag; sometimes, it was staticky and hard to make out, forcing us to wonder if what we experienced was really racism or if maybe our antennae were a little bent, out of tune, and not perfectly dialed in. The way someone looked at us, the volume at which they spoke to my parents, the compliments on the quality of my English: most of the time—no, all of the time—we nodded and smiled. We had to. It was easier that way.

My parents never used the word *racism* or *racist* to name the slights that befell us. In their minds, our occasional mistreatment rippled outward from a national animus toward the Vietnam War, the painful spasm of a country's collective memory. We, the Tràns, just happened to be the stinging reminders of that war, and that collateral prejudice was our lot—it was the price we paid to be alive. My parents were gracious and long-suffering in their journey, believing that people weren't racists—they just hadn't taken the time to know us yet. More than a dozen years after our arrival in 1975, they felt that our lives were better, and they were more comfortable in Carlisle. Better Englishing. Owning a home. Good jobs. Less staring. Things were improving for them, and Lou and I almost believed it, too.

But then the skinheads came. Sort of.

Not literal skinheads but the idea of skinheads stalked the punk scene. Lou (who was becoming a junior varsity member of the skate and punk crew) and I heard about these white power skinheads almost as soon as we learned about punk rock: what they looked like, what they listened to, what to do when you met one. The Dead Kennedys' song "Nazi Punks Fuck Off" deepened the mythology of fascism and racism in the punk scene.

White power skinheads. They had shaved heads, wore Doc Martens with white or red laces and braces (suspenders that never actually held their tight jeans up), and sported Iron Crosses (a World War II German symbol), swastikas, or other German nostalgia pinned to their flight jackets. There was a mythology about the colors of the laces and their braces, and every few months, we learned a bit more about the symbolism: red laces and braces meant that they were allied with the National Front, white laces and braces meant that they were white power, black laces and braces meant that they were unaffiliated, independent skinheads. All subcultures relied heavily on the symbolism of their uniforms, and skinhead culture was no different.

At keg parties and on curbsides, we all discussed what we would do if we ever encountered white power skins, which always resulted in some version of fighting them. We met some independent skinheads at a Doylestown show and learned about the non-racist, multiracial origins of skinhead culture in England.* Two friends in our group, Scully and Dean, shaved their heads and bought flight jackets, christening themselves skinheads. Scully was black and Dean was white and having a black skinhead (and a Vietnamese punk) in our crew made our politics clear. Our crew was not racist.

---

* Skinheads and skinhead culture originated with black and white working-class English youth in the sixties, a solidarity movement among the lower-class British who rejected the hippies in favor of Jamaican rude boy/ska culture because both groups were segregated from the middle- and upper-class English. In the seventies and eighties, a small number of white nationalists adopted skinhead fashion and music, leading to its association with white supremacists.

We'd heard about an organization of skinheads in the Philly and D.C. areas who actively fought the white power skins—they were called SHARPs (Skinheads Against Racial Prejudice). They drove white power skins out of their scene, beating the shit out of them at shows. Liam and I talked about how neither of us wanted to be skinheads, but we wanted a piece of that fight.

At punk shows, we were always on the lookout for white power skinheads, but the rumors that those skins would come always preceded their absence. We heard tales of white power shows in Lancaster, York, and Harrisburg, but in Carlisle and at our small shows of twenty-five or thirty kids, the skinheads were a story that we told one another to hype ourselves up, filling our minds with stories of a big bad wolf that never came. The actual fights at the shows were with other punks and asshole kids from other towns, teenage scuffles over ego and turf; the fights were never that primal fight against Nazis.

We called them Nazis, tapping into the allure of that last good war (even as we rejected all the other trappings of the Boomers). It was easy to hate Nazis. We could all envision punching Nazis, guilt-free. The Von Trapps did it. Indiana Jones did it. Surely a few skate punks in rural PA could do it, too, if the Nazis ever dared to goose-step their way into our sleepy corner of the Susquehanna Valley.

The subculture chatter about Nazi skins erupted into the national conversation when Geraldo Rivera hosted them on his talk show, conveniently airing after school on ABC. Lou and I watched, transfixed by seeing real-life Nazi skins on TV, espousing all the simplistic racist ideologies we expected. A fight broke out on the show and in the melee they broke Geraldo's nose. Geraldo came back from the commercial break, dabbing his swollen face, blood on his shirt. Nazis—fucking Nazis!—were real.

My imagination's gunpowder keg was stuffed full of myth and fear in addition to the real everyday racism I had endured. The Nazi skinheads were cardboard stand-ins, two-dimensional cutouts of the deeper and more complicated racism of our town, of our America. It was easy to imagine punching a Nazi and ending racism, like checking it off a cleaning list. Dust the curtains. Vacuum under the bed. Punch a Nazi.

It was against this entire backdrop that we encountered Mason.

That fall of 1989, a new kid moved in at the end of our block. He had the markings of a redneck: all denim all the time, mullet, wrestling sneakers, Metallica T-shirts, and Marlboros falling out of his pockets. He had big, boyish features on his man-sized head and a sparse hint of facial hair.

Lou and I didn't introduce ourselves. We kept our distance from rednecks in general, but we spotted an Iron Cross on his Levi's jacket, tucked in among buttons of Iron Maiden and Black Sabbath.

Mason hadn't said or done anything to me, and it was too early in the school year for me to decide who needed to be punched or not, but Lou—Lou decided that Mason was a Nazi. Mason was the proverbial Nazi whom we'd been waiting to punch.

"Did you see his Iron Cross?" Lou asked, determined.

"I mean, *maybe* he's a Nazi. We don't know for sure. I'm not gonna punch someone who I suspect is a Nazi. I mean, what are you going to do: Ask him?"

We had no plan for determining what or who was racist.

Lou, however, being in eighth grade, did not hear my question's ridiculous rhetoric. "Good idea. I will ask him. Plus, I heard from other kids on the bus that he *said* he was white power."

"What? Really? That seems made-up."

"I'm gonna ask him tomorrow. At the bus stop."

"And *then* what?"

"If he says *yes*, I'm gonna punch him." The logic, though simple, was airtight. Ask a Nazi, punch a Nazi. Whac-A-Mole fascism.

The next morning, Lou and I headed to the bus stop. Lou carried a roll of pennies in each hand because he heard that punching someone with rolls of pennies in your fists would hurt more. The air crackled with a late-November chill.

Mason, standing almost six feet tall, waited at the end of the street, headphones on, cheeks ruddy, his faded denim attire elongating an already thin frame, his hair still damp from a shower.

The neighborhood kids were queued up for the bus, which was still fifteen minutes away, and Mason leaned against the stop sign at the corner, his head hunched over, his Walkman blaring. Lou and I fell in line at the back, but Lou suddenly dropped his backpack and cut in front of the other kids. I followed him.

The kids protested the line-cut briefly, but when Lou and I flanked Mason, they instinctively drew a perimeter. Kids know when a fight is coming.

Lou reached up and tapped Mason on the shoulder. Mason slid his headphones off.

He looked at Lou. "Hey, what's up?" It was friendly enough. He didn't sound like a Nazi.

Lou wasted no time. "I heard you were a Nazi. Is that true?"

Mason seemed startled by the question's timing at seven thirty a.m. and its lack of preamble. Lou was not fucking around with the school bus only fifteen minutes away.

"So are you? Are you a Nazi?"

We expected *yes* or *no*. *No* would result in a peaceable retreat. *Yes* would result in a punch in the face.

Mason looked at us both. "Well, I used to be."

Used to be? What the fuck was I supposed to do with *used to be*? I had no idea. *Used to be* meant that he was no longer a Nazi, based on what I understood about verb tenses. Did that warrant a fight? I wasn't sure what to do, even as I stood by Mason, ready for a fight. The actual fight was now a grammatical fight in my mind about . . .

Thwack! Lou punched him as hard as he could—the blow made Mason totter. Catching him off guard, Lou landed a few more punches in spite of his being much shorter. Mason counterpunched Lou a few times awkwardly because of the height difference, and one blow split Lou's left eyebrow. Lou grabbed Mason's jacket sleeve and kicked him hard in the ribs, doubling Mason over.

Mason's nose was bleeding, and his face was red all over. Folded in half and clutching his side, he wheezed. "I don't want to fight anymore. . . . What the hell, man . . . ? What the hell was that all about?"

Lou's brow was pouring blood down his face, and I gestured to my own brow to alert him. "You should go home and get cleaned up—there's a lot of blood." He touched the side of his face and looked at his hand, drenched in red. We saw the school bus approaching from the top of the hill.

Lou picked up his backpack and scowled at Mason before heading home. The bus rumbled up as Lou slipped out of sight.

Mason gathered his backpack, and the half dozen neighborhood kids, a mix of middle schoolers and underclassmen, were still standing in the fight circle, shocked into silence by the dawn's early fight. Unsure of who was in the right, no one offered to help Mason or Lou, and they kept their distance from me, too.

The bus doors clacked open, and Carl, our bus driver, called out. "You kids okay?" We all nodded, but Mason's bloody nose and pummeled face told a contrary tale.

Mason and I nodded. "Yeah, we're fine." The other kids who were at the bus stop were terrified by the scene that had erupted. I scanned the line, but they all gazed at their shoes, refusing to meet my stare. Everyone filed onto the bus in silence, maintaining the strict kid-code of secrecy.

Mason sat in the seat in front of me on the bus, and we rode to school in a tense, contorted silence. I saw his brown hair matted in front of me, drying except for the lowest ends of his mullet. His headphones had come back on, but I didn't hear any music coming from them, and I suspected that Mason hadn't even pressed play on his cassette player. He turned around. "Your brother's a tough son of a bitch—he punched me really hard."

Was he complimenting me? Complimenting Lou? Or just making the most awkward school bus conversation ever? What were you supposed to say to such a remark? I had to say *something*. "Well . . . well, don't be a fucking Nazi." He turned around in his seat without comment.

When I got home later that day, my parents both yelled at me. Lou sat at the kitchen table, a bandage over his black eye. He looked worse than when I had seen him that morning, the fight having settled into purple and green splotches on his face; now he also had five stitches above his eye under the bandage. I learned that he had called my dad at work that morning and told him that he needed to go to the hospital, lying about falling down or something. Eventually, when Lou's injuries made it seem as though he had fallen down the basement stairs only on his face, he told my parents that he had gotten into a fight at the bus stop.

My mother's anger, rarely revealed, was pointed in contrast to my father's reticence. "Why didn't you help your brother?! You're his older brother! You're supposed to protect him!"

I protested. "Wait, what? Lou was winning the fight! He won that fight. I wasn't going to step in when he was winning!"

"That's not the point! He's in eighth grade! You're his big brother! His *big* brother! You don't let him get punched!"

"But he was winning!"

My father intervened. "It doesn't matter! You let someone punch him!"

"But Lou started it!"

"You let him get beat up!" My mother wouldn't let it rest.

Lou didn't say a word, sitting at the table, crestfallen, waiting for dinner, which would begin after my mother was done roasting me.

I looked at him, avoiding further argument with my parents. "Dude, you're a legend. Everyone heard about the fight. You beat up an eleventh grader! That's what everyone's saying." I didn't know how much of it my parents would appreciate, but I hoped they would take comfort in Lou's reputation. I was proud of him.

But he felt no pride. Lou avoided engaging me and mumbled a simple, "Oh, really?" He was angry—pissed that I hadn't jumped in with him to punch a Nazi. Betrayal. Lou had gone out there with his fists wrapped around penny rolls to crush a Nazi, and I, his older brother, stood dumbly by trying to parse the grammar Nazi.

We didn't talk after dinner—I had homework to do, and he watched *Perfect Strangers* and *Growing Pains,* alternately icing his knuckles and his purple eye. Growing pains, indeed.

What you don't think about when you're planning to punch a Nazi is what to do after you've punched the Nazi. We still had to ride the school bus every day with Mason. The following week, on the bus in front of everyone, Mason stood up in the middle of the aisle.

"Hey, Lou and Phuc! Look!" He showed off his backpack on which he had written in black permanent marker NAZI'S FUCK OFF.

We looked at it and shrugged. I noted the misuse of the apostrophe but didn't see the point in beating him up about his writing mechanics, too. "That's . . . cool." We still thought he was a dick for having ever been a Nazi, and now that he said he wasn't, were we willing to leave him alone or even be neighborly to him? We didn't know. This was far more complicated than the cartoonish justice of smashing him with the punk rock, and we didn't know how to talk about that complexity.

When I arrived at the high school, I found my way to our crew's meeting spot, which was across the street from the school so a few of them could smoke with impunity.

Philip, dragging hard to finish his breakfast Marlboro before class, broke off his conversation with the others. "How's your brother doing? I still can't believe he fucking beat up that Nazi prick. So fucking badass." The other boys nodded their assent.

"Yeah, he's okay. His face is still pretty busted up."

"You and Lou should just shave your heads and be skinheads. Join the SHARPs."

"Nah, that's okay. I mean, I like Oi!* just fine . . . but skinheads aren't for me."

Philip twisted his boot on the ground to extinguish the discarded butt, baring his teeth to grin. "Yeah, but you guys could be like Asian

---

* *Oi!* is a subgenre of punk rock specifically made by and for skinheads.

power skinheads." Liam chuckled at the idea, and Philip was pleased with himself at the joke. "Yeah . . . fucking Asian power skins! Instead of white laces and white braces, you could have . . . uh, you could have yellow laces and yellow braces!" Everyone laughed.

I shot back. "Why stop there? Why don't I just have noodle laces and noodle braces?"

The whole group erupted with laughter and gave me high fives. I had won the game by hating myself most.

The bell rang for homeroom, and we lumbered across the street. Philip put his hand on my shoulder. "You know we're just fucking with you, right? Fuck those Nazis. Racist assholes."

I assented silently. It was easy to hate Nazis because they were racists. But us? We weren't racists—we were the ones who fought racists. As we walked into school, I felt disappointed with myself and with my friends. If we wanted to fight white power skinheads, why did my friends also make racist jokes? And why did I have to make racist jokes about myself?

The truth was that we were against racists, but it felt like a lie sometimes, a lie that everyone told themselves—everyone including myself.

What was the lie and what was the truth?

JANUARY 1990

I walked across Dickinson's campus and found the professor's office. I had entered one of the grand limestone buildings, and it wasn't to vandalize or steal anything. I wasn't there to run any pigs. I encountered a large oak door with privacy glass and his name on a placard. *Professor Ralph J. Slotten. Religion.*

"Helloooooo?" The door was open, and I rapped on the glass.

"Hello? Yes?" Professor Slotten, in the flesh. Tall, Norwegian-looking, piercing blue eyes set wide, large brow, a shock of white hair, and a slouch in his shoulders that looked as though he had forgotten to take the hanger out of his blazer. "Hello, young man. How may I help you?" He looked exactly as I imagined a college professor would look, and for a moment, examining his desk and framed degrees on his wall, askew but prestigious, I wondered: What the hell was I doing there?

I gathered myself. "Hi. Ummm . . . I'm a junior at Carlisle High School. And, uh, I'm wondering if I could audit your course? I picked up a course catalog at the Hub building and saw that you're teaching a class on comparative Nordic and Celtic mythology. Could I audit that class?"

His glasses were so thick that I couldn't tell whether he was looking at me or not, but his eyes seemed to meander in my vicinity. He smiled. "Ah, well, that's interesting! I've never had a high school student audit a course. Why did you pick my class? Are you interested in comparative religion or mythology?"

"Well, I am definitely interested in religion and mythology. I'm interested in a lot of things—actually, I'm interested in pretty much everything. And I'm in the National Honor Society, so I'm a pretty good student, but to be honest, I just want to challenge myself more—see how I fare at the college level. I found out that a kid in my high school is taking an Ancient Greek class here at Dickinson, so I wanted to take a class here as well. But I am really curious about Celtic and Nordic mythology, and I don't know anything about comparative studies, and if you don't know anything about a subject, that should be the best reason to take a class on it, right?" He smiled and nodded as I rambled. "And to be *totally* honest: it's the only humanities class that fits with my high school schedule."

He laughed at my candor, flensing the truth from my shambolic introduction. "You want to keep up with that Greek boy, huh? You think you're just as smart as he is?"

"I don't know if I would say that. Honestly, I wouldn't even say I'm smart. Socrates said he was the dumbest person in Athens, but by virtue of acknowledging his stupidity, he was the wisest." I had recently read a synopsis of Plato's *Dialogues* and used my newfound knowledge to impress the professor.

Professor Slotten's face widened with delight. "Oh my goodness. Are we comparing ourselves to Socrates, then?"

"Oh God . . . not at all. I'm no Socrates. More like . . . Mediocrates."

Laughter. An auspicious omen. "Well, very good then. You may audit the class. What is your name, my witty friend?"

"Thank you so much. Thank you. I'm Phuc."

"Ah, Vietnamese?"

"Uh . . . yeah, actually. *Exactly.* I guess Vietnamese American, if you wanted to be totally accurate."

"Welcome to the class, Phuc."

He jotted down my mailing address, informing me that he would mail me a syllabus (I didn't know what that was) and a list of books that I would need to purchase at the campus bookstore before class started. I shook Professor Slotten's hand vigorously and thanked him again for the fourth time.

In the brittle blue of the faded January afternoon, I clomped across the Dickinson campus, whited out with piles of snow. College students, bundled and bustling to their rooms, crossed my path. I almost felt like one of them. The glow of the Hub building warmed the palette of an otherwise muted midwinter day.

I remembered the last time I went through the double doors of that building, feeling the memory's irony. The last time I had seen those doors, I was crashing through them as Pauly and I ran away from campus security. I was one of the barbaric townies, stealing clothes from dryers and vandalizing the campus, and now Professor Slotten let me enroll in his class. I made an impassioned and earnest appeal, and he seemed to understand what I was trying to achieve—or at least, the person I was trying to be. But who was that, exactly?

I was a Vietnamese. I was an American. I was an artist. I was a reader. I was the punk townie who stole jeans from the dryers. I was the punk townie who wanted to audit a religion class.

I began to wonder why I felt like I had to choose one thing over another. I was *all* of these things. I was a plurality. And I was one thing, one word. I was who I said I was. I had said to Professor Slotten: *I'm Phuc*. I circled back to my name, the only *Phuc* I had ever met and the only noun I had for who I was.

Phuc. That was enough to be the sum of who I was and who I would be. And it would never be a lie. I just had to find the courage to be him and ask myself why I was afraid to be Phuc.

THE AUTOBIOGRAPHY
OF MALCOLM X

Imagine if your whole life's work was squeezed into the blurb of a high school history textbook, into a paragraph totaling maybe sixty words—your life and its complexities pruned for word count and impact. The people you loved, the things you hated, your passions—all of these things condensed for the sake of historical concision. And that oversimplification sucks, but take heart: at least you're dead and can't be pissed about it.

I'm talking about Malcolm X.

When I learned about Malcolm X in Mrs. Romberger's AP US History class in eleventh grade, he was a bespectacled blur. I was being crushed under the avalanche of names, facts, dates: Adams, Madison, Quincy Adams, the Continental Congress, the Teapot Dome Scandal, the Bay of Pigs, 1791, 1812, 1945. Civil Rights marched by quickly, and Malcolm X was presented as a foil to the Reverend Martin Luther King Jr., but then we sped on. 1989 was also the year that the Berlin Wall fell, so Mrs. Romberger was especially keen to thaw the Cold War for us so that we could savor its delicious end.

When I read Malcolm X's autobiography myself, I felt disappointed in my high school's history book, let down by what I had been taught. We had not done him justice. He wasn't the opposite of the Reverend King as he had been portrayed, and he was more than the one-dimensional pro-violence, radical Black leader whom I had read about. Our textbook had taken a convenient and incomplete snapshot of who he was at a particular moment in his life to shoehorn him into the yin-yang paradigm of Civil Rights leaders, reducing his life's intricacy into a simple paragraph.

In fact, Malcolm X was complicated and evolving, and no one expressed that complexity better than he himself did. A year before his assassination, he wrote a letter home to his mosque detailing his epiphany about race relations, about his changing ideas of race and racism in America, about his movement *toward* white people as allies for civil rights. Malcolm X was changing, his name was changing—having rechristened himself El-Hajj Malik El-Shabazz—and his views on race were changing. "Even I was myself astounded. But there was precedent in my life for this letter. My whole life had been a chronology of *changes*," he writes.

But me? My views? It was 1990. I was a senior in high school. I was at my apex academically and socially. There was no need for me to change my views, and frankly, I didn't want to change. Everything made sense to me as it was—everything was in its place. I was poised to cross the finish line, sprinting to finish the race.

But what if the reality of life, what if experience and knowledge, went against what you thought? What if it went against what you wanted to believe? What if the race suddenly changed?

AUGUST 1990

The new decade had begun, but what novelties did the nineties have for us? There was no death knell for the eighties (unlike the DISCO IS DEAD implosion of 1979). 1990 felt like 1989, its metamorphosis only the matter of a split second, the *tick* of 11:59 p.m. to the *tock* of 12:00 a.m., with the immortal Dick Clark rockin' our New Year's Eve with his smooth, embalmed polish.

The summer's box office hits also suggested that 1990 didn't know what else to do other than to keep moonwalking back to the 1980s: *Back to the Future Part III*, *Die Hard 2*, *RoboCop 2*, *Young Guns II*, *Gremlins 2*, and *Another 48 Hrs*. Hollywood's coolest summer films were a reheated affair, microwaved entrées of recycled entertainment and regurgitated pabulum for the populous. In the face of this dreck, my friends and I dug our punk rock trenches even deeper and wider, erecting spikier bulwarks of biting cynicism and outré choices. Our punk umbrella had broadened to include the newly minted monikers of alternative music and independent films, whatever they were. I played Liam a cassette of the Pixies' new album *Doolittle,* and he found it weird. Meanwhile, Liam was descending into the industrial sounds of Ministry, and a few of us dabbled with the gangsta rap of N.W.A. and Public Enemy. Our crew was still, at heart, a punk rock crew, but our dogmatic adherence to the punk playbook was trying to rewrite itself: rap, punk, Britpop, Detroit techno, hip-hop. I loved the Pixies exactly because they were sonically all over the place, just like how *we* were all over the place. Defined more by what we were not than what we were—by our fuck-no's more than our credos—we pointed to the rednecks and jocks and preps, declaring that we were the opposite of them.

This opposition extended from music and movies to all matters of popular culture (going specifically against the notion of what *popular* meant). We didn't want *popular* culture—we wanted rarefied culture, the scribblings in the margins that were more authentic and raw and rebellious. If pop culture was the lecture in class, we were busy reading and writing the graffiti on the desks.

Conor had gone off to boot camp, and within a few months he would be on the dusty front lines of the Gulf War. Several other friends had also enlisted in the armed forces either by indecision or indifference. It was a ticket out of town, and if the military would pay the fare, it was a price that some of our friends were willing to bear. I was struck by the irony that our punk rock friends (rule-breakers and intrinsic, immutable iconoclasts) were hurling themselves into the hopper of rigid, rule-oriented institutions. It gnawed at me. We had spent countless hours listening to the Exploited singing "Fuck the USA" and Minor Threat railing against fascistic conformity, and now—now some of us were signing up for the army.

I was surprised and a little disheartened by their about-face, but I also didn't know what their futures could yield with high school transcripts that were dripping with the Cs and Ds of indifference, feckless documents that were hardly worth the time to print much less read. A few guys had dropped out of high school and rented squalid apartments, barbacking at the local taverns, landscaping, or dealing drugs. Conor, Scully, and Will all enlisted, emphasizing the opportunity to shoot guns and blow shit up, but their appetites for destruction seemed like a faint effort to distract from whom they were shooting (they didn't know) and what they were blowing up (they didn't care). Scully emphasized the irony of being in the military as if it were the ultimate prank. *Can you believe the Air Force took a fuckup like me? Just wait till I get in there.* As if one eighteen-year-old's bad attitude would be a punk rock wrench in the well-oiled gears of a war machine.

If I admired anyone, it was Philip. Philip followed in his older brother's footsteps, matriculating to NYU. It was a point of pride for our crew—another one of us had made it out of Carlisle—yet we didn't acknowledge that more of us would have made it if we had given two shits about school or grades or extracurriculars. That was our tragedy. Philip *had* cared and *had* made an effort at school (as did I), but his investment and academic successes were never a point of conversation or commentary. Dragging on his perennial Marlboro, Philip passed off his success as a by-product of effortless, genetic genius, and we were happy to celebrate his NYU admission as long as it appeared breezy and natural. A few of my honor society friends went to the far reaches of academia, schools which I had never heard of: Haverford (which I initially confused with Harvard), Bryn Mawr, George Washington, Carnegie Mellon. My only college plan was to get out of Carlisle.

In the middle of his basic training in Georgia, Conor came home to Carlisle on a week's leave. In addition to a Saturday barn party with two kegs of Yuengling, Nate and I suggested a drive to Philly on Sunday. Seven of us piled into Nate's VW Squareback station wagon and drove the two hours to Philadelphia to walk around South Street, where the record stores and punk rock boutiques seemed to be lifted straight from London by my rusticated estimation. Leather pants. Studded belts. Posters and T-shirts. Import-only, color vinyl pressings of rare singles. We cast our petty dollars around, excited small-town punks hoping to hook a big catch in Philly's flowing thoroughfares and waves of wares.

At home, I unpacked a few shopping bags from Skinz, Zipperhead, and Third Street Jazz and Rock. I didn't have a lot of money on the trip, but I made a few purchases after labored agonizing and *hurry-the-fuck-ups* from everyone.

"What'd you get?" Lou was curious about what spoils would have warranted a two-hour drive to Philadelphia.

"A couple of T-shirts. A poster. A few records. Check it out." I pulled out two black T-shirts that were bleached in the front so that the white part could be screen-printed. The bleach made the front image look as if it were exploding, with spots of white on the sleeves and neck. One shirt was screened with Albrecht Dürer's illustration of Christ's crucifixion. I bought this shirt to nettle my parents and anyone else I thought slavishly addicted to the opiate of the masses. My style compass, forged from irony, was oriented toward the slightly morbid and antiauthoritarian.

Lou shook his head at the T-shirt. "Whoa . . . Mom is going to freak out."

"Yeah, maybe. But she can't be *that* mad. I mean, it is Jesus."

"Yeah, but it's Jesus—*on a T-shirt*. That doesn't seem right."

I shrugged. My parents and I were locked in the churning cycles of offend and defend, provoke and react, ignore and annoy. The sacrilege of the Dürer T-shirt would irk them, but I also knew that they couldn't complain about the actual image, because it was Jesus.

I held up the second black T-shirt, screened and bleached in the same style.

"Who's that?"

"Malcolm X."

"Who's he?"

"Who's Malcolm X?! Jesus Christ, man . . ." I pretended that Lou was supposed to know better when I myself had only learned about him the previous year. I gave Lou the quick, basic rundown of Malcolm X and the Civil Rights Movement that I had read about in my history textbook. It was a sixteen-year-old's rehashing of what he remembered from the AP US History curriculum, and Mrs. Romberger would have been proud.

Lou looked more confused by the Malcolm X shirt than by the Jesus shirt. "Why'd you buy *that*?" Lou's question was childlike and hard to answer, his innocent queries foiling my sharpened ideology.

"Because it's cool. I mean: it's Malcolm X. He was a total revolutionary."

"I don't get why you'd get a shirt of him . . . and besides: they're just T-shirts." Lou shrugged and left my bedroom, overly perplexed by my clothing choices and bored by our conversation about T-shirts of dead martyrs.

I was stung by the barb of his naïve insight. He was right. They *were* only T-shirts, but for me they made a statement, drew a sociopolitical line in the sand, and maybe they would provoke a reaction. If I saw a Bad Brains T-shirt, I acknowledged an ally. If I saw a Confederate flag T-shirt, I perceived an adversary. And if I saw a United Colors of Benetton shirt, I knew that person was a lemming. In the stores, on the streets, in the hallways, our T-shirts were our nations' flags, chosen with care for the alliances they forged and the conventions they flouted. Jesus on a T-shirt? Malcolm X on a T-shirt? Maybe my T-shirts *would* offend someone. I was counting on it.

The rednecks had been offended by my being Vietnamese and by my hair and clothes. Now they could be offended by my T-shirt politics, too.

The shirts embodied my simplified take on politics and religion and everything else—T-shirt rhetoric for an image-obsessed age. You didn't have to articulate who you were if you could explain it by whom you wore.

I wore my Malcolm X T-shirt to school that September, and sure enough, it elicited comments. My peers were more curious than outraged. *Who's that? Oh, I see. Malcom X, huh?* I was waiting for a debate, ready to pounce, but no one took the bait.

Then in my AP European History class, Ms. Ganster saw the shirt and her mouth twisted into a slight pucker. I took surprising pleasure in her apparent disapproval, a pleasure that came from my general provocation rather than from a specific insult toward her. I liked Ms. Ganster.

"Ah, Malcolm X."

I nodded.

"What did you think of his autobiography?"

"His what?"

"You know: *The Autobiography of Malcolm X* by Alex Haley?" She seemed disapproving.

"Oh, uh . . . I didn't know he wrote an autobiography." I, lowly pawn, had been outmaneuvered by the History Queen. Check.

"Oh, it's quite compelling. Quite compelling. You should read it. Or at least, you should read it since you're flaunting the T-shirt."

The insult was subtle, but she knew that pointing out my ignorance smarted me. Checkmate. It turned out that she wasn't offended that I was wearing a Malcolm X T-shirt; she was offended that I hadn't read the book, and I pushed down my embarrassment, the so-called literature guy who hadn't read the book written by the guy on his T-shirt. Textbook poser.

That weekend at the Whistlestop Bookshop, I bought a used paperback copy of the autobiography—faded cover, stark in its red-black-and-white design, with a vivid photo of Malcolm X, finger jabbing the air, biting his lower lip. I was not going to let Ms. Ganster have the last word.

A few weeks later, I wore my Malcolm X shirt again and lingered after history class. "Hey, Ms. Ganster, I read the autobiography. Thanks for recommending it."

"Oh, you did? Really?" She seemed surprised but impressed that I had done it. Trained by Mrs. Ferguson, I rarely let a recommended book go unread, and even if I hated it, I at least tried to read it (sorry, James Joyce).

"Yeah, I just finished it."

"What did you think?"

"I'm still thinking about it. I mean: I think he goes a little too far in calling the white man the devil so much. That's kind of intense. I think we all need to live together, right? I guess I'm more aligned with Martin Luther King Jr. than Malcolm X. But Malcolm X seemed to be evolving right up to his assassination, so I'm not sure."

"That's great that you read it—his assassination was a tragedy in a harrowing series of tragedies in the sixties. And you're right that his autobiography depicts his evolution, his life. He was still growing and learning right up until he died. That in itself is an incredible lesson." Ms. Ganster was sincere, and I was surprised, having assumed ignorantly that my middle-aged white history teacher wouldn't be able to appreciate the radical stand of Malcolm X, but in fact, she viewed Malcolm X's death as a tragedy. She straightened the chables back into their forward-facing rows for the next period. "Did the book resonate with you at all, Phuc?"

"What do you mean?"

"Did his life or his writing connect with you and your experience?"

I didn't have a chance to answer as the bell rang for the start of the next period. I was late for calculus.

"I'll write you a hall pass for being late." She scribbled out a note for my tardiness. "Go on and get to class. We can talk more later."

I sprinted down the hall clutching my pass, flashing it to the hall monitors like an East German checkpoint and bursting into calculus with my half-open backpack. I threw myself into the nearest open chable.

Mr. Cook was unfurling the intricate turns of functions and limits as I pulled out my textbook, but my brain was still in the AP European time zone, mulling over what Ms. Ganster had asked me. I didn't know how to answer her question because I didn't know what her question meant.

Did Malcolm X resonate with me?

In that fall of 1990, if pressed hard, I would have said no. I couldn't comprehend it because of how I had compartmentalized my own experiences of bigotry. My parents had never talked to us about racism as a larger force at work, and we assigned prejudice, insults, and bullying specifically to anti-Vietnamese sentiment. In the long shadow of the war, I linked my personal travails to the war's aftershocks and couldn't see how our struggles were connected to a larger struggle for equality. We were not the descendants of slaves. Our people had not marched, sat-in, or been fire-hosed. It did not feel like our fight.

In high school, I understood racism as a thing that white racist people did and that Black Americans suffered, and our history books had the photos to prove it, in black and white. Racists were Klansmen and people who called Black people the *n*-word. Sit-ins. Bus boycotts. Rallies on the steps of Washington. Where did Vietnamese people figure into all of this? Nowhere, it seemed.

If I were honest, Malcolm's message didn't immediately resonate with me because his worldview about race and racism was flexible and responsive, and mine was static at best and cartoonish at worst. My understanding of racism hadn't evolved because I hadn't allowed it and didn't want it to. I didn't want the small, inscribed circle of racists to expand, because if it did, I was terrified it would include more people than just the Klan and skinheads.

It was the exclusive club in which no one wanted to have member-ship. If I put people who made racist jokes in that group, would all my friends go in that pile? Would I also be in that group? What would that mean to include myself in that group? It was a horrifying prospect to even consider that everyone I grew up with and my closest friends were racists if I broadened its definition, so I didn't.

Malcolm X wrote to his mosque, "I have been always a man who tries to face facts, and to accept the reality of life as new experience and new knowledge unfolds it. I have always kept an open mind. . . ." It was too much to consider and too hard to evolve my thinking about race as Malcolm had done. Malcolm's "reality of life" was too harsh to behold in the light of the truth. For my own survival and sanity, I kept the racists under their hoods and in the dark.

Was I ready to evolve my thinking about race and racism or was I going to cling to the narrow boundaries of who was racist? Did it matter whether I was ready or not? My evolution would begin regardless.

NOVEMBER 1990

I had quit the library job that summer, though I still volunteered there once a week as a page. I now worked at the Mobil gas station at the encouragement of Liam. One by one, during the spring of 1990, our crew of friends had applied for positions at the gas station, and by the end of summer, all the cashiers at the Mobil were our friends. It was the real-life cast of misfits tasked with running a gas station, and the upsides to the Mobil over the library were substantial: I got better pay ($4.25/hour!), worked with my friends when there were two of us on a shift, and when I had the closing shift at night, I perched on a rickety metal stool and did homework (which meant I didn't have to do it after work). With a demanding class load and a lot of homework, getting paid to do homework until ten p.m. seemed criminally convenient. Our sympathetic manager, Scott, was working toward his associate's degree at Harrisburg Area Community College, and he never complained about my reading on the job.

Saturday morning I sat in the fishbowl of the cash register office, flanked by a small steel rack of candy bars and a rotating display of merchandise: oil funnels, ice scrapers, air fresheners.

As I wended through my homework, the full-service customers had sharply dwindled. A few times an hour, a car came through full-service, setting off the pneumatic bell, alerting me to its presence and needs. Pavlov would have been proud. The bell jolted me up from the register, and I trotted out, metaphorical tail wagging with *yessirs* and *noma'ams*. Fill 'em up. Squeegee their windows. Check their fluids.

The mechanics clomped in and out of the office, making change, purchasing a Coke, avoiding the monotony of automotive maintenance. Dirty Dan (so nicknamed by us) ambled to the counter.

"Whatcher readin', boy? *I LAID*?!?! What the hell is *The I LAID*?!*"* Dan bellowed. He always called me *boy,* and I disliked Dirty Dan from our first encounter. His breath was a repellant cocktail of burps and tobacco. I ignored his question, but he persisted.

I refused to raise my eyes from the page. "ILL-LEE-ADD. It's actually pronounced *Iliad.* Like *The Iliad.*"

"Well, what the hell is *The Iliad*?" At least he said it correctly—that a boy.

"It's about the Trojan War. Greeks versus Trojans. I don't know. . . . I haven't gotten that far into it."

"TROJANS?! You mean like the RUBBERS?! Hawhawhaw . . . You know I'm jus' fuckin' with you, boy. Why the hell are you reading that book?"

"It's for class. Homework." I didn't want to get into it with Dan since I was actually enjoying *The Iliad,* and his idiocy punctured my reading.

"I thought *you people* were supposed to be good at *math!*" He laughed and slapped the counter several times with a greasy palm.

"Math? I'm doing that, too. Here you go." I lugged my AP calculus textbook out of my backpack. I had been procrastinating because calculus was killing me, but I felt the need to show him some identific-Asian. "This is my calculus textbook. See? Doing math. Big-time math."

"Calculus? Huh." He was suitably impressed. "Okay then . . . Enjoy yer book. . . . I LAID! Hahahahaha!" Hand-slaps on the counter again.

I finished up my shift and skated home, but I sat in my room unable to finish my homework because I was feeling too annoyed. And in the idle aggravation of not doing my work, I let loose and felt the full furnace of anger. I was actually furious.

Against a lifetime of small and large affronts, my humanity—my dignity—unhinged itself and swung open. I sat in my bedroom that night, fuming. Dan, a nincompoop by all measures, had looked at the color of my skin and the shape of my eyes and told me that I was somehow swerving out of my lane. Who the fuck was he to decide what lane I was supposed to be in? And what did it matter to him, anyway? My indignation rose up more as I felt like a punch line to some inside joke. That I was being laughed at, labeled, and pushed into a corner. I decided that I was going to get even with him.

I wasn't going to fight Dirty Dan, because he was a grown man and I would have gotten fired (and probably beaten up myself). And as I had seen from Lou's incident, punching racists was questionably effective. I was going to do what I could in the only context where I had any power: our high school newspaper. As the editor of the high school paper, I was given one editorial a month to write anything I wanted, and I decided that this was going to be where I'd serve my cold dish of revenge. I was going to write about the incident with Dan—I was going to humiliate him. I knew firsthand the power of words, and I was going to use that power to put him in his place (that is, if he ever read Carlisle High School's monthly newspaper and happened across the editor's column on the second page). Postponing my homework, I scratched out an eviscerating editorial in pencil on a yellow legal pad. My editorial unleashed a seething frustration: I was tired of the narrow path permitted to me because of how I looked, tired of the instant and lazy stereotypes that people applied to me. Did my friends suffer this bullshit?

On Monday at school, I handed it to Mr. Moyer, our school paper's adviser. During our newspaper period, he read over my editorial and called me to his desk. I took the chable next to his desk and asked him bluntly, "What'd you think? I think it's pretty direct. I don't think we've ever had an editorial like this." My anger over the incident was diminished slightly, but I was proud that I was taking a stand and calling it what it was: It wasn't Klansmen or skinheads, but my interaction with Dan was racism, and I dared to say its name. "Pretty shocking, right, Mr. Moyer?"

"Absolutely." Mr. Moyer shook his head. "Did this really happen?"

"Really happen? Uh, yeah, it really happened—happened over the weekend."

Mr. Moyer continued shaking his head, and I felt comforted by his empathy as he spoke. "I'm sorry that it happened. I'm glad that you wrote about it. But do you think that publishing this is the right thing? I mean, we're not the New York Times or even the Sentinel, and Carlisle is a small town. Someone might be related to or connected to Dan, and you don't know who you'll offend." My airy sense of comfort darkened at the realization that Mr. Moyer was trying to talk me out of the editorial.

I countered. "But that's the point."

"To offend Dan? Why?"

"So he knows he can't say that sort of thing."

"You think that it will stop him from having stereotypes or from saying ignorant things? He'll never read it. The editorial isn't a soapbox for your grievances. You're so smart, Phuc. Why don't you write about something that everyone can relate to, like the SATs? It's the college application season right now. Or this mess in Iraq? We might be going to war there. That involves the whole country. Those seem like things that everyone could relate to."

This made me doubly furious and even angrier with Mr. Moyer than with Dirty Dan. I was trying to comprehend what I was hearing. *Things that everyone could relate to?* I heard nothing but Mr. Moyer trying to protect Dan and to redirect me, telling me that my anger didn't have a place in a public forum. I was so angry that I almost wanted to seize my editorial and tear it up in Mr. Moyer's face, but instead I checked my frustration and spoke as calmly as I could. "This is really important to me, Mr. Moyer. No one reads the editorials or takes them seriously because they're always about nonissues. But racism . . ." My words broke off, and some of the other newspaper students hushed. I didn't want Mr. Moyer to tell me that racism only affected me, the Vietnamese kid, in a room full of white kids.

My assistant editor, Jenna, piped up. "Well, I think an SAT editorial would be good. I mean, I don't think the SATs are fair and—"

I whipped a stinging reply. "No one *asked* you, Jenna!"

"Phuc, she's just giving you some suggestions." Mr. Moyer lifted his chin as a sign to Jenna that we weren't done talking.

The whole room was silent, my verbal snap having stopped the small group work. I leaned closer to Mr. Moyer, knowing that I needed to salvage my position so that he wouldn't reject my editorial outright. I took a breath and collected myself. Pride swallowed. "I know this only affects me, but it's also really important to me. Maybe no one can relate to it, maybe you're right about that, but it's also an editorial. What editorials did you tell Laura she *couldn't* write?" Laura was the editor the previous year. "It's an editorial, Mr. Moyer—I know the difference between an article and an editorial. And I know this seems like a risk, but it's a risk I want to take, and I'm willing to write it and take full responsibility for it." I did the best I could in the moment to appeal to the logic and boldness of the situation, to downplay my rancor even as I hated feeling like I was groveling to be heard because I was, in fact, groveling to be heard.

Mr. Moyer looked at my yellow legal pad, his eyes scanning my editorial. "Well, it's too long, so you'll need to cut fifty words for the column. And you can't call Dan a *racist pig.* Leave it at *racist.* Lose the *pig.*"

"So I can run it?"

He nodded. "Yes. Yes, you can."

"Thanks, Mr. Moyer. Thanks so much." I would have shaken his hand, but I was nursing a broken trust. It was painful for me to endure bigoted remarks from the garage mechanic, but it was eviscerating—and felt like betrayal—for Mr. Moyer to ask me to think about offending others with the editorial. But at least in the end he allowed it, and in his acquiescence, it seemed like a self-inflicted win for me.

We ran the editorial at the end of the month. Simplistic because of its word count, my article was clear in its caricature of Dan: racism was bad. It was easy to hate caricatured racists as it was easy to hate Nazis, and the congratulatory feedback from my classmates was simple and frequent, but it didn't feel victorious. I had to beg for the editorial to be run, and none of my peers on the newspaper had come to my defense or encouragement when Mr. Moyer was trying to talk me out of it.

In my editorial, the takeaway was so palatable: racists were bad people, bad apples in the barrel. But bad apples were easy to spot. What Malcolm X was suggesting was that it was the whole barrel—America— that was the problem, but my teenage brain rejected that notion imme-diately. I didn't want to believe that the barrel itself was rotten because I was in that same barrel.

That fall I applied to three colleges with minimal assistance from my guidance counselor, Mr. Lebo, who was also the head football coach. His primary duty was coaching, and in the midst of the fall season, college guidance took the bench in favor of running plays and buttonhook pass options. We met once in his office, where he asked me a few times to help him pronounce my name, and then told me that I should definitely apply to Penn State because I had good grades. Afterward, he handed me a one-page handout with tips for writing a college essay and wished me luck.

I did apply to Penn State because I knew I would get in, and also because my parents (whose accents made it sound like Peng Stay) insisted on it because that was where my aunt had gone. Also, the in-state tuition for Penn State was affordable, and the three of us talked about additional financial aid and loans and grants. By this point, I seldom spoke with my mother and father beyond asking them for checks for the application fees or the use of a car to get to work. They had started taking classes at community college to earn their travel agent's licenses, and between my work schedule and their school schedule, we crisscrossed in our household, a weave of missed connections.

Mrs. Krebs and Mrs. Romberger wrote recommendations for me, and I felt as though I had an excellent chance for getting into college. That feeling, of course, was based on the faintest knowledge and understanding of the application process. I checked out the College Board's guide to colleges from the library, but its girth and its gray pages stifled even my breathy ambitions and aspirations. I knew I wanted to go to college in a big city, because—well, because fuck Carlisle. I had offloaded all my frustrations, all my grievances (real and perceived) upon the town, and it symbolized everything I wanted to leave behind. Carlisle, Pennsylvania: an easy symbol for narrow-minded bigotry and limited prospects for teenagers of all stripes—I couldn't wait to put Carlisle in the rearview. I wanted to be around music, culture, art, artists, punks, anarchists, socialists, girls who were well-read and promiscuous. None of that was in Carlisle.

I was shocked that some kids applied to Dickinson. Staying in Carlisle for college? No way. Fuck small towns. I felt like I was destined for the big city. The Big Apple. The big time.

I applied to New York University, mainly drawn to the idea of living in *the* big city and being in a city that seemed filled with more fun, more punks, and more people like me. I didn't know anything about its curriculum or the different departments. My parents seemed okay with NYU because my aunt and uncle still lived on Staten Island, and they envisioned my living there to save money. The only other big city that I had frequented and enjoyed was Philadelphia, so I applied to the University of Pennsylvania (which my parents and I thought briefly was the same as Pennsylvania State University). I heard about other colleges and universities to which my classmates were applying, and I skimmed their lists with no sense of where or what: Williams, Middlebury, Amherst, Skidmore, Swarthmore, Georgetown. They might as well have been rattling off Canadian territories, and I certainly had no sense of what a "good" college was. But I had started to hear the phrase "Oh, that's a great school" after some schools' names and not others. I had dumbly assumed that college was college and that what you did mattered more than where you were.

I requested the three applications for NYU, UPenn, and Penn State, and within the month I received their large, bulky white envelopes and the enclosed, polished prospectuses. My mother had gotten a discarded secondhand IBM Selectric typewriter from her insurance office so I could type out the applications instead of filling them out by hand. I filled out each application on the typewriter, one loud click after the next hard clack, the rhythmic sound of opportunity knocking.

I homed in on the personal essay and the opportunity to talk about what I loved, of course. I wrestled with what to write about. Don't talk about being an immigrant. Don't talk about race (Mr. Moyer's advice about my editorial stalked me as I thought about how I would present myself to the wider world). Don't talk about punk rock or running away or your fucked-up childhood. Universal. Relatable. Aspirational. Talk about your love of books, your love of art, your love of learning. Be funny. Be yourself. *No*—be better than yourself.

I took the SATs three times, and I thought my scores were fine. They weren't perfect, but my essay was propulsive. My essay would carry me. My grades were good (good enough for me to be in the National Honor Society for the last two years), but I leaned on my essay, my mission statement about the universality of literature, about my love of learning, proving that I was ready for college. Ready to be at an institution where they would see me for my intellect.

The UPenn application required four personal statements and supplemental essays. Undaunted, I wrote multiple drafts in Bic pen on my yellow legal pad. I scratched out edits and moved sections around, slogged through them, essay after essay after essay.

> Essay 6A. If you were given the opportunity to spend an evening with any one person, living, deceased, or fictional, whom would you choose and why?

I must have been feeling punchy or cocky or stupid. On the UPenn essay 6A I wrote about wanting to have dinner with God. I had been reading Woody Allen's collected essays, *Side Effects*, and fancied myself a satirist. I went in for the comedic kill, typing out the essay, so sure that I had slayed it with my irreverence and sacrilegious humor. I was the best-read kid in my class. I had audited a college course and gotten an A. I was the editor of our school paper and the literary magazine, and in a frenzy of adolescent hubris and ego, and for the first time, I was absolutely confident in my greatness.

Punchy. Cocky. Stupid. But that was me, unapologetically so, and if UPenn didn't want me, then fuck them.

Applications mailed.

DECEMBER 1990

I emerged from the gas station's bathroom, shoving the reluctant yellow bucket in front of me as I rounded the corner into the cashier's office. After some robotic mopping motions, I tipped it over outside as it made a foul, retching sound and heaved its gray water into the curbside drain. I rattled the wheeled bucket and mop back into the utility closet. "Okay, that's it—the bathroom's cleaned."

Liam gave me a thumbs-up. He and I worked the Friday shift because those shifts, between the full-service pump and register, bustled with customers and full-service patrons. "How much time is left? Do we have time to play quarters?" He rooted in his pocket for change.

"Yeah, it's like nine thirty. Let's do it—it's not that cold outside." I pawed around in my pants for quarters when a police car pulled up in the full-service lane.

Liam and I were immediately nervous, and all the petty villainy we had been committing sprang to mind: stealing lawn ornaments, mailbox baseball, trashing an abandoned farmhouse—that was what I conjured in the ten seconds while the patrol car idled outside.

The door chimed as the officer entered. Black uniform. Shaggy brown hair. Matching mustache. Middle-aged. Moderate belly. Shoes well polished but worn. He carried a large white three-ring binder under his arm. As the doorbell dinged, he glanced at me intently—the cop-look where you can tell they're measuring you up—and I stood in the corner with the oil display.

Liam stayed fixed behind the counter, and I watched as the cop approached him, the officer's wide frame blocking the width of the counter, and with his dark uniform, he eclipsed the space so that I saw only Liam's face and his recently shaved head. Liam had an incredible, gee-willickers-boy-next-door shtick that had saved our asses on several occasions, and I knew it was best to let him do the talking.

"Good evening, Officer. Can I help you?" Nice and polite—well done, Liam. His calm was inversely proportional to my anxiety. I was still adding several other misdemeanors to my mental list, including putting parking cones on top of the Dickinson gym roof, skating in a few pools illegally, and pushing over some cows one drunken night in Dillsburg. The police officer was definitely not there to give us any community service awards.

He drawled in his Carlisle accent, distinctly more Dixie than Yankee. *Yew boiz werrrked 'ere las' week? Las' Thurrrsday nat?*

"I did—it was just me." Liam nodded.

The officer continued. "Did you see the robbery?" The robbery was the talk of our Mobil station—the 7-Eleven across the street had been held up, and the perpetrator had gotten away. Scott, our manager, had posted a memo, and we all clucked about it (and about how robbing a convenience store was another level of criminality that we couldn't imagine). We were content to tip cows and steal lawn gnomes, but brandishing a knife to steal a store's cash was in another league of lawlessness.

Liam shook his head. "No, I didn't. I mean, we heard about it from our manager, but I didn't see anything. It's all the way across the street. . . . I can barely see it as it is from here."

"So you didn't see anything?" The officer wanted to make sure.

"No, sir." Liam's *golly-shucks* was working overtime.

"Did you see the culprit? He was a black male."

"I didn't know that. But I didn't see anything." Any dread that I felt dissipated once I had heard that the officer was inquiring about the robbery and not about any of our hooliganism. I pretended to arrange the oil quarts in the corner, unsure of what else to do but absolutely sure that I should stay out of the cashier area. Their exchange paused for a moment, and the white three-ring binder thudded on the counter, rattling aside the Skoal penny tray.

"Would you recognize the black male if you saw him?" The officer flipped open the binder. Over the officer's shoulder, I could see Liam's face as he looked down at the binder. A slight tremor recoiled across his face, but he forced his brow to smooth itself and feign an adolescent indifference.

"What?"

"Take a look at these pictures. Do you recognize him in these photos?"

Liam didn't look down. "No, I don't recognize him. I didn't see anything—like I said." Liam's insistence had gone from redundant to desperate.

"Are you sure?" The officer continued to flip the laminated pages.

"Yes, I'm sure." Liam's face went cold and ashen, and I felt his eyes straining not to look at me.

The officer spoke clearly. "Listen, son." He kept turning the pages of the binder, the word *son* hanging between them—dirty white laundry on the line. "Don't you want to get another nigger off the streets?"

My dread returned, exponentially terrifying.

Liam's voice almost cracked, but he persevered. "I'm sorry, I can't help you. I didn't see anything."

The officer finished flipping through the binder for another five pages, then closed the back cover. "All right, boys. You call the station if you think you remember anything." He pivoted and walked out, never glancing at me as I stood motionless in the corner, leaning into my sagging throne of oil quarts.

We were dumbstruck and waited until the patrol car was well away.

Liam stared out the glass office. "What *the living fuck* was that?!" We couldn't look at each other, and surveyed the station lot in the fear that he might return.

My whole being was rattled. "Dude. What was he showing you? In the book?"

"Mug shots, I think. I don't know. . . . It was pictures of the black guys in town."

"Seriously? Like pictures from when they were arrested?"

"I don't know, man. They had pictures of some guys we're in school with, too. Franklin Jefferson? His picture was in there."

"What? He hasn't been arrested, has he? Franklin? He's still in high school."

"I don't know, man. . . . I don't know. What the fuck just happened?" Liam shook his head.

We closed up the Mobil and locked the doors, the gloom of the office now a cave in which we had witnessed a terrible revelation. I wished we could have locked the whole incident in the office, in the dark of the night.

Liam gave me a ride home. Our usual loud, music-filled drive was instead somber mileage, more inward than homeward. Liam occasionally muttered *what the fuck*, and we'd rehash the events of the whole exchange. This was our first run-in with someone in a position of power displaying such blatant racism. This was beyond anything that I was ready for. I had accumulated a thick calculus from years of experiencing bigotry, but it was mostly at the hands of other kids whom I could punch or verbally lash back at. But this incident didn't involve Klansmen or skinheads or Dirty Dan. This was a police officer. He was sworn to serve and protect. He had a club and a pistol. He had authority. And he had a binder with pictures of black men in our town.

My narrow definition of what a racist was had to expand, and in the aftermath, the circle widened to include, apparently, some police officers.

The reality of life was forcing me to face a vile truth whether I was willing or not.

A letter from the University of Pennsylvania informed me that I was scheduled for an alumni interview with the vice principal of a nearby high school. After some deliberation, I decided to tone down the punk rock look. This was for all my future marbles, and I didn't want some small-town, anti-punk sentiment to scuttle my shot at Penn, so instead of spiking my hair on top, I pushed it over into the semblance of a respectable haircut. I wore a button-down vintage shirt that I tucked in, a black London Fog trench coat, jeans, and boots. I looked funky and stylish but serious and ready for college.

The vice principal, Mr. Daughtery, seemed nice. He was tall and athletic, and had a firm handshake, fading cologne, salt-and-pepper hair, and wore a gray suit. We met in an archetypal principal's office (flag, ferns, degree from UPenn on the wall). He talked at length about being a UPenn man and about his classmates, their business ventures, and their subsequent successes, all of which emanated ostensibly from the wide-ranging and munificent springs of UPenn. I thought it was odd that he was making the sales pitch to me—a kid who had already signed up to be a Penn man. I was ready to enlist in this fraternity, the lauded Pennmanship.

As he was delivering his UPenn spiel, he opened a manila folder and leafed through what seemed, upside down to me, to be my application: my transcript, my SATs, presumably my essays. I couldn't tell if he had already read them or was now looking at them for the first time.

"Tell me about some classes that you're really enjoying, Phuc."

"Oh, well, I really love my honors English class, but I'm really trying to push myself in all areas. I don't know what I'll be good at, but I love reading, writing, and visual arts. And I think it's important to have a broad foundation, so I took a class last year—well, audited it—a Dickinson College religion class, 200 level. I got an A- in that class. But I love learning and reading and the universal nature of great books."

"Tell me more about that." He looked interested, resonating with my connection to literature.

"Gosh—well, I think that discussing literature has been a chance for me to strip away all the unimportant things, the superficial things. We're all people—we all struggle and strive for the same things: love, acceptance, a sense of place and belonging. That's the universal struggle, the human struggle. If you and I can connect with each other through a book, we're really transcending the superficial things, the external things, the things that divide us."

He was nodding vigorously. I was on a roll. "That's great. I absolutely agree with you about the universal nature of great literature."

I didn't know if I was beaming or not, but I felt as though I had the widest grin on my face.

"Well, I have to say, Phuc: your grades are pretty good."

I caught his tone in the way that he said *pretty good* and mounted my own clarification. "Thanks. I mean, school is really important to me, and I've been working hard, and that's why Penn is so—"

He cut me off, looking over one of the pages in the file. "But Asian students, they're really the cream of the crop, right?"

I didn't know how to reply to his assertion about Asian students. I glanced nervously across his desk, not wanting to interrupt him.

He paused, holding one page in particular. "I mean, the best kids at any high school, if they have Asian kids, those kids are usually at the top of their classes. Your transcript is very impressive, but I expect it from students like yourself—your people are very diligent. We have some top-notch Asian students here. But I love what you said about the literature thing. That literature thing is good—I'll be sure to mention it."

Was he complimenting me or seeing me through the lens of some Asian stereotype? Was he making racial assumptions about me? But wasn't he saying that Asian students were awesome? I'd never expected anyone to say that being Vietnamese was an asset, and now I was wrangling with that statement in the midst of a college interview. My head spun as I tried to recover and redirect the conversation, but I didn't know if I was successful. The rest of the interview was a blur, I was so derailed by his remark.

I drove home and glumly ate dinner. My mood went unnoticed by my family, its foulness indistinguishable from any other cantankerous day for Phuc. I wasn't about to tell them that the interviewer said that my transcript would have to be better because I was Asian—it galled me even more so after I had told him that I was connecting deeply on the universal level of literature. I was trying to tell him that I *didn't* want to see race, that I wanted to get past it. But he told me that he *did* see race and that I'd have to do better.

My suspicions about who and what was racist, its Caucasian chalk circle, was widening to now include a UPenn alumni interviewer. He emphasized my race when all I wanted to do was ignore it, and in my ignorance, the circle widened to include myself, too. I just didn't know it.

It would be decades before I could acknowledge how our conversation was showing two ends of the same pendular swing. See race. Don't see race.

SUNDAY AFTER CHURCH

We motored home along Hanover Street, and at the red light near the Hardee's, we observed a couple fighting outside a brick apartment building. Even with the car windows rolled up, we heard their muffled profanities, saw their shivering gestures and middle fingers, their tank tops and undergarments far too thin for the December weather. Husband and wife? Boyfriend and girlfriend? Who knew? We could see that the fight had taken itself to the streets.

The man and woman were Black.

My father stared at them and defrosted the silence. "Geez . . . look at those Black people. Look at them."

Lou caught my eye and nudged me. For two years, I had been ignoring most of what my father said as part of my truce with him (it was easier for our family), but this remark, his use of "those Black people," outraged me.

I stopped him from saying any more. "What did you just say?"

"What? I just said look at those Black people."

"What's *that* supposed to mean?"

"I mean look at them. Fighting on the street. Half dressed. On Sunday."

"What does *Black* have to do with anything? You don't know them."

"Well, they *are* Black. That's just a fact."

"Your tone, Dad. That was racist."

Lou jumped in. "Yeah, you can't say, 'Look at those Black people.' What does that even mean?"

My father was shocked that Lou and I were both so agitated. We were calm but intense. It wasn't a fight. The light had turned green, and he kept his eyes fixed in front of him. "Are they *not* Black? Of course they're Black. That's all that I said."

"It's the context—it's what you were implying. There was no point to saying anything about them being Black."

"Geez, you're too sensitive."

"No, Dad. You're not sensitive enough. That's the problem. Jeeeesus f—" I swallowed the *fucking Christ* before it escaped my mouth.

"Phúc! Don't say *Jesus* like that!" My mother proved my point about tone and context.

"Oh, now you care about my tone? Well, don't say *Black people* like it's an insult. Do you really think that you guys are treated any better by white people? *Those* people that you just saw? We're on the same side."

"Same side of what? America is a great country! Americans helped us escape and gave us so many opportunities. Same side with Black people? Same side of what?" My father turned his head to look at us while we idled at another red light.

Lou jumped in. "The same side of RACISM!"

My father grimaced. "We are *not* the same as Black people. We work hard—"

I exploded. "ARE YOU KIDDING ME?!?! Are you telling me that Black people don't work hard?! That's insane!" I wasn't about to let him or my mother start spouting off their bigoted ideas, which we'd heard all our lives from nearly all our relatives.

This was it. In our Ford Fairmont on a Sunday morning. I took a stand, Malcolm X T-shirt or not. "Dad, you *cannot* make general state-ments about an entire group of people. I'm not going to allow it. We don't like it when white people do it to us! How can you do it to others?"

My mother reinforced my father. "But what people say about Viet-namese people is mostly true. We work hard. . . ."

Lou jumped in—it was a full-on yelling battle royal now, and I was surprised to see Lou tagging into the ring to throw some polemical el-bows. (Was this an inspired upside of his punching Mason?) "Mom, you can have your own opinion, you know? You don't always have to side with what Dad says!" Lou, who didn't even know what the patriarchy was, was criticizing the entrenched patriarchy of Vietnamese culture.

I backed him up. "Yeah, Lou's totally right! Mom, you should have your own opinions! You don't have to have the same ideas as Dad."

The conversation had careened from racism to sexism in a sharp angle, and my father defended himself. "Of course your mother has her own opinions! Honey! Tell them! Tell them you have your own opin-ions!"

My mother nodded. "It's true, I do." She said it so earnestly, so un-aware that my father had commanded her, that both Lou and I started

screaming, hitting each other with disbelief over the irony of it all, yelling *are you kidding me?* and covering our faces at my mother's insistence
of her own independence.

We argued all the way home, neither the front nor back seats budg-
ing, and by the time we pulled into our driveway we were a house
divided against itself. It was our Vietnamese civil war in a microcosm:
generational, cultural, and racial.

Our respective bedroom doors slammed, and before long, I headed
off to the Mobil station for my Sunday shift. Relieved at the chance to
have a break from my parents, I pumped gas and did my homework,
sitting at the counter and tuning in to the public radio station.

The doors opened, and a voice drawled. "Do you people have any
oil? 10W-30?"

"I'm sorry, what?" Did he just say *you people*?

"You people have any 10W-30?" But then my ear recognized that
this was a different context and a different tone. "You people" being
tossed about in a casual way, meant to address anyone who was sitting
behind the counter.

"Oh . . . right. Yeah—right over there."

Maybe my dad was right: Maybe I was too sensitive. *You people*
wasn't always a secret way of saying something bigoted. But I had heard
it from a mechanic. I had heard it from a University of Pennsylvania
alumnus. I had heard it from my father. In those instances, there lurked
a subtle judgment, yet I couldn't quite articulate it.

It was easy to spot racism when it shaved its head, drew a swastika,
and wore Doc Martens with white laces. But what about when it came
to your coworkers? Or during the college application process? The
police? Your parents? You and your friends who said the *n*-word without
flinching?

Who were the racists now? I suspected the answer and didn't want
to say it aloud. The answer slithered all around me, on the streets, in
the patrol cars, across the interview desks. It was even in the mirrors.

This was the real lesson I learned from Malcolm X, the one I had been avoiding, and like Malcolm, I had to evolve my own thinking. But for me, that meant confronting a hideous truth about who the racists were. This was the hardest thing he had written about. It would be a long time before I could begin to understand how big racism was and how it affected me, but I had to take the first step, to acknowledge the reality of life, to tackle the hardest truth if I wanted to fight it.

We all were the racists.

| II |

THE ILIAD

DECEMBER 1990, ENGLISH CLASS

Oh, for fuck's sake. I rolled my eyes back into my head, pupils rounding the full orbit, and I swore I saw the blackness of my own cranial cavity.

Grace and Sarah were arguing that *The Iliad* was pointless and had no relevance to their lives, their lives as two seventeen-year-old girls from Carlisle, PA. Homer vs. girls wearing Swatches and ponytails? It was what you would have expected teenagers to say about an ancient Greek bard, and I couldn't restrain myself.

I raised my hand, and finally Mrs. Ferguson called on me. "You guys, it's about greatness and power. It's about being the best at something and still not having power." I couldn't tell if Grace and Sarah were playing dumb or were actually just dumb.

Sarah shrugged. "I don't get it. We all know what it means to be the best at something. You win the contest or whatever. That's how we know you're the best. How does that not give you power?"

I nodded. "Exactly. That's the exact question that Homer is asking:

What's it mean to achieve greatness and to be powerless? What if you win the proverbial contest and you're still not the best?"

Grace jumped in, only tangentially picking up Sarah's point. She was doing that thing where kids just give a plot summary under the guise of analysis. "The Trojans steal Helen (sort of). The Greeks are mad about it. And the Greeks are also fighting with each other. This just doesn't mean anything to me. But it's my opinion, Phuc. You're entitled to yours, but you can't bully other people into thinking that something is a classic or a great book. We know you like it, and no one is trying to convince you that you can't like it. We're just saying that it's boring and irrelevant to us—*to us.*"

I pretended to die on my desk, thudding my forehead on my chable's top, crying out an epic groan worthy of a Homeric simile. My classmates laughed at the dramatics. I liked Sarah and Grace, but I was sure that they were so wrong. "That's fine to have your opinion. But I want you to see what you're missing. I'm not trying to convince you that your feelings are wrong. I'm saying that there's more work to be done on your part beyond reading a book and deciding whether you liked it or not. That's lazy Siskel-and-Ebert thinking. This is not about giving Homer one or two thumbs up—this is about asking: What is Homer trying to figure out? Okay, look: Let's take tennis, for example. Grace, you're one of the best tennis players on the team. And everyone says that you're the best, and you always beat your opponents. But what if you weren't allowed to be the team captain? And what if, even though you were the best, you got benched by the captain?"

"That wouldn't make sense. Why would the captain bench me?"

"EXACTLY! That's the conflict between Achilles and Agamemnon. Achilles has physical power, but Agamemnon, a freakin' idiot, is the one who has political power. So what do you do when the captain benches you and then the team is losing the game or the season? Do you quit the team? Do you argue with the captain that you should be put back in? Try to convince her that you're worth it?"

Sarah jumped in. "But everyone on the team knows that Grace is the best tennis player."

"Totally. You get it, Sarah—you just named the other problem. There's shame involved when, within the whole group, you're the best but not the most powerful." The girls nodded in agreement to my point, but I didn't stop. "These are some of the essential questions of *The Iliad*. Achilles's conundrum is complicated because he is the best fighter on the Greek side but not the leader of the Greeks and then he's shamed in front of the whole group. The MVP on the team but not the captain of the team. And there's this same issue between society and war—the underlying tension between political power and military power. It's a tangled, social mess that involves people, politics, and the power of the group. If the group decides that you aren't powerful, if someone else in power decides that you are not the winner, then *you are not the winner*. Too bad. And then you really have to ask yourself: What does it even mean to achieve greatness if that doesn't determine power or status? What does it mean, then, to be great or to be the best? Does it even matter? I don't know. . . . I don't know if it even matters, at least in society. In war, you kill or be killed, and it's simple for Achilles. But in the political system, Achilles can't figure it out—the system seems rigged. I mean, maybe it is all rigged."

Another one of my tirades in English class, one that left a burbling wake of quasi-nihilism, silent stares, and awkward book thumbing. Mrs. Ferguson nodded. "Okay, thanks for that, Phuc. Let's make some room for other voices, people we haven't heard from." I nodded at the irony of it.

I had finished saying my piece about greatness and power, and Mrs. Ferguson was subtly (and rightly) asking me to shut the fuck up so other kids could throw in their two cents—kids who probably hadn't done the homework, didn't care about Homer, or had no clue. I didn't want to say that I was Achilles, but I felt as though I were in a class full of Agamemnons. The system was all rigged. What did it matter if I was the best student in our English class? It didn't seem to matter in the college admissions process, because the candidate pool was so much bigger than I had anticipated, and the rules were not what I had thought they were. I was a good candidate, but apparently, not good enough for an Asian student.

My confidence was shaken by the alumni interview and left me feeling like maybe I wasn't really good or great at anything. Whatever blue ribbons or gold keys I had attained over the last few years felt like inconsequential tin badges. Those weren't the laurels of the battlefield—they were scholastic prizes doled out by a faceless committee, and the awards had no effect and bestowed upon me no special privileges, especially in the admissions process.

Earning good grades and the respect of my classmates, I was still hounded by a feeling of being the outsider, by a ghostly, piercing voice that told me I didn't belong there. And in my punk crew, in which we wore our outsider status proudly, I had to admit to myself: I didn't actually want to be an outsider anymore. My crew was bound by our ostracism, and my membership in our group was an ironic and short-lived salve to stanch my deeper wound, my gaping need to find my place.

And it wasn't just about achieving greatness in a vacuum—I wanted people to acknowledge it, too. *Star Wars* didn't end with Luke blowing up the Death Star—it ended with him getting a medal and having everyone clapping for him. The climax was his achievement of greatness *and* his public praise. In retrospect, my desire was so simple yet impossible to fulfill alone, as if I were trying to play tag by myself. I needed other people, and that need felt embarrassing; it felt weak to admit it, but it was true. I wanted to feel like a valued member of my school and my town even as I rejected my town and my school (punk rock, you're so confusing). I didn't even feel like a member of my own home, the place where I felt least safe and hardly regarded.

And atop those tangled feelings and desires was my own self-perception. Even if I were publicly celebrated, if my peers did value me, would I believe them? Would it be a futile effort to extol someone like me, who felt so low, eroded by so many insults and exclusions, large and small? How could I rise up from that? How could any feeling of agency or power bloom from such muck and mire?

The worries about greatness, power, and shame weren't just Homer's—they were my worries, too.

JANUARY 1991

When I worked at the Coral Reef at the mall, I had become friendly with a bookstore clerk, Damon, at Waldenbooks. He was working on his MFA in creative writing at Penn State, and I'd stop into the store even after I had left the mall job to chat about books, pick up discounted titles or a magazine. Damon always made time for a friendly debate even as his pile of reading or clerical duties mounted high to his left. We'd argue about Faulkner, James, or Proust, and he'd tell me about his MFA program in graduate school, about which I knew nothing.

Our talk that January turned to my college applications, and I mentioned the three schools to which I had applied.

"Did you look at Bard College?"

"Bard?" I'd never heard of it, but he could have listed off all the Ivy Leagues and top-tier liberal arts colleges, and I wouldn't have recognized half of them, either. "I haven't heard of Bard. What's it like?"

"Oh, it's a funky school. Artsy. Punky. You'd love it. I mean Hampshire, Reed, St. John's, they're all liberal arts schools. But I think you'd really love Bard." I was sold as soon as I heard *punky*. A college for punk rock kids? I sent away for the prospectus and when I got it two weeks later, I felt a shiver of shared humanity. The brochure read *BARD COLLEGE: A Place to Think.*

Fucking *yes.* A place to think. A place that cherished and nurtured the process of intellectual pursuits. This wouldn't be a college that would check my jockstrap or fail me for gym class or make me get hall passes whenever I was late.

But then I saw that it was in a small town. The description of Annandale-on-Hudson was idyllic and, for me, revolting. Annandale-on-Hudson was not the metropolises of New York or Philadelphia. It appeared to be the splinter of an outpost, one hundred miles north of New York City. But everything else about Bard sounded like it would be a haven for me, so I convinced myself that this seemed within the orbit of the city and that New York State was still closer to New York City than anywhere else.

I filled out the Bard application last minute and convinced my reluctant parents to write a fourth check for the application fee. They wondered who needed to apply to four colleges, but once I explained to them that Bard offered a special scholarship for students who graduated with a top-ten GPA of their high school (matching their state school's tuition for their four years), they relented. That seemed like an incredible opportunity. I put the Bard brochure at the bottom of the stack.

I still had all my urban university hopes pinned blindly on UPenn or NYU—despite the fact that I had not visited either of those campuses—and if my first two choices denied me, I would maybe go to Bard. If all three options failed, I would go to Penn State and transfer somewhere else later. And regardless, any of those college selections were better than the armed forces, whose recruitment officers were harassing me weekly because Conor—thanks, you dick—had jokingly listed me as a likely candidate. The recruiters called often, and my parents panicked that I would be drafted and flown off to Operation Desert Storm to fight for Kuwaiti freedom and cheap oil. Sometimes the recruiters would even come to our house, knocking on our door in full dress uniform. If I had taken a moment to empathize, to pull my head out of my own ass, I would have seen real dread in my parents' eyes, a dread that was stitched with their old-world experience, dyed by the blood of drafted brothers and cousins, and sewn into a long, unwinnable war.

In retrospect, I realized how my parents draped the hopes of college and greatness upon me, their eldest born. They snuffed out their own ambitions, exchanging their dreams for their children's, hoping that our lives would be full of possibilities and free from devastation. My vague but lustrous potential would be built upon the heavy shards of their broken futures.

FEBRUARY 1991, FRIDAY NIGHT

Our band, Squareback (named after Nate's Volkswagen Squareback), had finished practice. Rehearsal was winding down in Liam's basement, and we were fooling around, taking turns on the bass, guitars, drums, and the mic. Byron was really good on drums, but the rest of us were equally bad on vocals, guitars, and bass, and you couldn't tell if the right person was playing the wrong instrument. Liam's parents, long-suffering of skateboard sessions and impromptu parties at their house, were happy to support the band—a relatively safe, zero-crime enterprise—and to tolerate the five of us rehearsing in the basement because it meant that they knew we were not getting into trouble. We had all had various encounters with Carlisle Police at this point (tickets, summonses, license suspensions). So there we were in the basement—Nate, Liam, Byron, Gabe, and I—rehearsing our eight songs for an upcoming show at the Mifflin High School gym.

I had traded guitars with Gabe, and we switched our effects pedals. "Hey, do you guys want to try something a little different? I've been listening to My Bloody Valentine, and they have a really cool sound. It's not exactly our sound, but it's got a lot of distortion and noise. Let me show you." I detuned his guitar to an open E chord, turned up the volume and reverb, plugging in the delay and distortion pedals. I struck a sequence of chords that made a woozy, minor-key progression, up and down, churning and throbbing. It was slow and simple enough that Byron starting playing along on drums, and Liam jumped in on bass, and Gabe started playing a riff on top of the noise. We churned on the chord progression for a while, and Nate started yelling some lyrics.

I shouted out to Nate over the music, which didn't sound half bad.

"YOU DON'T REALLY YELL TO THIS. . . . I MEAN . . . IT'S NOT EX-
ACTLY A PUNK SONG. . . . JUST SING . . . LIKE SING SOMETHING IN-
STEAD OF YELLING IT. . . ."

Nate had never properly sung anything, and we didn't know if he'd
be able to carry a—nope. Totally off-key. Terrible. After a few minutes,
we all knew it wasn't working with the vocals and we stopped playing.

Nate shrugged. "That's not really my thing, dude. Singing, I mean."

Gabe couldn't resist. "Oh, 'cause you thought lead *singer* meant something else? Or was our flyer for a lead singer misleading because you
have the literacy of a third grader?" Laughter and an exchange of middle fingers. Gabe gave me a thumbs-up. "That sounded cool, Phuc. We
should do more songs like that." Byron nodded from behind the drums
and assented.

Nate shook his head. "That's cool if that's what you're into, but it's
not what I signed up for. I ain't singing, at least not like that."

Liam nodded. "Yeah, it's not exactly sounding like what we said we
were going to play."

"No, I get it. That's cool—we have a harder sound. The songs we
have are good. The Mifflin show'll be cool." I said it nonchalantly, but I
was disappointed as we were bumping up against the limits of punk and
arguing about what our band was supposed to sound like. Why couldn't
punks play something other than punk? Did that mean we weren't punks
anymore? But what would be more punk than being authentic to yourself? I decided it wasn't worth bringing up as I unplugged my guitar.

As we all spooled our amp cables and helped Byron break down his
drum kit, Liam and Nate discussed getting food at a truck stop. "Let's go
to the All-American. You guys in?"

Gabe and I shook our heads.

Byron needled me and Gabe. "The fuck you guys doing? Too cool to
hang out with the boys on a Friday night?"

"Oh no, you're very handsome, all of you, but, uh . . ." I paused. "I
have plans to hang out with Molly." I had started hanging out with a
girl in the eleventh grade, Molly, whom I had met on a National Honor

Society field trip. It was the most fucking nerdy way to meet a girl, but there we were now, dating and making plans for a Friday night.

Nate high-fived me. "Nice, Phucster. Good choice. I'd *totally* choose getting my dick sucked over hanging out with us, too."

I frowned at his remark. "It's not like that."

Nate looked horrified. "No suckee-suckee?"

"Dude, no. We don't do it like that," I said, ignoring Nate's fake Asian accent in his joke.

"Oh, kinky! Tell me what it's like then? I'm all ears!"

"We just hang out. Talk."

Liam jumped in. "Talk?! What do you talk about? About the lack of blow jobs happening?"

These guys were my crew, so I decided to just be honest. "We talk about movies, music, books, whatever's on our minds. It's nice— actually, it's really cool. She's cool—I'll bring her around."

Nate piped up. "Does Molly have any friends who will suck dicks?" We all groaned.

I shook my head. "Jesus, man. At least have the self-respect to use the phrase *my dick*. The plural *dicks* is gross. She's not on the fucking turnpike handing out blow jobs like candy."

Nate snorted. "*Excusé moi*, Professor AP Literature. Does my use of the plural offend you? Let me rephrase the question: Does your Molly have any friends who will suck my singular dick?"

I laughed that even my crew had picked up on my reputation as the literature guy. "Professor AP Literature? Nate, come on. We all know you don't even know how to spell AP. And no, Molly does not have any friends who will suck dicks or dick. And not your dick."

Byron packed up his kick drum. "Well, she sounds very reasonable if she ain't sucking down bags of dicks at the turnpike. You should bring her to a Squareback show sometime." I shrugged a *maybe*, and everyone turned their attention to Gabe.

"Okay, Gabe—Phucster's got an excuse. What's yours? We *know* you don't have a date. Not going out with us to the All-American? We can show you a good time, big boy. . . ." Nate reached up and cupped his own chest, caressing it like a pair of breasts to emphasize the enticement of *big boy* while Gabe shook his head.

"Nope, sorry—I gotta finish the intake on the Nova. It's the last thing to do and then she's up and running. You guys are gonna fucking love how fast she is." Gabe lit up as he talked about his car, his prized possession—a maroon '71 Chevy Nova restoration he was doing with his brother and dad.

Outside, Nate, Liam, and Byron piled the amps, drums, and themselves into Byron's car. "Okay . . . suit yourselves. We'll give you guys a call tomorrow night?"

"Totally—Gabe's giving me a ride home. I'll see you guys later." Gabe and I gave quick waves as he and I got into his parents' car. On the ride home, we talked about forming a side project to play different music, although Gabe was reluctant about playing just acoustic guitars, which was too much of a departure, even for him.

In my driveway, he popped the trunk for me to grab my guitar. "So what movie are you and Molly going to watch while she's *not* giving you a blow job?"

I laughed. "You guys and your fucking blow jobs. There's more to life than sex, you know?"

"But not much more."

"Anyway, you're going to love the title then. *Sex, Lies, and Video-tape.*"

He shrieked in disbelief. "WHAT? How are you NOT going to get a blow job from this movie?"

"It's not like that! I just like talking to her, and yeah, we make out and shit, but it's different—like we enjoy similar things, but not exactly the same shit. It's fun to talk to Molly. She's got a brain and she's cool. . . . I don't know."

Gabe got quiet. "It does actually sound awesome."

"It *is* awesome, actually."

"But you have to agree: it'd be better with blow jobs."

"I'm not answering that."

"I'll take that as a yes." Gabe laughed and patted my back sympathetically as I headed into the house.

Molly was my first official girlfriend in high school, and she wasn't a covert after-school affair like Charlotte was in ninth grade. Molly wasn't into punk or so-called alternative music, but she was funny and smart, and as a junior, she blushed in the attention that I, a senior boy, lavished upon her.

My parents liked Molly—a nice Irish Catholic girl who went to Saint Patrick's, played the cello, and waved to them at mass. In turn, Molly's parents were kind, a bit wary of me, but ultimately warm and loving. At first, they didn't know what to make of our dating. Who was surprised that teenage boys were foulmouthed and single-minded in their pursuits? But between Molly and me, my heart wasn't drawn to easy sex. And it soon became apparent to even her parents that I really cared for her and that our relationship wasn't wham-bam-thank-you-ma'am. If anything, it was a bonnet-upon-it-I-wrote-you-a-sonnet.

In our kitchen, she made small talk with my parents about school and her parents and last week's homily at mass, and then my parents retired to their bedroom by nine p.m. Lou had a sleepover at a friend's house, and in the living room, we put in the VHS cassette that I had rented from West Coast Video.

As the piracy warning flickered, she nuzzled into my shoulder. "So what's this movie about?"

"Well, the title might tell us since it's *Sex, Lies, and Videotape*."

"Clever title. So subtle. It's a porno then?"

"Jesus, you couldn't pay me to watch porn with my parents down the hall. Also, how dare you insinuate that I would make you watch porn? I would definitely tell you first. And the title wouldn't be so obvious— porn titles have weird puns in them like *Flesh Gordon* or *Little Whores on the Prairie*. Classy titles like that. This is an indie film. It's supposed to be . . . ahhhht." I stretched out the word *art* in a British accent and pretended to adjust a monocle and stroke my imaginary beard.

Molly rolled her eyes. "I'll be the judge of that. Speaking of real art, I finished the Ibsen play. Thanks for the recommendation—I loved it."

"Right? It's so good, right? Fuckin' *Doll's House*. So brutal and honest."

She nodded. "Definitely. It's feels so modern—the feminism in it."

"I know, right? But also surprising that a man wrote it . . ."

"Shhhhh! Save it for another time. Movie's starting."

I pecked her on the top of her head, her French braids still smelling faintly of shampoo. "Oh, Byron asked at band practice if . . ." But Molly shushed me again before I could invite her to the show, and I changed my mind. She probably wouldn't enjoy it, and I didn't want the crew to meet her and then later reduce her to tits and ass and the predictable blow job potential, which they would have done. Our relationship felt private, and I wanted to keep it for myself.

If Norman Rockwell had painted an idyllic romance between a punk rock Vietnamese kid and an Irish Catholic girl, we were that *Post* cover. We spent weekends watching movies on the couch or debating books, movies, and music in a booth at one of the many truck stop diners that dotted Route 11. We talked endlessly over fries steaming with gravy, ordering more cups of coffee to rent our table for another forty-five minutes. Lovebirds, late-night hawks at the diner, conjuring the most magical, grandest ideas that we could summon. There was a purity, an innocence, that I didn't want defiled or sullied by my friends who sexualized everything and everyone.

And even among my friends, there was developing a complexity and nuance for our punk scene. I saw change in all of us. Our definition of what was and wasn't punk was evolving and we would need to evolve with it or we would be choked by it. The crew couldn't allow ourselves to be ostracized by our own punk fundamentalism. We'd been together too long and been through so much—we were brothers in arms, besieged and beset. At the end of high school, my needs and interests had grown (and changed), but all our friends were intellectually and emotionally in different places and wanting different goals.

Thankfully, my friends were my friends, and we cheered one another on, regardless of how we dressed, what we listened to, and what our other goals were besides getting drunk and going to shows. The rednecks and jocks were still dicks, and we still had to stick together. By a wordless decree, we chose one another and supported our friendship, celebrating whatever we were doing, whether it was the military or the university or the mediocrity.

Did the crew care that I was the editor of the paper, editor of the literary magazine, a member of Quizbowl, and other nerdy shit? They didn't. Instead of getting shit about it, I got a nod and a "Fuck yeah—I'm glad one of us got in there," as if I were a double agent. To them, the punk rock Phuc was the authentic Phuc, and the nerdy, bookish Phuc was doing what he had to do to infiltrate the system, a punk rock Trojan horse snuck in behind the ivory walls of academia. I had recently written an editorial that satirized the desire to be cool, mocking the pursuit of popularity, and my friends read it as a social grenade hurled across enemy lines. "Dude, first the racism editorial, and now this? You are fucking shredding on people." They were right. I *was* on a rampage, but it was in *every* direction, sarcastic shrapnel hurled indiscriminately by an insecure boy who wanted so badly to belong and to feel that he was achieving greatness.

MARCH 1991

I found out that I was waitlisted at UPenn, but I didn't call or write the university to say that I wanted to matriculate there. It was called the waitlist, not the beglist. I didn't know whether my alumni interview had helped me or not, and the UPenn waitlist was hopeful enough for me to keep my big city dreams bustling.

I got into Penn State. While I was relieved that I would be going somewhere, I was indifferent to the prospects of the biggest state school in PA. My parents and Lou roundly congratulated me for my first college acceptance.

But then I got a large white envelope from NYU the next week. It was after school, and I tore it open, and I saw the word: *Congratulations*. I had gotten into NYU.

I called *everyone*, did a crazy dance—that whole celebratory montage that you see on TV when someone hits the jackpot. NYU was my first choice, far beyond UPenn, and I was finally heading to *the* city.

I told Mrs. Krebs and Mrs. Romberger at school and thanked them for their support, and they hugged me in congratulations.

"NYU's a great school—you're going to love New York! You think New York is ready for you?" Mrs. Krebs beamed, and in her accolades, I was radiant, knowing that I had attained some measure of greatness, that the college application process validated it.

But the celebration was short-lived. Two weeks later, my parents sat me down, the purple NYU folder splayed out in front of them. My father resuscitated his long-dormant law degree to make their case, dispassionate and impartial. They'd done the math and scrutinized the financial aid. The numbers did not lie, and I wasn't supposed to take it personally. The mathematics of it said *no* even as my emotions wailed *why*. "Phúc, we can't afford NYU. They didn't give you enough financial aid, and we still need to plan for Lou's college in three years." The blows were mercifully short because of how volatile my parents' relationship was with me—a powder keg that could be ignited with a few sharp words sparked against fragile egos. My father was monotonous and direct in his delivery. Just the facts. I couldn't be mad at Lou, but I felt no ripples of emotions, or empathy, from my parents. "At least you're still going to Peng Stay."

"Can't I take out loans?" Holding out for some sleight of miracle, some financial Three-Card-Monte, my chest heavy at the news. I couldn't look at my father in the kitchen, me sitting in my seat, him sitting in his. This was where he had tried to kill me with scissors. For a moment I wished that he had succeeded, my disappointment was so unbearable.

"You don't want to graduate college with so much debt—it will be terrible for you. And if you default on your loan, we will have to pay it." Classy of him to assume that I would default on my debt.

"Jesus, Dad. I won't default on the loan."

"Don't say God's name in vain." That was all my mother said as they were immolating my NYU dreams: not to take God's fucking name in fucking vain.

"We can't cosign for you." *Can't or won't?* I wondered. It was semantics. I mumbled a weak assent.

I had told everyone at school—my peers, the crew, my teachers—that I was going to NYU. Molly gave me a card to congratulate me, writing in purple pen: "NYU will be so lucky to have you!" Everyone told me what a great school it was. Everyone told me how they saw me fitting right in in New York City. Fitting in—that was the dream.

And in addition to *not* going to NYU, I now had to tell everyone that we were too poor to afford it. Some group somewhere—some committee with the power of admission—had decided that I was great enough to get in, but not that great. Or at least not as great as I had hoped I was, and the public backtracking was humiliating for me.

My father concluded, "We can look at Bard's financial aid if you get in. But at this point, it'll be Peng Stay unless Bard is the same price. Then you can decide." I nodded and left the table wordlessly.

I didn't have tears for this disappointment. Crying seemed a small measure for getting into the college of my dreams but not being able to pay for it. Crying would change nothing. In my room, I looked at the Penn State paperwork, the brochure, the statistics. Tens of thousands of kids, all smiling, wearing their Nittany blue and cheering on the football factory that was Joe Paterno's Nittany Lions. Penn State's size, its student body, was epic, and their winning legacy was legendary. But football and a campus that worshipped sports with papal reverence? That didn't seem ideal for me, but it was a pill that I could swallow. I had hoped for something bigger and better after Carlisle. Penn State only seemed bigger.

I looked at Bard's brochures again. The course catalog had interesting classes. One thousand students—that was even smaller than Carlisle High School. I reexamined the tagline for the brochure: a place to think. I didn't get a sweaty whiff of sports or jocks or anything like that. The team mascots were the Blazers, whatever the hell that was. Bard didn't even have a logo—unlike Penn State's slicked-back lion head. Between Bard and Penn State, it seemed like a no-brainer—and I remembered Bard's top-ten scholarship. It would cost me the same as Penn State if I were in the top-ten GPA of my class.

The next day, I stopped by the guidance counselor's office.

"Hi there . . . could you tell me what my class rank is?"

"Do you need an official transcript?"

"Oh no—just my class rank. My last name is Tran."

A secretary shuffled about in a filing cabinet, pulled out a manila folder, and jotted a number down on a scrap of paper, sliding it across the counter as if it were unseemly to say it aloud, like a chlamydia test result.

I looked at the square scrap for a moment, thinking of the ten numbers that would guarantee me state-school tuition at Bard. I panicked: What if I were number ten? Did being number ten mean that I was still within the top ten? Or did tenth place mean that I was not within the top ten? Did the scholarship say *in* or *within*? It couldn't possibly mean *within*, could it? I thought about Casey Kasem's top ten lists, MTV's top ten lists, which always included numbers one through ten. I was overthinking it. This was stupid. Of course even tenth place would be top ten.

But it didn't matter, because I turned the paper over and saw the number 14. The fourteenth best GPA in a class of 313. Fucking fuck. Without top-ten GPA status, Bard's tuition would not be as affordable as Penn State's tuition. I would have to go to Penn State.

I kept this information all to myself, allowing the aura of NYU matriculation and the UPenn waitlist to halo myself with the corona of supposed greatness. It felt good for people to think that I was going to

NYU, that I was a good student, even if the perception was a shanty, bundled together with half lies and wholehearted hopes.

APRIL 1991

During last period, AP Calculus, Mr. Drake burbled in over the intercom to make an announcement. "I'm pleased to announce that the class of 1991 has voted for its graduation speakers. Congratulations to the following students: Matt Crum, Sam Miller, Latrice Hebron, and Phuc Tran."

Holyshitholyshitholyshit. I tried not to smile—I thought it would have looked arrogant—but an irrepressible smile broke my stoicism. "Whoa . . . oh man . . ." Everyone in the room clapped and smiled at me.

Greg turned around in his seat to shake my hand. "All right, Tranman! Congratulations!" He was beaming as brightly as I was shining inside. I tried to not let my classmates know how much it meant to me, but they could all see it from the look on my face. I felt exposed, but in their recognition, they caught me and held me up.

It was the affirmation I had wanted. This was my Luke-Skywalker-getting-his-medal moment.

"Thanks, Greg. I'm *really* surprised."

"Surprised? No way! People *love* you!" Greg said it so quickly, I was sure he didn't even think about it, but those words—*people love you*—spread over me in a molten flow, warming every extremity. *People loved me?* Could I let myself believe it? The people had spoken. And voted. And loved. They wanted me to speak at graduation. My heart was buoyed by Greg's sincere excitement for me.

My head was full of nothings for the last few minutes of class as the announcement about graduation speakers was still replaying itself in my mind. I had hoped—wildly dreamed—that in my most far-flung aspirations, the senior class would vote for me to speak for them. *And they had.* I would walk up on that stage and command the microphone for a few minutes. Me. The kid who had started out in this country with one shoe and a weird name—I was going to be a graduation speaker.

In my fog, I forgot to write down the homework assignment and was slow to pack up my books. Mr. Cook pulled me aside as kids trickled out of class. "Hey, Phuc! I knew you'd be one of the speakers." He pumped my hand and grinned.

"Thanks, Mr. Cook." My face tightened as though tears were imminent. He kept pumping my hand for a few moments after we stopped talking, smiling widely.

If my election as graduation speaker was an Achilles moment, my conversation with my father was an Agamemnon moment. At dinner that night, breaking from my usual routine of sharing nothing with them, I told my parents about being elected to be a graduation speaker. My mom didn't understand fully the honor or the validation of it, but she did her mom thing. "That's great, honey!" she Vietnamesed.

My father was mid-chew, dipping some beef into hot sauce. "Oh, so you'll give a speech?"

"Yeah, I'll be speaking at graduation."

"Why you?"

I could tell he was asking to annoy me, but I wasn't going to be goaded into an argument with him; I was not going to let him have power in this moment. "Well, I'm the editor of the newspaper. Maybe they think I have something to say."

"And do you? Do you have anything to say?" He kept eating, shoveling rice into his mouth, his comments tossed off haphazardly.

"Well, I have to think about it." I was starting to get annoyed.

"You can't think of anything for your speech?"

"I will, Dad. Oh my G— Just forget it." I regretted bringing any of it up and stuffed my mouth full of beef and bok choy. His only power was to aggravate me, and I was not going to let him have it.

My father wouldn't let it drop. "How many other kids are speaking?"

"Four. Well, four kids and the valedictorian. Just forget it."

"So five? That's a lot of speakers. Who's the valedictorian? Not you, right?" His tone implied that it wasn't special to be one of five speakers, and he reminded me that I was not the valedictorian.

"Jacob Royal. He's the valedictorian."

Lou jumped in. "What's a valedictorian?"

My father cut me off before I answered. "The best student in the graduating class."

I shot back. "Good grades don't necessarily mean that he's the best student."

Lou looked at me. "So you got voted to give a speech even though you're not the valedictorian? That sounds pretty good to me."

I nodded. "Thanks, Lou. I'm really excited." I didn't want to say anything more about it at dinner, given how my father was shitting all over my moment of greatness. I had brought up being graduation speaker because I wanted to share it with my family. Why? Because no matter how alienated I felt from my parents, I kept returning to a deep and undeniable need for their praise and approval. What would have made being graduation speaker better? Knowing that my parents were proud of me, really proud, and feeling that they really saw me. It was a gamble I took, and I was poorly rewarded by my mother's reflexive praise and my father's cutting inquiry. Another failed connection for our history books.

After dinner, I sat in my bedroom and made some notes about my speech. I wanted to deliver a great one—that much I knew. I assumed that this was my first and probably last moment to address so many people, and the graduation speech had to be my best effort. I had to seize my moment of greatness, my *aristeia*.

Aristeia in ancient Greek means "moment of greatness" or "moment of being the best." In *The Iliad* there are countless episodes where a warrior has an *aristeia*. Video-game kids would call this beast-mode. It's the highlight reel of battle, full of lopped-off limbs and gnashing of teeth and another foe biting the dust. It was a manifestation of what I yearned for—my peers' recognition in the spectacle of a singular feat, a synthesis of greatness and accolades.

My graduation speech was going to be my *aristeia*.

I came home from the gas station on Wednesday evening, and my parents *and* Lou were waiting for me at the kitchen table. Surprised, I immediately scanned my conscience for what I was in trouble for (still such a long list), but that inquiry stopped quickly.

"You got mail from Barg College." My father's accent (the difficulty of switching from *d* to *c*) made a phonetic fun-house mirror of Bard College.

"Oh—I guess that must be the admission decision and maybe financial aid stuff."

My mother pointed only to the most obvious things as indicators of good news. "Yes. It's a *big* envelope. So big. That's good news—I know it." Classic Mom.

"It doesn't mean anything, Mom." I tore the edge without fanfare. *Congratulations* . . . blah . . . blah . . . blah . . . *welcome to Bard College* . . . blah . . . blah . . . blah . . . I had gotten in. "Dad, how much is Penn State?"

"About five thousand dollars. How much did you get from Barg College? What will it cost?"

"Well . . ." I looked at the numbers and various line items. "I got accepted. It costs about twenty thousand a year, but they gave me fifteen thousand in aid. So it's . . . it's going to be the same as Penn State?" I didn't dare to say it as a declarative statement.

"*Really?* That's good news for you. I guess you'll have to decide between Barg College and Peng Stay."

Bard had granted me the top-ten scholarship, even though I was fourteenth in my class. Some group, somewhere—some committee—had decided that I was worth it. I was graduating and would attend Bard. I was going to speak at graduation. With a few weeks of school left, I was going to make it. For a moment I felt great.

I got to school the next day, and a different group decided that I was *not* great.

When the morning bus spewed me forth into the parking lot, I was met by a phalanx of the auto shop kids. Grease. Denim. Mullets. Travis stood at their fore and brandished his cigarette pack.

Travis and I caught each other's eye. We hadn't had any scrapes since middle school and had reached an unspoken détente, but maybe he felt that our time was slipping away, that he had a narrowing window to be a dick to me. Once more for old time's sake.

Travis looked right at me. "HEY! GO BACK TO 'NAM, YOU FUCKING FREAK!" Guffaws ensued, hand-slapping and high fives.

I stared at them all. "Fuuuuuuuuuuck you." Both of my middle fingers for the hearing impaired.

They fired back. "No, fuck *you*, you fucking gook!" More guffaws.

It was 7:45 a.m., and all the other kids in my bus procession pretended not to hear our exchange, even though it echoed across the lot. Travis's announcement in the parking lot brought me back to reality. With the leaden weight of *gook* slung around my neck, I was dragged back in my place at the familiar bottom. Back to 'Nam. It didn't matter that I was going to speak at graduation or going to Bard or that I was on the prom court or any of that crap. I had felt an uneasiness at the top, an unfamiliarity—I knew what the bottom felt like. I was still, shocking even to myself, a gook no matter how hard I tried not to be. Their admissions committee had decided.

Outnumbered, I stormed off to meet up with my crew, my face burning hot and my eyes welling. I had been humiliated in front of everyone in the parking lot. While the other kids had ignored Travis's insults, there was no way that they hadn't heard them. I felt a sharp and white pain like never before. This was the pain of the fall. I had just been celebrated, supposedly, by everyone, and in less than a day, I had been belittled in front of everyone.

When I got to our meeting spot, I was enraged. I had snapped, and my wounded ego was now just blindingly enflamed. The feeling of belonging—the feeling of being loved—capsized, its flimsiness all too apparent. Could you sink a whole ship with one hole? Apparently, you could. My fears and insecurities weighed so much heavier than anyone's love and light.

Liam, Nate, Stephen, and a few others were milling around. I threw my bag down. "Fucking Travis. Fuck him. I'm going to fight him right now—can you guys come and get my back? Make sure none of his friends jump me?" *Everyone* stood up without hesitation, as I knew they would.

"What happened?" Nate asked.

"I got off the bus. Fucking Travis yelled out 'Go back to 'Nam' and called me a gook. Fuck him. I'm gonna fucking kick his teeth in."

Liam, who was always down for a fight, strangely spoke up against my plan. "You can't fight Travis, Phuc."

I shook my head. "I'm not letting this bullshit go and let him think he can get away with it. If I don't do anything now, as a senior? What does that say? What does that look like? Fucking bullshit." I started to head toward Travis and his chain-smoking, ash-hole friends.

Nate grabbed my arm and held me in place. "Liam is right. You do this and for what? You know what'll happen."

He and Liam were referring to our school's draconian fight policy. If you were caught fighting at Carlisle High School, you were automatically suspended for two weeks. All school assignments given to you during those two weeks were recorded as a zero. The net effect was that you would fail most, if not all, your classes for that grading period with a two-week suspension. Thanks, Reaganomics and your zero-tolerance policing. I did know the policy, but my fury overpowered any reasonable assessment of the insult and a measured response. I wasn't going to write another editorial. Words were a useless currency in this exchange of pejoratives and blows. I didn't care about suspension, failing, or college. In that moment, I only felt hurt and angry, humiliated and defeated.

Nate held me in place, Liam and Stephen lined up behind. "Listen: you're going to graduate soon. Don't fuck that up. Travis's an asshole. Always has been." He paused for a second and thought aloud. "What the fuck am I doing? I'm going to summer school again as it is. Where is Travis?" I understood the gravity of what he was suggesting: Nate was going to fight Travis for me.

"He's at the bus drop," I told him, stunned.

"Okay—*nobody* come with me. You guys will be late for class. I'll take care of this. See you tomorrow, maybe." Nate sped off, and Liam and Byron kept me from following him. The seriousness of Nate's act unfolded on me. I felt buoyed by Nate's selfless, kind, and loyal gesture. I vacillated between my still surging rage for Travis and my disbelief at Nate's sacrifice. Even after the bell rang for first period, I chose a chable by the window, straining to see if maybe Nate had managed to get away or to not even fight Travis. He was a good friend—no, he was a great friend.

We didn't see Nate or Travis for the rest of the week. I didn't call Nate (he lived with his grandparents and they never answered their house phone), but Liam confirmed for me that they had both been suspended from school; ironically, Nate wasn't grounded by his grandparents, because he had told them that he fought Travis in defense (leaving out in whose defense he fought). It was just another fight, and no one in our crew gave Nate's suspension more thought other than an added caginess around the auto shop kids in case they decided to retaliate. But for me, Nate's fight was so much more than a typical fight between punks and rednecks. He was willing to literally take a hit for me so that I wouldn't fail my classes or get suspended. Nate saved my graduation and graduation speech. Because of him, my moment of greatness in front of our school still awaited me.

I saw Nate that weekend at a party. I didn't have the right words to thank him for keeping me from failing classes and torpedoing my future in a senseless fit of anger. It was the loyalty and kinship that had kept us together as a crew, and in the fading weeks of our senior year, that iron-forged kinship glowed as bright as it ever did. At the party, I patted him on the shoulder. "Dude, thank you."

It was Nate's *aristeia*, and I had failed him as his bard, unable to better herald his greatness.

JUNE 1991

My father stood at my bedroom door. "You're cleaning up your room. That's good. Geez, that's a lot of books on the floor. You're picking them up?"

"Obviously. I mean, they're going to take a picture and stuff." The Carlisle *Sentinel* was sending a reporter to interview me for a profile that our town's paper was doing on area high school seniors.

"Why are they interviewing you? Tell me again? Did you do something special?"

"Jesus, Dad, for the last time, I don't know. They contacted the high school to ask for a list of kids to interview, and someone gave the *Sentinel* my name. Maybe it's because I'm the school paper editor or a graduation speaker or . . . I don't know."

"You don't have to be so emotional about it—I was just asking a question. And don't take the Lord's name in vain."

"Forget it—let me finish picking things up, okay?"

The reporter, a thirtysomething man named Dan Miller, came by at noon. My mother asked him four times if he wanted tea, and my father hovered around awkwardly in the kitchen while Dan and I talked in the living room. Dan asked me about my love of art and literature, who nurtured my passions, what my future plans were. I kept my parents sequestered as much as possible, worried that my mother might say something stupid and/or unintelligible; and that my father would say that he figured I wouldn't amount to much because of my interest in literature and art and not in a practical degree like engineering.

Finally, with my father unable to give us any berth of privacy, Dan asked him, "So, Chanh, tell us what little Phuc was like. Any good stories?" I held my breath but could feel myself recoiling, bracing myself for my father to say something backhanded or embarrassing. My father smiled as I had never seen before, his eyes lighting up. He was unrecognizable. Most strange, my father said my name not as we Vietnamesed it in our house (*Phúc*) but as it was Americanized (*Fook*). "Oh, *Phuc*? He loved books even as a little kid. When we lived in Sài Gòn, his favorite thing was to look at books, and if you turned a picture book upside down, he would scream and turn it around again. So smart! He was only one year old and he knew when a book was upside down. And when we came to Carlisle, we took him to the library so much and read him so many books. For his good English, you know."

I was speechless. A warmth, a latent pride, exuded from my father's recollections of me as a child while he recounted my passion for reading at an early age. In his exuberance, I was surprisingly hurt, stung by its dormancy and now-sudden awakening. Where was this warmth, this pride, for the last few years of high school? Where was it even five minutes ago? Was he trotting out his pride in me because there was a stranger in the house and he was trying to save face, or did my father really feel this way? I felt embarrassed and confused, uneasy from his praise and attention, feeling the tension of our relationship crack with his heartfelt recollections of my childhood. A blinding flash went off in the corner of my eye—my father had taken a camera out and snapped a picture of me and Dan, punctuating his reminiscence with a paparazzi pop of the camera flash.

"Say *chee*! This is a special day!" he cried out—this from the man who had earlier been privately grilling me about why anyone would want to interview me but was now publicly my number one fan.

With the flash still in our eyes, I suggested that we move to my bedroom to talk uninterrupted. Dan looked at my Smiths posters, my walls redecorated with random collages of pictures cut out from magazines, and my collection of discarded library books.

Eyeing my shelves, he said, "Tell me about these books—it's unusual to see so many books in a teenager's room."

"Oh, I discovered that I really love literature." That was absolutely true, but I wasn't going to tell him that I started reading books to sound smart. "I love connecting with people over great books. It bypasses the superficial stuff, the stuff that divides us."

"I interviewed your English teacher, Mrs. Ferguson, earlier this week. She said that you are the best-read student she's ever taught."

"She did? Really?" I was surprised to hear that, since she had never said it to me. "That's . . . nice. She's a great teacher. I've been so lucky to have so many great teachers. Mrs. Krebs, Ms. Ganster."

"You said that you'll want to teach someday?"

"Definitely. Once, when we had a sub for AP European History, Ms. Ganster told the sub to have me teach the class. Left me the lesson plans and everything. Oh man, I loved teaching—sharing something I love with the class. But I love school and the classroom—it's where I'm happiest. I'd like to get a PhD in literature. Teach at the college level. But I love art, too—painting."

"So you'll have to decide between those things?"

I pushed back. "Why? I love art and literature so much. Why do I have to decide on only one?" I felt this pressure to sacrifice one for the other, and I hated it. If I had the vitality to pursue both things, who was going to make me choose only one? Dan was jotting down my answers, and the interview by our town's newspaper felt like an acknowledgment of me—of my greatness. "No one made Leonardo da Vinci or Michelangelo choose between painting and sculpture and engineering and architecture. Why can't I be a Renaissance man as well?"

Dan smiled and scribbled into his notebook. "Ah, that's great . . . a modern-day Renaissance man?"

I didn't flinch. "Yes."

"That's quite ambitious."

"That's the whole point, right? I mean, I'm not saying I'm going to achieve it, but those are my passions, and I have to try. I mean, I got scholastic gold keys for art *and* writing this year, so academically, no one is telling me to stop either one. There's a whole world out there of people telling you what you can't do or who you can't be. That's the world I live in. And who are those people who think they know me and know who I can be? And why do they care? There's only what I do and how hard I work at being great at it. That's all there is for me because no matter what I do, to some people I'll only be . . ." I stopped myself from filling in the blank, because it felt corrosive. I could feel the insult of Travis and his assholes still eating away at me, and I wanted to focus on the positive, shifting the topic to being a graduation speaker.

Dan didn't push me on my line of thought, and allowed me to trail off. Instead he moved on to ask me about my family, our journey to Carlisle, my plans for college. We talked a lot about our favorite books, bands, movies. I ended the interview by complaining about modern poetry—especially e e cummings—and free jazz. He thanked me and my parents for our time, and said that the article would run the following weekend right after commencement.

The Carlisle *Sentinel* had documented the Trầns, for better and worse, over the last fifteen years—from our arrival in 1975, the follow-up articles chronicling Ông Bà Nội's arrival as boat people, to the fire that killed my great-grandmother and my uncle's murder-suicide. I would not have named those events as highlights for our family, but here I was, garnering some acclaim because of my accomplishments, not because of tragedy or infamy or history. If I had anything to say about my aspirations, anything about my personal goals, I was going to say them aloud, in print, for the whole world to see, to show people that I was striving for greatness. I wasn't going to be defined by a war or race or my family's story, holding forth to the reporter with equal parts insecurity and arrogance, as if they were so different. *I was a Renaissance man*, I declared.

I didn't know if I would achieve those goals, but that was the very nature of having goals. They were aspirational, hopeful—not predictive. The potential for failure did not lower my hopes. My hopes were pinned and melted to my waxy dreams, soaring upward. After the interview, I sunned myself in the warm public recognition of my *aristeia*.

But when I read the article a week later, I knew I had soared too high. I felt profoundly embarrassed. I cringed at my public hubris and arrogance, for comparing myself to Renaissance greats, for believing that I had anything worthwhile to say as a seventeen-year-old. In my mind, I was an Achilles, but in the harsh light of my local newspaper, in the blinding black-and-white of print, I saw that I had behaved like an Agamemnon.

My aspirations for greatness were the antithesis of punk, and I knew it. And for the first time I realized that the most punk thing for me to do was to be who I was without pretention or preamble or grandiose posturing. I had read it in Nietzsche but didn't know what it really meant: become who you are. But becoming who you are required throwing away who you thought you were, unloading expectations both internal and external.

In this mind-set of unburdening myself as the horizon line of graduation drew nearer, I thought about the fresh start of college in three months. No one would know me, no one would have preconceived notions of who I was, no one would know my family or our history. They would only know what I told them. Who was I, anyway? I had spent all this time trying to figure out who I should be for acceptance, for protection, for prestige.

When the graduation speakers met to choose a theme, I was still feeling wounded from the whole Travis incident, wounded because everything was for naught. I had tried so hard to fit in at school, establish myself inside and outside of the classroom, and the effort had been rendered pointless for me. There would always be kids and adults out there in the audience, looking at me and thinking whatever horrible shit they wanted. And I cared about what people thought, but I felt too pained to say that I did. I wanted to throw it all away, to leave everything behind, all the emotional baggage, and to start over.

In the speakers' meeting, I impertinently suggested "baggage" or "luggage" as our theme (in response to the other kids' cliché suggested themes of the future or our hopes), and the group improbably agreed. The theme for graduation speeches would be "luggage."

It was time to get rid of my emotional baggage.

JUNE 5, 1991, GRADUATION NIGHT

In keeping with Carlisle High School tradition, the boys and girls wore the green and white of our school's colors, boys in green and girls in white. The National Honor Society students got an additional golden stole that draped our shoulders, a visual distinction from our rank-and-file classmates. I was the only one in my crew wearing one.

Liam and Byron flipped the stole in my face before shaking my hand warmly. "Way to go, Phucster—we're stoked for your speech!"

"Thanks—we made it, guys. We *fucking* made it." They whooped, and no one mentioned Nate, who had been permanently expelled for shaving SUCK IT into the back of his head and would not graduate with us.

In my pocket, I had my speech folded up and damp. We were all sweating under our polyester gowns, and Mr. Drake vigilantly watched us to make sure that no one inflated a beach ball or did anything to puncture the grandeur of the processions.

A stage had been erected in the middle of the football stadium at the fifty-yard line. Early concerns about a late-afternoon thunderstorm dissipated, and the low front had moved on, leaving clear skies and a muggy warm glow over the end zone as we lined up at seven p.m. Parents, friends, teachers, well-wishers gathered in the aluminum bleachers, clanging around to find seats. Lou sat with my parents and both sets of grandparents. Molly sat with some of her friends. I could see Mrs. Krebs, Mrs. Ferguson, and Mr. Shirk, my favorite art teacher, and most of the high school faculty.

Jacob Royal, our valedictorian; Elizabeth Rousek, our class president; and the four graduation speakers led the procession, taking our seats nearest the stage. I fingered the corner of my speech back and forth, looking out at the sea of waves and smiles.

In the days leading up to graduation, I worked with Mrs. Krebs on the speech. She had asked me how I was feeling about graduation and what I wanted to say to my classmates. Her advice was to say how I was feeling, but truthfully, I was not feeling my greatness. I was thankful that I had survived high school, but I didn't think that my teachers or peers wanted to hear me say that. At the end of high school, I was exhausted, frustrated, and angry that I had spent so much of my time in Carlisle trying to be seen, understood, and accepted, and I just wanted to forget it all. I was done rolling the boulder up the hill. I knew that my real feelings wouldn't fulfill the expected, celebratory tone of a graduation speech, so I told her I wanted to write a speech about souvenirs, and she agreed to it.

And now it was graduation.

National anthem on a trumpet. Welcoming address. Elizabeth's introductory remarks. The other speakers gave their five-minute addresses, and we all clapped.

Mr. Drake read my name out: PHUC TRAN. I mounted the stage, and took the microphone. The early evening lowered a deep indigo over us all, and stadium lights had buzzed on with fluorescent fanfare. I could still make out the bleachers, but the audience was blurry and indistinguishable. My classmates clapped as I approached the mic, and I heard Liam yell out, "YEAH, PHUCSTER!" which caught a fiery glare from Mr. Drake. I took a breath and leaned into the microphone.

I wanted to prime my audience for the imagery to follow, so I started out with some jokes about souvenirs, and waited for the laughter to subside, knowing that I had begun with some easy and disarming humor. That was my universal defense, but I was going to turn it on its side now.

"Anyway, I guess most of us buy souvenirs to bring back the memories that are associated with them, and I think that's okay. But here's a thought that I don't think everyone has thought. What are you going to do when you become senile and can't remember where New York City is, much less why you have twenty commemorative statuettes of liberty? Let's face it: we can only accumulate so many commemorative things."

Was I holding on to things, having forgotten why I had them in the first place? I looked at my friends seated down below to my left. My crew. My classmates. Lab partners. Quizbowl teammates. Yearbook staff. Newspaper staff. They would only be with me if I remembered them.

"I just never understood the logic behind buying souvenirs. After all, it's the memory we want, not the souvenir, and once the memory goes, what meaning does the souvenir have? That's like keeping training wheels on your bicycle. I think most of us spend far too much time looking back at our past anyway and not worrying enough about the future without an attic full of old prom dresses, dried corsages, books, toys you don't play with anymore and photo albums of pictures we had thought were long gone."

I looked out to the bleachers and wondered if my parents understood that part. My parents had fled from a place too painful to remember yet too precious to forget—they had lugged around old photos that they never looked at but couldn't bear to throw away until the flood.

My family didn't have old prom dresses or corsages. We came with nothing. My toys had been thrown away long ago. My classmates had basements and attics full of heirlooms, bronzed baby shoes, treasure boxes full of firsts. I only had my story, but none of it sounded like their stories. I wondered: How would my classmates have reacted if I had told them about my *real* experiences? Who would believe me if I gave a speech about my father trying to kill me because I didn't make honor roll? Who would care if I told them about how I tried to change my name to Peter because I wanted to fit in? Who would be able to relate to me if told them about my family's harrowing escape from Sài Gòn?

"Leave your souvenirs behind. The ones of Carlisle, the ones of the beach, the ones of your friends. Put away your yearbooks, hide your seashells, and forget the pictures, because if these things mean nearly as much as you say they mean, you'll never forget them.

"I don't need souvenirs, and I don't want souvenirs. None of you need souvenirs either. As long as you laugh, won't you carry all the good times with you? And as long as you cry, won't you carry all the bad times with you? So wherever we all end up and wherever we are all going, I know we don't need souvenirs because laughter will always be laughter, and tears will always be tears."

I stepped away from the microphone to signal the end, making sure the last word *TEARS* could ring out. That was my final word: *TEARS.* I had planned not to say *thank you* at the end of the speech, thinking that its omission would be a small, symbolic gesture that I wasn't the typically thankful, gracious immigrant, but I slipped up and reflexively said it anyway. *THANK YOU.* So fucking Pavlovian and contradictory.

Clapping. Singing from the chorus. Hats in the air. I sighed. It was over.

My parents and grandparents had made a late buffet dinner at our house after the ceremony, and my mother had printed out a giant dot-matrix banner that had a sixteen-bit illustration of a graduation cap and the words CONGRATULATIONS, PHÚC! My father shook my hand and said *good job*, and my mother told me that she thought my voice sounded nice on the PA speakers. What else could they have said about the speech?

Bà Nội reached up and pinched my cheek, Vietnamesing, "You did a great job! That sounded so nice, but you know I have no idea what you said!" She cackled at the joke/not-joke and handed me a red-and-gold envelope with a crisp fifty-dollar bill in it.

"Thanks anyway, Bà Nội." I kissed her on the cheek before she went to everyone at the dining room table.

My parents and both sets of grandparents hadn't been together in years, and they were equally happy to catch up with one another. I shoveled some eggrolls and rice vermicelli into my mouth and took the earliest opportunity to excuse myself. I changed my clothes and took our car to pick up Molly at her house.

She slid into the front seat. "Hey, Mr. Graduation Speaker. Nice job. That was great!"

"Oh, thanks . . . I was super-nervous."

"It was great. Really."

"Thanks, really. So there's a graduation party at Scully's apartment. And there's a party at Derek Linker's that we should go to. Those are the only parties I know about. Seem okay to you?"

"Yeah, of course. It's your graduation night—we do what you want."

We showed up at Scully's dank apartment downtown and found graduation mayhem. Kegs. Weed. A giant American flag hung in the living room. I took a few celebratory hits from a bong, and we laughed about the improbability of Liam having actually graduated. After an hour, we left to go to Derek's house, a grand suburban home (his parents were both physicians). Derek and I were in AP Calculus, and we'd been in school together since Mooreland Elementary. Kids milling around, watching TV, and fishing their fingers in the Chex Mix to reel in their favorite bits. Juice, mixed with ginger ale, in giant crystal punch bowls. The opposite of mayhem. Ho hum.

Still high, I leaned over to Molly, who smiled with equanimity in both polarizing expeditions. "Hey—wanna just go to the All-American? Gravy fries and coffee?"

"Really? That's what you want to do?" She shook her head.

"Yeah, kind of." We left the party.

In the car, in honor of graduation, I ironically played Depeche Mode's *Black Celebration*. I did want to go to the truck stop to eat gravy fries and drink coffee. I had recently read *The Fountainhead* and was still ruminating over its themes. I didn't know much else about Ayn Rand but was so eager to talk about the book with Molly—just another Friday night of spirited literary critique. I started telling her about it but paused as we pulled into the truck stop diner.

Glowing with tubes of neon, sparkling with chrome, the All-American Truck Stop on Route 11 was a garish sight that was familiar and comforting to me—our favorite of all the truck stops along the I-81 and I-76 corridors. After late nights partying, after punk shows, after driving around aimlessly, my friends and I had eaten, puked, and passed out in its maroon vinyl booths for the last four years of high school. The All-American's waitresses were direct, surly, and fast. The truck drivers, weary from miles at the wheel, filled the booths. It seemed fitting to celebrate at the truck stop on my graduation night, the eternal returns on an endless stretch of country highway.

As the hostess led me and Molly to a booth, we passed exhausted truckers, too tired to look up, as they ate their breakfast, lunch, or dinner—all of it served with the ambrosia of coffee.

"What'll you have, sweetheart?" The word *sweetheart* never sounded so world-weary.

"Fries with the gravy on the side. Brown gravy, please. And two cups of coffee. Black. Thank you."

As we waited for our fries, sipping on our coffees, encased in red and silver and the low chatter of interstate stories, I plinked a quarter in the table-side jukebox. It was our game at the All-American to play the most annoying country or classic rock song, and we were well versed in Dolly, Loretta, Merle, ELO, and Elton. But you didn't pick a good Elton John song like "Tiny Dancer"—you picked an annoying one like "Crocodile Rock."

I flipped the lever at the top of the jukebox and froze. "*No. Fucking. Way.* They have R.E.M.?" The tiny placard trumpeted R.E.M.'s "Losing My Religion." I had never thought I would ever, in the course of a million plates of fries and cups of coffee, see R.E.M. on the truck stop jukebox, but there they were.

R.E.M. had a hit record that spring of 1991, and "Losing My Religion" played everywhere. Radio. MTV. Blaring from random cars in the middle of Carlisle. Gone were the days of my bootleg cassettes of *Reckoning* and *Chronic Town*. Good for them, I guess. They had made it.

As the song's mandolins started up, I grumbled about sellouts and corporate rock, sipping my first cup of coffee. Molly squared herself to me at the table, leaned in over her coffee. "Sooo? How's it feel to graduate? You did it, Mr. Carlisle High School Graduate. *And* you gave a great speech!"

"Oh, I don't know about that. It was okay. I messed it up a little from my nerves, I guess. I feel . . . I feel weirdly let down. So much hype around everything, you know?" I reflexively shrugged at Molly's compliment, deflecting praise as I always did because I was so unaccustomed to hearing earnest accolades. Any kind remark made me feel vulnerable, forced me to confront myself and my purported excellence, a task that felt impossible and undeserved. The fall from Travis's insult had apparently kept me grounded, pinned me down.

She shook her head. "Well, *I* thought it was great. And it seemed like your family was proud of you."

I scrunched my face. "Seriously? My family? You don't really know my parents. And I doubt they knew what I was talking about anyway, so if they were proud, they didn't know what they were proud of."

Molly pushed back against my dismissiveness. "But your grandparents were all there—all four of them! That was nice to see them all, right? Your dad's parents drove all the way from Oklahoma—that seems like a big deal."

"It is a big deal. But . . ." I paused as our order of fries landed on the tabletop with a clatter, followed by a small bowl of steaming rich gravy.

"But what? It's not enough for your family to show up and cheer for you?" Molly nibbled on the still-too-hot fries.

"I guess it is." I plunged my fries into the gravy and thought about what Molly said, then changed my mind. "Actually, *no*. No, it isn't. It's not enough for me to have them just show up. I worked really hard on the speech, and I don't think that they understood any of it—okay, maybe my dad did a little—but it sucks that they didn't really get it. It sucks that my grandparents and mom don't know enough English to get it, and my dad doesn't really know enough about the idea of metaphors and symbolism to get it, never mind my high school experience. And Lou? He's in ninth grade, so he doesn't get it yet either. I'm bummed that they don't get it, because it confirms that they really don't understand me."

Molly shook her head. "But you've always said that your family didn't get you. How is this new to you?"

"I know, I know. But now that we're talking about it—*really* talking—I guess I had always secretly hoped that it wasn't true. I *did* want them to understand me because they're . . . they're my family. It feels good to be understood, and I imagine that it would feel really good to be understood by your family because they've got the most mileage with you. They made you. But I don't know what that understanding is like."

"But they still could connect with you, right? Someday? It sounds like you're writing them off."

I shook my head at her suggestion. "I suppose that they could change, that they could come around and know me as a person. But I'm about to go to college. We're not going to write each other letters. I mean: they still don't understand why I want to major in English and art, and I can't explain it to them in a way that they'll get it. I feel like the door is closing on me and my parents, and this is as good as it's going to be—my relationship with them. They literally can't understand me because my Vietnamese sucks as much as their English. And there's a cultural and generational barrier, frankly. And who knows what else?" I was cratered by a deep sadness at this realization that I hadn't expressed before—the barriers felt insurmountable, each of us alone on our sides. My heart ached with the thought.

The song had ended, and I ordered a second coffee. Molly was always so optimistic, circling back to the beginning. "Well, to my original point: I thought the speech was great. And other people thought it was great too, so that's got to be something. That recognition must have felt good."

"It did." I conceded her point, still pained by the idea that my parents and grandparents sat in the audience with hardly a clue as to what I had said while total strangers understood every word (even if they didn't understand the intent). At my most public, my most exposed, I felt most alone. "Yeah, it was nice that people applauded. I thought the speech and graduation were going to be this big, triumphant moment of greatness, but it wasn't. It was a weird mix of different feelings and expectations. But I see what you're saying. The audience liked it, maybe most of my classmates liked it. Good for me. Ugh—I don't mean to sound like an unappreciative asshole. . . ." I trailed off, wanting to pivot from my melancholy, which was squeezing itself, uninvited, into our celebratory booth. I looked around at the truck stop diner and its patrons, and a revelation lighted upon me, pushing off my unwelcome gloom. I surveyed everyone under the diner's fluorescent glow. "You know something? You and I, we have something in common with these truckers."

Molly laughed. "Oh really? Are we done psychoanalyzing you and your family? We've moved on to ourselves and the truckers? Well, I'm pretty sure neither of us have beards or know how to drive an eighteen-wheeler."

"No, seriously. You know, for the last four years, my friends and I chose the All-American diner because we thought it was funny to come here and mingle with redneck truckers at one a.m. I mean, we wouldn't openly fuck with them, but we'd laugh at how they stared at us or shook their heads, but I realize something now."

"What's that?"

"Teenagers and truck drivers: *We're all on our way to somewhere else.* We're all sitting at these booths, knowing that we're not at our final destination. This is not the last stop for any of us. We're all en route to far-off places, but our arrival? Who knows? Our arrival will be dictated by things we both *can* and *can't* control, unforeseen things. I'm going to college to study English and art, but who knows if that'll happen? Conor's joined the army, but what if he gets killed in Iraq? What about you or my brother? What's next? And we might get to our destination directly, but maybe it'll be in a roundabout, crazy way."

Molly nodded. "Interesting point." As she slid a quarter into the jukebox and clicked through the song selector, I mulled over the living metaphor of sitting at the truck stop, waiting to get on the road, longing to see Carlisle in my rearview, to look out at an unexplored horizon. The past in a mirror, the future in a window, the present behind the wheel.

The rural highway of Route 11 outside the truck stop brought me back to the beginning, back to our beginning in Carlisle.

One of my earliest memories flickered in my mind. My parents, me, and Lou, joyriding in the first car we owned, the sage-green Pontiac. My parents would take us out on Route 174, a long, narrow stretch of hilly swells surrounded by high corn and lowing cows. Lou and I would lie on the back seat, unbuckled, as my father pinned the accelerator. We crested over the hills, the engine rattling and wheezing, and Lou and I would go flying in the air as the car rocketed for a moment, hovering with an aerial magic before crunching back down. In the back seat, we lurched upward and then collapsed into the upholstery, banging our elbows and knees, laughing hysterically and begging him to go faster over the next hill. When we reached Shippensburg, he'd turn the car around and we'd drive back faster, flying higher than before. In Carlisle, we cried out to do it again, and the car turned around and roared down the road, all of us exhilarated and cheering from the simple, brief pleasure of driving on a country road with nowhere to go and nothing to do.

I smiled at the recollection, waiting for Molly to pick a song for our soundtrack.

From the diner booth, I squinted at the glorious, blinding lights of Carlisle's famous truck stop. Its Olympian-sized eagle, shining red, white, and blue, loomed over us, and in the glass, I saw two images simultaneously: myself reflected in the diner window, and the star-spangled sign soaring aloft in the night air, pointing the way, winking at me again and again.

All-American.

All-American.

All-American.

ACKNOWLEDGMENTS

I want give my deepest, undying thanks to so many people who have cheered me on in this memoir-writing process. Who does this writing thing for a living? Good God, you writers are amazing. Writing the book has been an incredible, challenging, and rewarding journey, and I am immeasurably grateful to all my literary Sherpas who pushed, dragged, and portaged my ass up the mountain. I feel humbled and so very lucky.

Sue Tran: Where do I even begin? You've read every single word I've written, a hundred times over. Your keen insights and sensitive reading of every sentence, paragraph, and chapter made my writing and book better. And beyond your literary prowess, you soldiered on alone on weekends with nary a complaint while I hid myself away to write and edit. The kids were fed, dressed, and cleaned; the laundry was done; dinner was cooked—all this happened while I sat on my ass, writing and psychoanalyzing my childhood. You're the Mary to my George Bailey. Thanks for finding me in this wonderful life. I love you more than my words can express, but I will spend the rest of my life trying to tell you.

Sarah Levitt: You get all the credit for ferreting me out from under my teaching and tattooing and motorcycle riding. You saw something that was worth saying to the world, and from day one you've understood me and how I wanted to tell my story. Your patience and cheerleading have propelled me and kept me focused. As the card says: You're fucking awesome. And it's your fault that my Honda CB350 restoration is *still* unfinished. *Now* can I go back to working on it?

Jasmine Faustino: Thank you so much for your eagle-eyed edits, patience with my schedule, and your boot-camp approach to my flabby, wide-ranging story. You gave my book its beach bod with your love and enthusiasm. I appreciate so much that we have a shared experience and common touchstones, and I can't imagine anyone else who could have teased out the threads of the story as you've done. So how about that tattoo of yours?

Thanks to *everyone* at Flatiron Books for your patience, precision, and professionalism (especially Bryn Clark, Christopher Smith, and Ellen Pyle). "Oh, can I see another version of this? How about now? No, move this? Can we make it more punk rock looking?" Good grief, you were nice about it all.

Lou Tran: You were the first person who ever said to me, "You should write a book." And I laughed at you for like ten minutes. "Yeah, right." Thanks for believing in me and for being the Chewbacca to my Han. It could not have been easy to be my brother, but you've borne it with grace and kindness—maybe it wasn't all terrible? There's a reason that you're the hero in my story. We clocked long miles together, and hopefully we have many more. Time to rent that RV! And we still have a motorcycle trip to take!

Chanh and Chi Tran: Mom and Dad, we all did our best, and I know that you tried. I know that the book's complexity might be lost on you, but I want you to know that I am grateful for the sacrifices that you both made. They are immeasurable, and I know that you did it for me and Lou.

Lewis Robinson, Seth Rigoletti, and Taffy Field: You guys had *no reason* to be so excited about and supportive of my writing, but you all were unfailingly full of enthusiasm and love for me. Lewis, remember when you had the flu and still let me come over at nine p.m. to talk to you about some New York agent (Sarah) who had emailed about representing me? And then you asked me to be on your writing podcast long before I was writing anything. You knew before I knew! Seth, you wanted to hear my story before I wanted to tell it, and every time I said some bullshit or deflected, you called me on it. I've admired and emulated your vulnerability and honesty. Taffy, my favorite colleague, your unending efforts to be a better human being have inspired me. It's been a highlight of my career to teach with and learn from you.

Team LRG: Y'all are the best book club ever—thanks for the lively conversations and good cheer at every chapter. Please don't choose my memoir to read for book club.

Paula Chu: Thanks for being my Yoda. Your deep wisdom, humor, and empathy have changed me profoundly and for the better. That change made possible the writing of this book (the dredging up of a lot of sad and painful memories).

All my teachers, but especially Jane Krebs, Lorene Ganster, Sue Hench, Marsha Mentzer, Jim Shirk, Robert Moyer, Michael O'Hara: You cultivated the best that you saw in me with your gentle and firm teaching. You endured my full-sail, pissy adolescence (arrogance, anger, moodiness, and depression) with such love and empathy. I became a teacher because of you all, and I can only hope that I've been half the teacher that you are.

My crew: You guys saved my life. What a crazy high school experience it was. RIP our friends who didn't live long enough to see that it could get better. Because of the book's focus, so many people, stories, and relationships ended up on the cutting room floor—you know who you are. Long drives, Shakespeare Troupe rehearsals, hikes in the woods, cemetery walks, endless phone conversations: I just didn't have room to get it all in there, and I am saddened that I wasn't able to tell the world how much you meant to me, but to me you meant the world.

So much love to Josh Paynter, Julie Fogliano, Ric Loyd, Val White, Sonya Tomlinson, and Jay Merritt: I start the new year with you all, and you set the benchmark for joy, laughter, and friendship.

Adam Burk and the TEDxDirigo team: Thanks for taking a chance on my crazy idea for a TEDx talk.

Brendon Whitney: Rest in power—we all miss and love you, buddy.

To all my aunts, uncles, and cousins—the Wu Tran Clan: you all were that proverbial village that it took to raise a roughneck like me, and you kept me close and loved me at my most unlovable. Special thanks to my aunts Cô Hai, Cô Tu, Cô Sáu, and Cô Bảy—you're the best. In telling my story, I realize how much I want to hear yours, and I hope that we have the time. I'm all ears.

Last but certainly not least, Phoebe Tran and Beatrix Tran: You're five and eight at this writing. I'll try to control my dread when you read this book (YOU CANNOT READ THIS BOOK UNTIL YOU'RE SIXTEEN). I hope that you can see me as a person who had many struggles and persevered all while seeing humor and beauty in the world and drawing strength from my friends, family, and teachers. I was a teenager once, too, and not the overbearing, protective, and sarcastic person that I am now. Well, I was always sarcastic. And probably overbearing, too. I was not always protective, but I didn't have anything I wanted to protect until you were born. You girls make me want to be the best version of myself, and I fail every day. But every day, I try again. I love you both so much. Thanks for letting me be your father.

ABOUT THE AUTHOR

PHUC TRAN has been a high school Latin teacher for more than twenty years while simultaneously establishing himself as a highly sought-after tattooer. He has a BA in classics and received the Callanan Classics Prize. His 2012 TEDx talk, "Grammar, Identity, and the Dark Side of the Subjunctive," was featured on NPR's *Ted Radio Hour*, and he is an occasional guest on Maine Public Radio. He owns Tsunami Tattoo in Portland, Maine, where he lives with his family.